THE COMPLETE
Scottish Terrier

by JOHN T. MARVIN

ILLUSTRATED

1971

HOWELL BOOK HOUSE

845 THIRD AVENUE

NEW YORK, N.Y.   10022

Cave Canem. Beware of the Dog. From a mosaic at Pompeii.

*To my
Grandchildren,
Gretchen and Charlie,
both lovers of
dogs*

Scotch Terrier, 1840.

The Dog and his Shadow. Landseer, 1826.

Contents

PART II

Preliminary Training, Care, Feeding, Breeding, Medical

v

A Landseer vignette, 1824. Note old type of Terrier at the left.

Foreword

*If a man has once owned a Scottie, he
will never want to own any other dog.*
—F. W. BARTON

As a lover of all Terriers and especially of the
Scottish breeds, I consider it a rare privilege to write this book. The
research and information between these covers have given me real
and lasting pleasure since they have brought me into close contact
with many people interested in and dedicated to the Scottish
Terrier.

I have tried to trace the history of the breed from dog's early
beginnings through the derivation of the Terrier breeds and to the
development of today's Scottish Terrier. I have mentioned many
names in this chronological progress of the breed but space limits
their number. I had to concentrate upon the persons and their dogs
who hold the more important places in the long and interesting
narrative of the breed. While some may not agree with my choices, I
hope all will understand my position.

I wish to thank those who helped me gather information for this
book in this country and in England. Particular appreciation goes
to those who obtained important photographs which add so much
to any compilation like this. To Miss Alice Exworthy I give special
thanks for the use of her charts and statistics on the production of

champion Scottish Terriers in this country, which will mean much to the student who wishes to delve more deeply into the subject and will certainly be a source of amazement to the tyro.

It is hoped that all of the information presented here is accurate and in proper chronological order. Any errors are unintentional. The very immensity of the task involved lent opportunity for error. I trust that the readers will derive as much pleasure from this effort as I have gained in writing it.

JOHN T. MARVIN

Courtesy, *Dog News*

A famous pair: Harry Lauder and the great Ch. Heather Realisation, 1936.

1

Introducing the Scot

"ALL Dogs are good; any Terrier is better; a Scottish Terrier is the best." So said William Haynes many years ago. Today, no fancier of the Scotsman will disagree, which proves that the statement is still true and that the breed attributes have been maintained throughout the intervening years. This love of the strain may be traced directly to its character. This is not a superficial breed or one with lavish tongue and a quick-to-forget approach. Rather, the Scot is a bit on the dour side, as might be expected from his heritage, sometimes solemn but always loyal to his master. The Scottish Terrier is dignified, slow to react and show affection, and steadfast whatever the circumstance.

The Scot melds such virtues as prudence, enthusiasm, stability and selective affection into every act of his small and vital life. These qualities are cherished by those who understand him and by his master most of all, for he *is* his master's dog. In this respect I can say without fear of contradiction that there never was a promiscuous Scottie, or one that loved everybody. Many of the breed will tolerate others, particularly when these persons have their master's blessing. But for absolute adoration concentrated upon one or two people, the Scot has no rival, which is why his following is legion and loyal.

S. S. Van Dine, a noted novelist and himself a Scottie devotee and breeder, once wrote:

> A quality of the Scottie is his aloofness. He has a sense of bashfulness, and despite his vigorous nature, he is highly sensitive. Like all well-bred people he hates to be stared at. If you look straight at him in a critical way he will turn his head and attempt to act indifferently. He dislikes to have his privacy invaded and, like any gentleman, resents being the centre of attraction.

Lest some may think the breed lacks sparkle, let it be said that Scotties will play as any other dog; they will chase a ball, plunge in a lake for a swim and in general act like all Terriers. But their attachment to their master and his family is different and more profound than with most dogs. This difference is the major quality that draws and holds so many to this small and intense breed.

The Scottish Terrier is a wary dog that will observe a provocative situation with smoldering and often averted eyes and without evidence of any great interest. What is he thinking? Why does he suddenly decide to enter the fray with enthusiasm? I believe it is because the Scottie, like his human counterpart, is a canny individual that never acts without reflection and consideration of the consequences. Once the decision is made, however, he enters the melee with authority and abandon.

A compilation of compliments paid to this breed by its many admirers would fill volumes. Two of the most revealing of these add insight into its basic character. The first was written by S. S. Van Dine:

> A Scottie's character is hard to analyze, as are all colorful personalities; and it may perhaps best be described as an ever-blazing internal fire, both physical and temperamental, that shines forth from his eyes, vitalizes his expression, invigorates his body and animates his activity.

Dorothy Gabriel wrote:

> The character of the Scottish Terrier is wonderful. He is essentially a one-man's dog, loving his home and owner and having absolutely no use for outsiders. He never forgets—his heart will break with grief, but he will not yowl about it. He is absolutely honorable, incapable of a mean or petty action, large hearted and loving with the soul and mind of an honest gentleman.

These tributes sum up the many fine qualities of the Scottie, and they may constitute the reason why the late Vinton Breese said: "Once a Scot owner, always a Scot owner, for no other breed can fill his unique place."

2

The Scotch and the Scottish Terrier

Most authors before 1800 agreed that there were two varieties of the Terrier but none offered definitive names for them. Long-legged and short-legged they remained, and in short and long coats of many colors. This indicates that early Terriers were not always of pure blood but historically there is evidence of pure ancestry at that time.

With the coming of the 19th century, sportsmen and others became increasingly aware of the need for special abilities in dogs and because of this began to reproduce such animals by breeding techniques that progressed with each passing year. The Terriers were separated into strains which later became distinct breeds each with a conformation and temperament that was tailored for a given purpose.

The fact that the original Terrier variants were bred in specific areas and localities was not mentioned in most early sporting books. This was to be expected, for the majority of the authors were not dog men but sportsmen who knew that dogs existed but who cared not for their derivation. The flood of dog books of the early 19th century attempted to explain the origin and conformation of the several varieties known at the time. *Cynographica Britannica* by Sydenham Edwards (*circa* 1800) was the first of these. This was issued in quarterly sections but never completed. Nevertheless, the colored plate of Terriers together with a description thereof offers some interesting information. Five widely different varieties of Terriers are depicted. The Manchester or Black and Tan is easily identifiable. The rather typical Scotch Terrier is of a reddish wheaten color. This plate proves any that there were different Terrier breeds in 1800, and it suggests that earlier authors neglected to give proper descriptions of them. Thomas Brown in his *Biographical Sketches and Authentic Anecdotes of Dogs* (1829) made a great contribution to the study of the Terrier breeds. Here the student finds the first real breakdown of the Terrier kind. Brown said:

> There are two kinds of Terriers,—the rough haired Scotch and the smooth English.
> The Scotch terrier is certainly the purest in point of breed and the English seems to have been produced by a cross from him. The Scotch terrier is generally low in stature, seldom more than twelve or fourteen inches in height, with a strong, muscular body, and short, stout legs; his ears small, and half-pricked; his head is rather large in proportion to the size of his body, and the muzzle considerably pointed; his scent is extremely acute, so that he can trace the footsteps of all other animals with certainty; he is generally of a sandy color or black. Dogs of these colors are certainly the most hardy, and more to be depended upon; when white or pied, it is a sure mark of the impurity of the breed. The hair of the terrier is long, matted, and hard, over almost every part of his body. His bite is extremely keen. There are three distinct varieties of the Scotch terrier: The one above described. Another, about the same size and form, but with hair much longer, and somewhat flowing, which gives his legs the appearance of being very short. This is the prevailing breed of the Western Islands of Scotland. The third variety is much larger than the other two, being generally from fifteen to eighteen inches in height with the hair very hard and wiry, and much shorter than that of the others.

The description of the Scotch Terrier offered a useful delineation with the first mentioned variety apparently the forerunner of what we now know as the Cairn, West Highland White, Dandie Dinmont and Scottish Terrier. The second variety unquestionably defined the Skye and the third variety, now extinct, was probably the progenitor of the Irish Terrier and was also a useful cross with fighting dogs of the Bull Terrier strain.

This description was copied by a host of later authors, generally

4

without credit, and was modified in terms by many others, often to its detriment. Thus, the term Scotch Terrier found in books after 1829 did not necessarily indicate the dog we now know as the Scottish Terrier but was generic to at least three other varieties, to wit, the West Highland White, the Cairn and the Dandie Dinmont. This variation was narrowed down rather quickly to two other breeds since the Dandie gained early independence, probably at a date even before the publication of Brown's book.

The indiscriminate use of the term Scotch Terrier as a designation for Cairns, West Highlands and Scottish Terriers continued for many years. The Scottish Terrier was the first to gain autonomy through club and show activity, followed by the Westie and finally the Cairn, which still bears the closest resemblance to the early Scotch Terrier. In spite of the emergence of separate breeds from the basic blood, there was much interbreeding of these strains even into the 20th century.

The late Walter Reeves, a great Terrier man and all-breed judge, told me that in England and Scotland, around the turn of the century, all three breeds often came from a single litter according to what the buyer wanted. It is also a known fact that West Highland Whites were often classed and shown as Scottish Terriers and were in great demand because of their distinctive color. Cairns, too, fell in this category and records will show that registered dogs of all three breeds often could be found in a single pedigree. Actually, Westies and Cairns were not fully separated until about 1917 through a Kennel Club decree which prohibited interbreeding.

Thus, claims of first birth by proponents of any of these breeds of Scotch descent are ill-founded since students have difficulty in tracing pure blood in any of them before about 1875–1880. The distinct characteristics of Scottish, Cairn and West Highland White Terriers as we know them today are, however, quite different. The conformation of the Scottish Terrier, as will be shown, has been changed the most through the years while the Westie may possibly be a larger dog than his progenitors. The Cairn is gradually being shortened in back but most nearly resembles the early Scotch Terrier, although the ears are now always upright.

The first real move towards breed autonomy by the Scottish Terrier branch from the more generic Scotch Terrier family came about through dog shows, which began in 1859. At this time, those inter-

5

ested in exhibiting their dogs began to realize the need for greater uniformity of type. Then as now, the requirements for a dog to win were determined by the judges who placed the dogs at the shows according to their opinion of what a good 'un should be.

The Scotch Terrier made his first appearance in the show ring at Birmingham in 1860, the second year of organized dog shows. Here there was a classification for "Scotch Terriers." The winner of the class was a "White Skye" which adds to the early confusion brought about by the generic breed name. As time went on, dog shows increased the problem of separating the breeds or strains. The classes for Scotch Terriers disappeared and classes for such breeds as Rough-haired Terriers, Aberdeen, Paisley, and Highland Terriers were provided, and dogs of several breeds were entered indiscriminately. According to Gray, Paisley Terriers were silkies and the Rough-haired Terriers were a nondescript lot. To compound the problem, many Scotsmen preferred to call all of their dogs Skyes and frequently exhibited Scottish Terrier types in the Skye Terrier classes. Mr. Gordon Murray was one of these, and when he entered his "Otter," which according to advice was a proper Scottish Terrier, as a Skye at Swindon in 1876, the judges were bitterly denounced for not recognizing it as "a genuine Skye." Thus, the Scottish Terrier had many an alias which caused difficult times. In 1879 the Kennel Club revived separate classes for Scotch Terriers which were quickly assailed by fanciers of the Aberdeen strain who wanted additional classes for their breed. The effort failed, and by 1881 the several varieties were engulfed by the more popular Scotch Terrier classification. About the same time, proponents of the "pure," "genuine," and "hard-coated" Skye became reconciled to call their dogs Hard-haired Scotch Terriers and the turmoil gradually subsided.

This stormy period certainly retarded the growth and widespread recognition of the breed and the Scot's determination to "make a point" did not hasten the solution. By 1881 the die was cast and the following year, 1882, saw a loosely knit group of Scotland's most prominent fanciers form a club to support the breed. (The Scottish Terrier Club of England came into existence in 1887.) It did not flourish; by 1887, according to Gray, "The spark had fled." Through its initiative, however, a breed standard was drawn which was accepted by the majority of the group who appended their

6

signatory approval. This was indeed a milestone in the breed's forward progress; it did much to stabilize and improve the fortunes of the Scottish Terrier.

The breed standard was actually the work of Vero Shaw, author of *The Dog* first published under his name in the *Field*. It will also be found on page 79, October 1883 issue of the *American Kennel Register* and reads as follows:

Points of the Hard-Haired Scotch Terriers

Skull—(Value 5) proportionately long, slightly domed, and covered with short, hard hair about ¾ in. long, or less. It should not be quite flat, as there should be a sort of stop, or drop, between the eyes.

Muzzle—(5) very powerful, and gradually tapering toward the nose, which should always be black and of good size. The jaws should be perfectly level, and the teeth square, though the nose projects somewhat over the mouth, which gives the impression of the upper jaw being longer than the under one.

Eyes—(5) set wide apart, of a dark brown or hazel color; small, piercing, very bright, and rather sunken.

Ears—(10) very small, prick or half-prick (the former is preferable), but never drop. They should also be sharp-pointed, and the hair on them should not be long, but velvety, and they should not be cut. The ears should be free from any fringe at the top.

Neck—(5) short, thick and muscular; strongly set over sloping shoulders.

Chest—(5) broad in comparison to the size of the dog, and proportionately deep.

Body—(10) of moderate length, not so long as a Skye's, and rather flat-sided; but well ribbed up and exceedingly strong in hindquarters.

Legs and Feet—(10) both fore and hindlegs should be short, and very heavy in bone, the former being straight, or slightly bent, and well set on under the body, as the Scotch terrier should not be out at elbows.

The hocks should be bent, and the thighs very muscular; and the feet strong, small, and thickly covered with short hair, the forefeet being larger than the hind ones, and well let down on the ground.

The Tail—(2½), which is never cut, should be about 7 in. long, carried with a slight bend, and often gaily.

The Coat—(20) should be rather short (about 2 in.), intensely hard and wiry in texture, and very dense all over the body.

Size—(10) about 14 lb.–18 lb. for a dog, 13 lb.–17 lb. for a bitch.

Colors—(2½) steel or iron gray, brindle, black, red, wheaten, and even yellow or mustard color. It may be observed that mustard, black, and red are not usually so popular as the other colors. White markings are most objectionable.

General Appearance—(10) the face should wear a very sharp, bright and active expression, and the head should be carried up. The dog (owing to the shortness of his coat) should appear to be higher on the leg than he really is; but at the same time, he should look compact, and possessed of great muscle in his hindquarters. In fact, a Scotch terrier, though essentially a terrier, cannot be too powerfully put together. He should be from about

Teaser, an early winner.

Scotch Terriers at work. By James Robertson, 1835.

9 in. to 12 in. in height, and should have the appearance of being higher on the hind legs than on the fore.

Faults

Muzzle either under or over hung.
Eyes large or light-colored.
Ears large, round at the points, or drop. It is also a fault if they are too heavily covered with hair.
Coat. Any silkiness, wave, or tendency to curl is a serious blemish, as is also an open coat.
Size. Specimens over 18 lb. should not be encouraged.

Having read the above standard, and considered the same, I am prepared to express my approval of it, and will give it my support when breeding or judging hard-haired Scotch Terriers.
David Adams, Murrygate, Dundee.
J. A. Adamson, Ashley Road, Aberdeen.
Alex Barclay, Springbank Terrace, Aberdeen.
H. Blomfield, Lakenham, Norfolk.
James Burr. M.D., Aberdeen.
J. C. Carrick, Carlisle.
John Cumming, Bridge of Don, Aberdeen.
W. D. Findlay, Portlethen, Aberdeenshire.
Wm. Frazer, Jasmine Terrace, Aberdeen.
John L. Grainger, Summer Street, Aberdeen.
D. J. Thomson Gray, South George Street, Dundee
Pat Henderson, Tally Street, Dundee.
Mary Laing, Granton Lodge, Aberdeen.
P. R. Latham, Tween Terrace, Bridge of Allan.
H. J. Ludlow, St. Giles Plain, Norwich

Gray's book elaborates upon the standard and offers some additional important comments. For example, "An all-white colour is much prized; but white markings which often appear on the forefeet and chest, are very objectionable." This is another indication that dogs of the West Highland strain were present and acceptable as Scottish Terriers in the ring. However, the early fanciers most valued the "sandy" color for it has been said that "no other word is so expressive of colour, and will readily be understood by all Scotsmen." In spite of all the "points of beauty" insisted upon by fanciers, the working man ignored them if the dog could work, if not, he was a "guid-for-naething useless brute."

Of considerable interest to students of the breed's development is the description of a Scotch Terrier offered by Hugh Dalziel of Kirkcudbrigdeshire and author of *British Dogs*. He gave it from memory and referred to dogs known to him in his childhood, about 1840. He described the "true" Scotch Terrier as follows:

9

AMERICAN
Kennel Register

Copyright, 1884. Entered at the Post Office as Second Class Matter.

PUBLISHED BY THE FOREST AND STREAM PUBLISHING CO., 39 & 40 PARK ROW.

P. O. Box 2832. **New York, August, 1884.** VOL. II—No. 8.

SCOTCH TERRIERS.
Miss Mary Laing's "Foxie" and Mr. J. A. Adamson's "Roger Rough."

American Kennel Register title page, August 1884.

A stoutly built dog, leggy in comparison with the Skye, or Dandie, varying in size, as all breeds little cared for do, but easily to be kept near to a standard of 15 pounds to 18 pounds, which I hold to be the most useful for a working "varmint" dog, even if he is not wanted to go to ground.

The head rather short and the skull somewhat round, the jaws being strong and also short—more or less bearded; long, lean punishing jaw, as the phrase goes, is a modern feature in terriers of any variety, and the idea is often carried to great excess. The eyes bright and keen, piercing through short, shaggy hair. The ears small, covered with soft, short hair, semi-erect, falling over at the tip. The neck short and strong.

The chest moderately deep, ribs strong, the back ones fairly developed; the back short as a fox-terrier's with strong loins and good muscular square buttocks. The legs stout, well covered with hard hair, stifles only moderately bent; forelegs straight, all covered with hard hair; the feet compact and hard in the sole and the claws strong. The tail, if undocked, 8 in. to 10 in. long, brushlike, not fringed, the covering being hard hair. The prevailing colour sandy, sometimes a dark grizzle, and I have occasionally seen them brindled. The coat hard and very dense, from one inch or rather less than two inches in length at the greatest.

Dalziel's description is of utmost interest when compared to the first accepted standard of the Scottish Terrier. The head differs since it appears that Dalziel describes the head of a Cairn or West Highland more accurately than that of a Scottish Terrier. The tail is relatively long and sometimes docked while the standard emphasized "never cut." The most interesting comment in Dalziel's description, however, is the suggestion, "the back short as a fox-terrier's." The standard suggests that the body be of "moderate length." Both specifications note the ears to be small and while Dalziel's requires a semi-erect ear, the standard prefers a prick ear.

Since the breed had never really become autonomous until after the standard was adopted, it is understandable that few dogs of merit were recorded before that time. Several, however, did gain mention and these were complimented by Shaw in his article that included the standard. Woodcuts of Miss Laing's Foxie by Sharp ex Fan, and Mr. Adamson's Roger Rough by Fury ex Flo, were used and these were later the subject of the frontispiece of the August 1884 issue of the *American Kennel Register,* reproduced here. Shaw's article also gives credit to Messrs. Blomfield and Ludlow's, Bonaccord and Splinter II, both good dogs of the day.

Passing to Gray's *The Dogs of Scotland,* published in 1887 (first book on the breed), we find that Ch. Dundee was considered by the author as the best to that time. He was owned by the Gourock

11

Kennels of Messrs. Mackie and McColl of Glasgow. Dundee, the biggest winner of his day, ruled the shows in Scotland and England from about 1884 through 1886. Dundee carried a stud book number of 16,818 and according to Mr. McColl, one of his breeders, was by Dunotter out of Glenorchy, Dunotter being by Bodach out of Callack and Glenorchy by Dunolly ex Calliach (See Gray's *The Dogs of Scotland,* 1887). Dunolly was also considered a very good specimen at the time.

The interesting point of this pedigree set forth in 1887 is the disparity between it and the lineage offered by Mrs. Dorothy Caspersz in her book, *Scottish Terrier Pedigrees,* compiled in 1934. Mrs. Caspersz, who was one of the greatest modern authorities on Scottish Terrier pedigrees, used an entirely different background. According to this later authority, Ch. Dundee was whelped December 30, 1882; bred by Captain Mackie and by Rambler out of Worry, he did not finish his championship until about 1888. Since Gray's book was published in 1887 and perforce had to be prepared before that, it is evident that Dundee finished before 1887. The major deviation however is found in the breeding, where entirely different parents are given. Mrs. Caspersz undoubtedly followed the same authority as C. J. Davies who in his book *The Scottish Terrier* (1906) said "the statement made in *Dogs of Scotland* (1891 ed.) that the bitch, Glenorchy became the dam of Ch. Dundee is incorrect." Why it is incorrect he does not say. In any event, the "error" was carried forward in Gray's book from the 1887 edition into the 1891 edition without apparent comment from the many readers. Whatever the answer, this situation points to the many stumbling blocks and pitfalls that confront later authors who wish to present accurate findings. Suffice it to say that Dundee was the third Scottish Terrier to gain the title, according to Mrs. Caspersz, having been preceded by Syringa and the aforementioned Dunolly, bitch and dog, respectively. Mr. McColl writes interestingly of "Old Syringa," which he says liked the water and had been seen to stand "in a burn for hours, her head and neck only being above water, watching a rat hole in the embankment."

Some interesting measurements of the two dogs Dunolly and Dundee together with those of a bitch Glengogo, all of the 1880's, are found in *Dogs of Scotland:*

12

RT I,   **PRICE ONE SHILLING.**

THE
OGS OF SCOTLAND:

THEIR VARIETIES, HISTORY, BREEDING, EXHIBITION, AND MANAGEMENT.

ILLUSTRATED.

By D. J. THOMSON GRAY ("Whinstone").

Editor of " The Scottish Fancier and Rural Gazette."

DUNDEE: JAMES P. MATHEW & CO., 17 and 19 COWGATE.
LONDON: L. UPCOTT GILL, "THE BAZAAR" OFFICE, STRAND, W.C.
EDINBURGH AND GLASGOW: JOHN MENZIES & CO.

1887.

Cover of the book, *Dogs of Scotland,* 1887.

	Dunolly	*Dundee*	*Glengogo*
Occipital bone to eye	4⅞ inches	5 inches	4½ inches
Inner corner of eye to nose	3 "	3 "	3 "
Shoulder to root of tail	15 "	15 "	16 "
Length of tail	—	7 "	7½ "
Round muzzle	6⅞ "	7¼ "	6½ "
" skull	11½ "	11¾ "	11½ "
" chest	17¾ "	17½ "	17½ "
" loin	14¾ "	15 "	15 "
" arm	4⅞ "	5 "	4½ "
Height	10 "	10 "	10 "

These measurements indicate that the old Scots were considerably longer in back than present day breed representatives. Surprisingly enough, however, the head measurements indicate substantial length, about seven and one-half to eight inches, while the skull was rather broad in comparison to the muzzle; which should have given the dogs a rather snipy outlook on the Cairn order. Since these dogs weighed from 16 to 18 pounds and had about the same height at the withers as today's specimens it is apparent that the bodies were shallower and the dogs more up on the leg in order to maintain the weight-height proportions. Also the bodies were not as full, and had more of a flattish side appearance of the type now seen on Westies and Cairns.

This was the hectic history of the breed during the long and harried quest for recognition. Known and shown under many names, the breed finally reached its goal with the designation Scottish Terrier which still is accepted, used and respected by all.

He was a gash an' faithfu' tyke
As ever lap a sheugh or dyke.
His honest sonsie, baws'nt face
Ay gat him friends in ilka place.
ROBERT BURNS

3

Scottish Terrier Bloodlines

ALL Scottish Terriers descended from common blood, but through the years certain dogs have exerted more than their share of influence on the breed. This is indicated by repeated notice of a given sire or sires in the pedigrees of quality dogs.

Because of the excellent pedigree delineations published by Mrs. Dorothy Caspersz (British) and Dr. Kirk (American), together with numerous articles by Alice Exworthy on the bloodlines of the breed, there is little use of going into an exhaustive exposition of the subject here. Those who have a genuine interest may trace families and pedigrees in great detail by referring to these expansive efforts. However, to offer a perspective of the immensity of the task, Miss Exworthy has prepared some vitally interesting charts that show the influence of certain dogs together with a compilation of champion American progeny of the main line of descent. This material will be found at the end of this chapter. It is hoped that this exposition will whet the appetites of all to probe further into the study of background, an interesting and useful adventure if one is to progress in the art of breeding Scottish Terriers.

15

Landseer's Comical Dogs, 1836. Note early Scotch Terrier.

Caricature by Frank Paton, 1893, showing an early Scottish Terrier.

Basically, there are two lines of descent which are accountable for the great majority of all Scottish Terrier champions. The first is the Ch. Dundee line, the second the Ch. Alister line. According to Miss Exworthy the first of these two male strains produced a total to date of 142 American champions, while the second is responsible for the amazing total of 1,674 American champions. The Dundee line is of disputed origin as noted in the preceding chapter. It may have begun with the dog, Bright, as Mrs. Caspersz suggests, or it may have come from a different origin in accordance with the early book, *The Dogs of Scotland*. In either case, starting with Ch. Dundee, the blood passes down through such dogs as Seafield Rascal, Laindon Lockhart, Ch. Albourne Beetle, etc. Thereafter the influence weakens and today the line is of minor importance when compared to the Alister branch of the family tree. This, beyond dispute, came from the aforementioned Bright through Bonaccord to Rambler which begot Ch. Ailsa II, Ch. Glengogo and possibly Ch. Dundee. Rambler's best known son was Ch. Alister which came from the bitch Ch. Lorna Doone sired by the aforementioned Dundee.

Alister sired many great dogs in the early days of the breed's development including the first American champion, Tiree; Ch. Kildee, Ch. Mirza, etc. However, the most illustrious of his sons was a dog named Whinstone, probably after the breed authority D. J. Thomson Gray who wrote under the pen-name "Whinstone." This dog's direct male line was propagated through Heather Prince to Claymore, sire of Ch. Claymore Defender. He in turn sired Ch. Seafield Blossom, winner of 26 Challenge Certificates, thus tying the record previously held by Ch. Bonnaccord Nora; Ch. Tighnavarloch, J. Dean Willis' great and productive stud Ch. Bapton Norman (a black with an extremely short body for the day) which sired six English and ten American champions and also had the distinction in 1912 of siring more litters in the United States than any other American or British stud; and last but by no means least, Bapton Noble, a brother to Norman, whose great grandson, Ch. Laindon Luminary, became a key dog in the Alister line.

Luminary produced a number of champion get but it was his son Albourne Joe that carried on through a son, Ch. Albourne Adair. This dog was prolific as a stud but two of his get will always be remembered because they were the fountainheads of bloodlines that

17

Ch. Dundee, the third recorded British titleholder.

Skittles, an early Scottish Terrier of about 1882.

are of greatest importance today. These two dogs were Ch. Albourne Scot and Ch. Albourne MacAdair. The first produced Ch. Albourne Barty through a union with Albourne Jennifer. Barty became one of the great dogs of the breed; he was whelped on September 17, 1925 and his breeder was the master of Albourne Kennels, Mr. A. G. Cowley. More will be offered about this great dog and his influence upon present day bloodlines later.

The second, Ch. Albourne MacAdair, sired a dog named Harton Highlander which in turn produced the incomparable Ch. Heather Necessity (whelped on September 14, 1927). The facts leading up to this event are of considerable interest since they demonstrate that all great dogs do not necessarily come from carefully planned breedings. It seems that a Mr. Herbert Bains, known as a breeder of several Terrier breeds, bought a bitch named Harton Holdfast. She was said to have been a good one, well bred but no flyer. He showed her nonetheless at Manchester with indifferent success. While at the show he discussed her future with William McCandlish, the famous judge and a good breeder, who advised that she be mated. Since she was in season at the time and since Ch. Albourne MacAdair had won the breed on the day and was available, the mating was arranged on the spot. The litter produced five puppies including one dog. He was named Harton Highlander and was later sold to Sam Wilson, a breeder and judge who held the dog at stud. Highlander was later bred to a biggish bitch of good quality named Skerne Scotch Lass and the result was Necessity, originally named "Snooker's Double."

Robert Chapman ultimately acquired the dog that turned out to be one of the all-time greats, a 20-certificate winner and the sire of some 18 English and 12 American champions together with a host of other fine Scottish Terriers. Chapman, after buying Necessity, demonstrated a breeder's instinct and purchased Skerne Scotch Lass. She too proved to be an excellent investment as will be seen.

It is interesting to observe that many of Necessity's best offspring came from bitches closely line-bred to Ch. Albourne Barty. This is understandable upon study of Necessity's pedigree, which defies all the precepts of good breeding practice and presents a host of unrelated ancestors in a pedigree devoid of any semblance of line breeding. In spite of his background, Necessity had something that few dogs own, that illusive quality, "prepotency." Many will say that

19

there is no such thing. On the other hand, Necessity was bred to many bitches that, according to principle, should not nick because of background, but these same bitches produced offspring that made history.

Take for example, Ch. Lonkley Larkspur, Ch. Heather Enchantress, Ch. Heather Fashion Hint and Ch. Ortley Elegance, to name a few; all were by Necessity but in no case can a common ancestor be found within the first five generations of their pedigrees, which certainly is contrary to all accepted principles of line breeding. The fact remains, Necessity had so much quality, so much to give, that he carried over in spite of the bloodlines. No one can ever say that this dog lacked prepotency because the record proves the statement false.

In addition to the above noted offspring, Ch. Heather Necessity was responsible for such dogs as Ch. Rookery Adair, Ch. Heather Essential of Hitofa, Ch. Sandhey's Silvertip, Ch. Rouken Rogue, Ch. Heather Ambition, Ch. Albourne Royalist and Ch. Crich Certainty of Deephaven. Certainly these names are widely known today as each did his share to bring the breed to its present position. Ch. Heather Essential of Hitofa, exported to the United States, sired among others Ch. Hillcote Laddie which in turn sired some 15 titleholders including Ch. Deephaven Warspite, a great show dog that led the breed in the United States in 1945 and 1946.

Ch. Heather Ambition did his part to maintain the family's blood by siring among others Ch. Ortley Pilot, Ch. Heather Beau Ideal, Ch. Heather Independence (whose great-grandson, Ch. Shieling's Signature, sired 22 champions and in addition won the Garden in 1945) and Bradthorn Banker, sire of the great Ch. Bradthorn Bullion, one of the stalwarts of the once famous Relgalf Kennels.

Ch. Heather Fashion Hint, Necessity's most prolific son, sired 14 English and 26 American titleholders. These included Ch. Radical of Rookes, Eng. Ch. Masterpiece of Rookes, Ch. Dandy of Docken, Ch. Walsing Wallet, and Eng. Ch. Heather Realisation, which proved to be a prepotent stud with such get as Ch. Walsing Warrant of Marlu, the grandsire of Ch. Deephaven Red Seal (sire of 24 U.S. Chs. including Ch. Goldfinder's Admiral and Ch. Marlu Clincher), Heather Benefactor and Heather Herald. This last named dog produced Kennelgarth Blacksmith; he was responsible for Reanda Roderic, the sire of Eng. Ch. Reanda Roger Rough that

20

Ch. Ems Chevalier, whelped 1904.

Ch. Heworth Rascal, painted by John Emms, 1902.

Ch. Bonaccord Peggy.

produced many good ones including the Barberry Knowe Kennel's Ch. Walsing Wild Winter.

Heather Benefactor, by Realisation, sired Walsing Wizard which in turn fathered two great sons, Walsing Watchtower and Westpark Masterpiece. The first of these is behind such widely known winners as Ch. Walsing Lomond Lancer of Hampton Hill, Ch. Glendoune Gauntlet, Ch. Reanda Rheola, Ch. Bardeen Boy Blue, Ch. Wyrebury Woodnymph and Ch. Glendoune Gaytime (dam of five champions), to name a few. Masterpiece was even more prolific, with Eng. Chs. Roskeen Banner, Westpark Masterman, Westpark Achievement, Am. Ch. Trevone Tartar of Bothkennar, a great sire in America, and the redoubtable Eng. Ch. Westpark Rio Grande. The last named sired 21 American titleholders in addition to Eng. Ch. Westpark Romeo, father of the great Ch. Westpark Derriford Baffie which proved to be an outstanding producer both in England and the United States. Another great and prolific son of Westpark Rio Grande, the dog Ch. Wyrebury Wrangler, produced three great bitches in Chs. Wyrebury Water Gypsy, dam of five champions, Niddbank Ladybird, Walsing Winoway and the dogs, Ch. Crescent Hill Ace O'Spades and Ch. Wyrebury Wilwyn. The latter fathered Ch. Special Edition, sire of Ch. Scotvale Sunshine and Ch. Wycheworth Wizard, among others.

To enlarge further upon the progeny and family of Ch. Heather Necessity would amount to dedicating this book to his achievements, since the list is never ending. Many great dogs have not been mentioned and many tie-ins with present day winners have not been noted. Suffice it to say, Ch. Heather Necessity was one of the greatest of Scottish Terrier sires and his efforts undoubtedly were responsible for a major part of the success of the breed as we know it today. In fact few pedigrees can be extended without noting Necessity in the background. Possibly this may be explained by discussing the dog briefly.

Necessity has been described as a "new" type Scotsman for the day. He represented a transition between the old and the new types. It has been said that never before had a Scottish Terrier had such length of head, compactness of body and straightness of leg. He was lower to the ground than his forebears, owned a short back and a short, inverted carrot-shaped tail that was always carried stiffly erect, even when the dog was sitting. Some said that he could never do the

The great Ch. Heather Necessity.

```
                                                          Albourne Joe
                                     Eng. Ch. Albourne Adair
                                                          Eng. Ch. Albourne Dinkie
                   Eng. Ch. Albourne MacAdair
                                                          Ruminantly Rocket
                                     Albourne Matron
                                                          Albourne Snap
  Harton Highlander
                                                          Biddick Boy
                                     Loyal Boy
                                                          Loyal Ann
                   Harton Holdfast
                                                          Claymore Conqueror
                                     Glenbrae Betty
                                                          Monnyruy
ENG. CH. HEATHER NECESSITY
(Whelped 9/14/1927                                        Romany Monk
Breeder: Mr. Walker)                 Ornsay Chieftain
                                                          Tantallon Vixen
                   Eng. Ch. Ornsay Brave
                                                          Misty Morning
                                     Eng. Ch. Bellstane Lassie
                                                          Meadow Lass
  Skerne Scotch Lass
                                                          Romany Bishop
                                     Abertay Aristocrat
                                                          Abertay Darkie
                   Meg
                                                          Abertay Brigadier
                                     Fanny
                                                          Tattle
```

Ch. Heather Fashion Hint.

```
                                                        Eng. Ch. Albourne Adair
                                        Eng. Ch. Albourne MacAdair
                                                        Albourne Matron
                    Harton Highlander
                                                        Loyal Boy
                                        Harton Holdfast
                                                        Glenbrae Betty
        Eng. Ch. Heather Necessity
                                                        Ornsay Chieftain
                                        Eng. Ch. Ornsay Brave
                                                        Eng. Ch. Bellstane Lassie
                    Skerne Scotch Lass
                                                        Abertay Aristocrat
                                        Meg
                                                        Fanny
ENG. CH. HEATHER FASHION HINT
(Whelped 6/2/1929                                       Eng. Ch. Laurieston Leaper
Breeder: J. Donald)                     Eng. Ch. Laurieston Landseer
                                                        Garnqueen Gertrude
                    Laurieston Ladeside
                                                        Garnock Bertie
                                        Carmel Kate
                                                        Carmel Betty
        Innerkip Irma
                                                        Ornsay Ranger
                                        Garnock Bob
                                                        Garnock Jean
                    Innerkip Nanette
                                                        Ornsay Bannock
                                        Garnock Ura
                                                        Garnock Kate
```

work for which the breed was intended and many decried the radical change in type that this jet black dog presented. Nevertheless most of his critics bred their bitches to him in hope of obtaining something that would look, produce and win as he did. From his list of accomplishments it is easy to say that many of these breeders were not disappointed in the results. Necessity was surely one of the greatest studs the breed has ever known.

Returning to Ch. Albourne Barty, we find that while he was not as prolific as Necessity he nevertheless sired some great dogs and a host of important bitches that helped establish quality and wide breed recognition. In fact the Barty line is equally as important as that of Necessity. He sired among others the brothers Ch. Albourne Brigand, in whose line we find Ch. Blanart Barrister, sire of some 14 U.S. Champions, and Ch. Albourne Reveller, both out of that great brood bitch Albourne Annie Laurie. Reveller gained fame by producing Ch. Heather Reveller of Sporran, a great winner in this country and a dog that gained an excellent press because of his record and the prominence of his owner, the late S. S. Van Dine. Surveying Heather Reveller's pedigree we see that the dog was out of Skerne Scotch Lass, which was also the dam of Ch. Heather Necessity. Here we find that Chapman's foresight in quickly buying the bitch after he acquired Necessity was a very smart and useful move. In Reveller the two branches of the Albourne Adair blood were reunited and the effort proved to be quite productive for he was not only a great show dog but a good sire. Albourne Binge Result, another son of Albourne Reveller, was responsible for one of the all-time show greats in Eng. Ch. Albourne Admiration. This dog was a 20-certificate winner and the only Scottie to tie Necessity's record to that time. He was the result of a half-brother–half-sister breeding since his dam, Elspeth Judy, was also sired by Reveller. Thus the blood behind Admiration had a heavy Barty influence blended through both sides of his genealogy. Admiration founded a line that extended through his grandson, Ch. Malgren Juggernaut to Ch. Walsing Winning Trick of Edgerstoune. Winning Trick was the top winning Scottie in America during 1949 and was the winner of the Garden in 1950. He sired 23 titleholders in this country including Ch. Edgerstoune Troubadour, sire of 35 champions, one of the greatest of modern-day studs. Troubadour's name appears in the pedigrees of such dogs as Ch. Rebel Raider, Ch. Fulluvit Festive

25

Ch. Edgerstoune Troubadour, painted by C. C. Fawcett.

```
                                           Albourne Samson
                               Malgen Juggernaut
                                           Malgen Jerusha
                  Walsing War Parade
                                           Walsing Winebibber
                               Walsing Wishing
                                           Walsing Wishbone
         Ch. Walsing Winning Trick of Edgerstoune
                                           Walsing Wizard
                               Walsing Watchmaker
                                           Glencannie Sonia
                  Walsing Whymper
                                           Hillhead Ambassador
                               Walsing Wildwind
                                           Kilette
CH. EDGERSTOUNE TROUBADOUR
(Whelped 7/13/1949                                   Ch. Ortley Ambassador of E.
Breeder: Mrs. J.G. Winant)      Ch. Heather Resolution of E.
                                                     Desco Dream
                  Ch. Heather Commodore of Edgerstoune
                                           Walsing Winebibber
                               Walsing Wishing
                                           Walsing Wishbone
         Ch. Edgerstoune Orphan
                                           Ortley Matador
                               Ch. Ortley Ambassador of E.
                                           Ortley Bibby
                  Edgerstoune Ophelia
                                           Heather Beau Ideal
                               Ch. Heather Ophelia of E.
                                           Gaisgill Vanity
```

Fling, Ch. Rebel Invader and Ch. Fulluvit Fieldmouse, among others. In addition to his siring ability, the dog won some of the largest shows in the country during his long and fruitful ring career, a worthy son of the great Winning Trick.

While the foregoing has been limited in a large degree to the accomplishments of selected stud dogs from two main lines of descent, several outstanding bitches of the past have also been mentioned. Admittedly, there are many, many more, but because of the limited number of offspring that any one bitch is capable of producing, the importance of the distaff side of the pedigree is difficult to document with proper credit to the many that have contributed to the success of the breed. For these reasons, no extensive digression into the female's part in the breed's development will be offered. However, two bitches from the present day stand out so completely that they bear mention among the all-time greats since each one has productively outdistanced all of their forebears. These are Ch. Blanart Barcarolle and Ch. Gaidoune Gorgeous Hussy.

Barcarolle's pedigree offers an interesting blend of producing blood. Her sire, Cabrach Caliper, goes back through the tail male line to the aforementioned Ch. Albourne Barty with a double cross of Ch. Heather Necessity included. Her dam, Hi-Scott's Clipper, goes through Ch. Heather Realisation to Necessity; whereby both sides trace back directly to Ch. Albourne Adair. With such a background it is little wonder that this bitch did so well. When bred to Diehard Toby she produced Ch. Blanart Barrister. A glance at Barrister's pedigree will show that Toby represents a double cross of Diehard Fashion blood, the grandsire of Barcarolle. Thus three of the four great-grandsires of Barrister are Diehard Fashion, which surely intensifies the line. Ch. Blanart Bewitching, a great show bitch and winner of two Garden Terrier groups, has strong Barcarolle blood, as she was by a son and out of a granddaughter of Barcarolle's. Thus, it is apparent that good breeding tells and intensification of prepotent blood more frequently than not leads to success.

Possibly Barcarolle's best known son was Ch. Blanart Bolero, sire of 20 U.S. titleholders, which was sired by Ch. Barberry Knowe Rascal. Rascal was a good nick with Barcarolle and represented a double cross of Ch. Albourne Barty blood to further intensify this prepotent line. In all Barcarolle produced ten champion offspring.

27

Ch. Blanart Barcarolle.

```
                                                         Cabrach Reek
                                      Ch. Cabrach Calibar
                                                         Cabrach Cheetah
                    Diehard Fashion
                                                         Heather Romancer
                                      Diehard Viola II
                                                         Diehard Viola
   Cabrach Caliper
                                                         Ch. Cabrach Tanner
                                      Cabrach Poker
                                                         Cabrach Classic
                    Cabrach Dot
                                                         Ch. Cabrach Calibar
                                      Cabrach Glamor
                                                         Tower Hill Glamor
CH. BLANART BARCAROLLE
(Whelped 6/20/1947                                       Eng. Ch. Heather Fashion Hint
Breeder: Blanche E. Reeg)       Eng. Ch. Heather Realisation
                                                         Gaisgill Sylvia
                    Flornell Real Fashion
                                                         Eng. Ch. Heather Fashion Hint
                                      Bradthorn Black Berry
                                                         Arns Ruby
   Hi-Scott's Clipper
                                                         Ch. Bradthorn Bullion
                                      Blanart Bomber
                                                         Hi-Scott's Penny Wise
                    Black Eyed Susan IX
                                                         Dalreoch Resounder
                                      Franfield's Sweet Heather
                                                         Franfield's Merrymaker
```

Ch. Gaidoune Gorgeous Hussy again lends proof that "blood will tell." She is by Ch. Rebel Raider ex Ch. Glendoune Gaibonnie. Raider was by Troubadour bred to his half-sister, Marlu Cute Trick. Thus, Raider offered a double cross of Walsing Winning Trick on the sire's side to team up with Walsing Watchtower blood on the dam's, which intensified the influence of Necessity. This again proves that line breeding is the surest means of producing good stock. Hussy, when bred to Ch. Todhill's Cinnamon Bear, whelped top show dogs on two different occasions. The first was Ch. Gaidoune Great Bear, one of the great show Terriers of the time, and the second, Ch. Gaidoune Grin and Bear It, is presently winning well. These of course are but two of her champion whelps, now numbering twelve. The twelve titleholders came from four litters by three different studs. The reason for the success of the Cinnamon Bear breeding is not surprising since he was by Ch. Friendship Farm Diplomat ex Todhill's Beeswing and is line bred to Necessity on both sides.

This short discourse on the accomplishments of two great bitches could be extended to include many more worthy females. In each instance however, it would be found that strong line breeding is and always has been the surest way to produce quality animals. In the chapter on breeding an explanation of the reasons for this statement will be found.

In order to consolidate the records of stud dogs and producing matrons, a listing of all males that have produced ten or more American champions and all bitches that have whelped five or more American champions follows. Unquestionably, other Scotties have had a serious impact upon the success of the breed but listing of dogs with lesser records would be prodigious and unwieldy.

Dams of Five or More Champions

Ch. Gaidoune Gorgeous Hussy   12
(Ch. Rebel Raider x Ch. Glendoune Gaibonnie)
Ch. Blanart Barcarolle   10
(Cabrach Caliper x Hi-Scott's Clipper)
Blanart Bit of Bitters   7
(Ch. Blanart Barrister x Blanart Bittersweet)
Ch. Fran-Jean's Bridie Mollie   7
(Eng. Am. Ch. Glendoune Gauntlet x Ch. Glendoune Gesture)
Ch. Garthright's Dark Sorcery   7
(Ch. Carnation Coolie x Kinclaven Golden Earrings)
Ch. Shieling's Gracious   7
(Ch. Walsing Whirlwind x Ch. Shieling's Winsome)

Ch. Gaidoune Gorgeous Hussy.

```
                                                  Walsing War Parade
                                    Ch. Walsing Winning Trick of Edgerstoune
                                                  Walsing Whymper
                    Ch. Edgerstoune Troubadour
                                                  Ch. Heather Commodore of E.
                                    Ch. Edgerstoune Orphan
                                                  Edgerstoune Ophelia
      Ch. Rebel Raider
                                                  Walsing War Parade
                                    Ch. Walsing Winning Trick of Edgerstoune
                                                  Walsing Whymper
                    Marlu Cute Trick
                                                  Ch. Deephaven Warspite
                                    Ch. Marlu Sassy Lassie
                                                  Marlu Miss Heather
CH. GAIDOUNE GORGEOUS HUSSY
(Whelped 9/30/1956                                Eng. Ch. Wyrebury Wonder
Breeder: Helen Gaither)             Eng. Ch. Wyrebury Welldoer
                                                  Wyrebury Dream of Dockindee
                    Glendoune Gay Boy
                                                  Glendoune Galcador
                                    Glendoune Gadabout
                                                  Glendoune Gorgeous
      Ch. Glendoune Gaibonnie
                                                  Rosehall Enchanter
                                    Ch. Rosehall Toryglen Tam O'Shanter
                                                  Rosehall Miranda
                    Eng. Ch. Glendoune Gipsy
                                                  Medwal Midshipman
                                    Rosehall Brocade
                                                  Judy of Tapton
```

Gaisgill Vanity   6
(Eng. Ch. Heather Fashion Hint x Gaisgill Sylvia)
Ch. Glendoune Gwenda   6
(Glendoune Gregor x Glendoune Galina)
Marlu Lady May   6
(Ch. Deephaven Waispite x Marlu Lady Godiva)
Ch. Barberry Knowe Wyndola   5
(Ch. Syl-Von's Sirius x Ch. Hampton Hill Whim)
Blanart Barcee   5
(Ch. Blanart Barrister x Ch. Blanart Barcarolle)
Blanart Barcee's Trey   5
(Ch. Blanart Bartender x Blanart Barcee)
Carnation Dark Lady   5
(Carnation Stowaway x Ch. Carnation Dark Secret)
Ch. Crisscot Canterbury Bell   5
(Ch. Blanart Bartender x Ch. Blanart Bellflower)
Deephaven Dahlia   5
(Ch. Heather Gold Finder x Ch. Deephaven Fair Damsel)
Ch. Edgerstoune Betty   5
(Ch. Edgerstoune Spitfire x Eng. Am. Ch. Heather Benefactress of
Edgerstoune)
Eng. Am. Ch. Glendoune Gaytime   5
(Glendoune Gregor x Glendoune Gaiety)
Glad-Mac's Sally   5
(Ch. Glad-Mac's Sailor of Seaglen x Glad Mac's Stardust)
Eng. Am. Ch. Heather Benefactress of Edgerstoune   5
(Eng. Ch. Heather Realisation x Heather Annie Laurie)
Marlu Cute Trick   5
(Eng. Am. Ch. Walsing Winning Trick of Edgerstoune x Ch. Marlu
Sassy Lassie)
Eng. Am. Ch. Wyrebury Water Gypsy   5
(Eng. Am. Ch. Wyrebury Wrangler x Midnight Dancer)

Sires of Ten or More Champions

Ch. Edgerstoune Troubadour   35
(Eng. Am. Ch. Walsing Winning Trick of Edgerstoune x Ch.
Edgerstoune Orphan)
Eng. Ch. Heather Fashion Hint   26
(Eng. Ch. Heather Necessity x Innerkip Irma)
Ch. Deephaven Red Seal   24
(Ch. Marlu Crusader x Deephaven Mary)
Eng. Am. Ch. Walsing Winning Trick of Edgerstoune   23
(Walsing War Parade x Walsing Whymper)
Ch. Shieling's Signature   22
(Ch. Shieling's Salute x Ch. Shieling's Symphony)
Eng. Ch. Westpark Rio Grande   21
(Westpark Masterpiece x Westpark Bubblin' O'er)
Ch. Blanart Bolero   20
(Ch. Barberry Knowe Rascal x Ch. Blanart Barcarolle)
Ch. Heather Gold Finder   20
(Eng. Ch. Albourne Reveller x Black Lady)
Eng. Am. Ch. Westpark Derriford Baffie   19
(Eng. Ch. Westpark Romeo x Derriford Tam O'Shanter)

31

Ch. Alister won prizes both as a drop-eared and prick-eared exhibit.

Ch. Alister
|
Heather Prince
|
Claymore
|
Ch. Laindon Luminary
|
Albourne Joe
|
Ch. Albourne Adair————Ch. Albourne Scot
| |
Ch. Albourne MacAdair   Ch. Albourne Barty

American champions in line of descent exclusive of those through Barty and Necessity total 142.	Harton Highlander | Ch. Heather Necessity	This line produced 377 American champions. See Chart 4.
Seventeen sons and and their progeny produced 154 champions. See Chart 1.	Eng. Ch. Heather Ambition line produced 286 champion descendants. See Chart 2.	Eng. Ch. Heather Fashion Hint line produced 708 champion descendants. See Chart 3.

American champions descended directly through Eng. Chs. Heather Necessity and Albourne Barty through December, 1965, total 1,537.

American champions descended from Ch. Alister, except for those noted above, through December, 1965, total 142.

American champions tracing their bloodline back to Ch. Alister through December, 1965, total 1,674.

The Male Line of Descent from Ch. Alister to Chs. Albourne Barty and Heather Necessity together with the Producing Records of these two Great Scottish Terriers and their Progeny.

Ch. Special Edition 18
(Eng. Am. Ch. Wyrebury Wilwyn x Wyrebury Watersprite)
Heather Asset 16
(Eng. Ch. Heather Beau Ideal x Heather Honeysuckle)
Ch. Trevone Tartar of Bothkennar 16
(Westpark Masterpiece x Trevone Tres Bonne)
Ch. Glad-Mac's Rolling Stone 15
(Ch. Reimill Radiator x Leading Wren of Seaglen)
Ch. Hillcote Laddie 15
(Eng. Am. Ch. Heather Essential of Hitofa x Henshaw's Gloaming)
Ch. Blanart Barrister 14
(Diehard Toby x Ch. Blanart Barcarolle)
Ch. Gold Finder's Admiral 14
(Ch. Deephaven Red Seal x Gold Finder's Bess)
Ch. Cantie Captivator 13
(Ch. Fran-Jean's Bokor x Ch. Schlenker's Bridget)
Eng. Am. Ch. Wyrebury Wrangler 13
(Eng. Ch. Westpark Rio Grande x Eng. Ch. Wyrebury Maigarth Mazurka)
Eng. Ch. Heather Necessity 12
(Harton Highlander x Skerne Scotch Lass)
Ch. Balachan Agitator 11
(Ch. Cantie Captivator x Ch. Fran-Jean's Bridie Mollie)
Ch. Friendship Farm Diplomat 11
(Ch. Friendship Farm Midshipman x Ch. Marlu Sparkle)
Eng. Am. Ch. Ortley Ambassador of Edgerstoune 11
(Ortley Matador x Ortley Biddy)
Ch. Trojan of Elm Hall 11
(Ch. Edgerstoune Troubadour x Ch. Jane's Grey Wonder)
Ch. Bapton Norman 10
(Eng. Ch. Claymore Defender x Ch. Bonaccord Nora)
Eng. Am. Ch. Bardene Boy Blue 10
(Eng. Ch. Happy Kimbo x Bardene Beau Peep)
Eng. Ch. Crich Certainty of Deephaven 10
(Eng. Ch. Heather Necessity x Crich Coffey)
Ch. Relgalf Rebel Leader 10
(Ch. Gillsie Dictator x Relgalf Rebel Lass)

Chart 1

The Alister–Necessity producing line composed of 17 sons of Eng. Ch. Heather Necessity which, with their descendants, produced a total of 166 American champions through December 1965. The total includes Necessity's twelve champion get.

Eng. & Am. Ch. Heather Essential	57	(includes 49 through his son Ch. Hillcote Laddie)
Eng. Ch. Sandhey's Silvertip	19	(includes 10 through his son Ch. Gaisgill Nosegay)
Firebrand of Ralc	18	(through descendants Lambley Sandboy and My Ideal of Glenview)
Ch. Drum Major of Dochen	16	

33

Eng. Ch. Crich Certainty of Deephaven	12
Glenisla Sterling of Scotsward	6
Heather Romancer of Diehard	5
Sandhey's Solomon	4
Eng. Ch. Tremont	4
Eng. Ch. Albourne Royalist	2
Ch. Flornell Soundfella	2
Ch. Wilfield Necessity	2
Claddoch Necessity of Briarcroft	2
Rosehall Rip	2
Cabrach Carouser	1
Inverdruie Scaramouche	1
Ch. Walnut Aristocrat O'Briarcroft	1

Chart 2

The Alister–Necessity producing line through Necessity's son, Eng. Ch. Heather Ambition, whose eight sons and their descendants produced a total of 286 American champions through December 1965. This total includes Ambition's five champion get.

Eng. Ch. Heather Beau Ideal	87	(includes 67 through his son Heather Asset)
Eng. & Am. Ch. Heather Independence of Edgerstoune	48	(includes 46 through his son Ch. Heather Criterion and his great-grandson Ch. Shieling's Signature)
Ortley Observer	103	(includes 2 by his son Ortley Matador and 101 through his grandson Eng. & Am. Ch. Ortley Ambassador of Edgerstoune)
Ch. Catterthun Model	22	
Bradthorn Banker	16	(includes 15 through his son Ch. Bradthorn Bullion)
Redlington Ian	3	
Eng. Ch. Ortley Pilot	1	
Walnut Royalist	1	

Chart 3

The Alister–Necessity producing line through Necessity's son Eng. Ch. Heather Fashion Hint, whose twenty-one producing sons and their descendants were responsible for a total of 708 American champions through December 1965. This total includes Fashion Hint's 26 champion get.

Eng. Ch. Heather Realisation	544	(includes 43 by Realisation; 33 through Realisation's son, Eng. Ch. Walsing Warrant; 146 through Warrant's

A classic assembly of the Heather stud before the home at Glenboig.

```
                                                        Eng. Ch. Albourne MacAdair
                                   Harton Highlander
                                                        Harton Holdfast
              Eng. Ch. Heather Necessity
                                                        Eng. Ch. Ornsay Brave
                                   Skerne Scotch Lass
                                                        Meg
  Eng. Ch. Heather Fashion Hint
                                                        Eng. Ch. Laurieston Landseer
                                   Laurieston Ladeside
                                                        Carmel Kate
              Innerkip Irma
                                                        Garnook Bob
                                   Innerkip Nanette
                                                        Garnock Ura
ENG. CH. HEATHER REALISATION
(Whelped 1/17/1934                                      Harton Highlander
Breeder: R. Chapman)               Eng. Ch. Heather Necessity
                                                        Skerne Scotch Lass
              Eng. Ch. Sandheys Silvertip
                                                        Albourne MacAndy
                                   Albourne Annie Laurie
                                                        Eng. Ch. Mischief of Docken
  Gaisgill Sylvia
                                                        Albourne MacAndy
                                   Marksman of Docken
                                                        Eng. Ch. Mischief of Docken
              Gaisgill Ling
                                                        Eng. Ch. Laindon Lancelot
                                   Crogsland Bess
                                                        Crogsland Queen
```

grandson Ch. Deephaven Red Seal together with other descendants as follows:

Ch. Trevone Tartar of Bothkennar	43
Ch. Cantie Captivator	27
Ch. Reimill Radiator	9
Ch. Glad Mac's Rolling Stone	16
Eng. Ch. Westpark Rio Grande	28
Ch. Wyrebury Wrangler	45
Ch. Special Edition	26
Eng. Ch. Westpark Romeo and his son Ch. Westpark Derriford Baffie	43
Rosehall Enchanter	76

together with an additional 9 through the efforts of Heath'er Benefactor, Walsing Wizard and Westpark Masterpiece and their descendants)

Eng. & Am. Ch. Radical of Rookes	51	(includes 33 through Ch. Relgalf Rebel Leader and 6 through Ch. Relgalf Rebel Dictator)
Eng. & Am. Ch. Walsing Wallet	16	
Ch. Hallcrest Black Lancer	14	
St. Margaret Subaltern	10	
Eng. Ch. Masterpiece of Rookes	10	
Ripper of Rookes	6	
Ch. Hitofa Chief	5	
Eng. Ch. Dandy of Docken	4	
Eng. & Am. Ch. Rakish of Rookes	3	
Ch. Bothkennar Fashion Plate	4	
Glentworth Chic	2	
Cabrach Carnac	2	
Ch. Walnut Dandy	2	
Walsing Welldoer	2	
Ch. Ortley Michael	1	
Ch. Rosehall Roamer	1	
Ch. Rosehall Scotch Pickings	1	
Maccrystal Beau Brummel	1	
Ch. Hallcrest Buccaneer	1	
Ch. Heather Premier	1	

Chart 4

The Alister–Albourne Barty producing line composed of two branches that were established by Barty's sons, the brothers Eng. Ch. Albourne Reveller and Eng. Ch. Albourne Brigand which, with their descendants, produced a total of

36

377 American champions through December 1965. This total includes Barty's five champion get and two additional champion descendants.

Eng. Ch. Albourne Reveller 186 (includes descendants through his son Albourne Binge Result as follows:

Eng. Ch. Albourne Admiration	1
Eng. Ch. Malgren Juggernaut	10
Eng. & Am. Ch. Walsing Winning Trick of Edgerstoune	43
and Ch. Edgerstoune Troubadour	119)

74 (through his son Ch. Heather Reveller of Sporran including 64 through a grandson Ch. Diehard Reveller)

42 (through his son Ch. Heather Gold Finder)

Eng. Ch. Albourne Brigand 68

```
                                                    Eng. Ch. Laindon Luminary
                                   Albourne Joe
                                                    Eng. Ch. Laindon Lightsome
                   Eng. Ch. Albourne Adair
                                                    Eng. Ch. Albourne Beetle
                                   Eng. Ch. Albourne Dinkie
                                                    Albourne Young Gyp
      Eng. Ch. Albourne Scot
                                                    Eng. Ch. Ruminantly Raven
                                   Binnie Boy
                                                    Abertay Maud
                   Fragments
                                                    Baltimore
                                   Florida
                                                    Albourne Finesse
ENG. CH. ALBOURNE BARTY
(Whelped 9/17/1925                                  Abertay Brigadier
Breeder: A. G. Cowley)      Eng. Ch. Laindon Luminary
                                                    Abertay Luna
                   Eng. Ch. Laindon Lumen
                                                    Claymore Commandant
                                   Eng. Ch. Laindon Lightsome
                                                    Abertay Bliss
      Albourne Jennifer
                                                    Eng. Ch. Albourne Adair
                                   Eng. Ch. Albourne Adonis
                                                    Albourne Matron
                   Albourne Free Love
                                                    Eng. Ch. Albourne Adair
                                   Eng. Ch. Albourne Alisa
                                                    Albourne Huffy
```

Pedigree of Eng. Ch. Albourne Barty.

```
                                                    Eng. Ch. Albourne Adair
                                   Eng. Ch. Albourne MacAdair
                                                    Albourne Matron
                   Harton Highlander
                                                    Loyal Boy
                                   Harton Holdfast
                                                    Glenbrae Betty
      Eng. Ch. Heather Necessity
                                                    Ornsay Chieftain
                                   Eng. Ch. Ornsay Brave
                                                    Eng. Ch. Bellstane Lassie
                   Skerne Scotch Lass
                                                    Abertay Aristocrat
                                   Meg
                                                    Fanny
ENG. CH. HEATHER AMBITION
(Whelped 9/30/1931                                  Eng. Ch. Albourne Adair
Breeder: Mr. and Mrs. A. M. Robb)   Eng. Ch. Albourne Scot
                                                    Fragments
                   Eng. Ch. Albourne Barty
                                                    Eng. Ch. Laindon Lumen
                                   Albourne Jennifer
                                                    Albourne Free Love
      Eng. Ch. Albourne Romance
                                                    Eng. Ch. Albourne Adair
                                   Eng. Ch. Albourne MacAdair
                                                    Albourne Matron
                   Albourne Athene
                                                    Eng. Ch. Albourne Adair
                                   Albourne Unity
                                                    Albourne Mode
```

Pedigree of Eng. Ch. Heather Ambition.

4

British Breeders
and Kennels

In the preceding chapter on early history and bloodlines many famous breeders have been mentioned because of dogs they owned or bred which became landmarks in the progress of the Scottish Terrier. This chapter will enlarge to some extent upon the breeders and kennels in Britain from the beginning of the breed's recognition until the present, and will also attempt to offer some interesting sidelights to supplement previous information.

As designated heretofore, it all began with the early recognition of the breed in the 1800's when such men as Captain Mackie, co-owner with Mr. McColl of the famous Gourock Kennels in Glasgow; John Adamson of Aberdeen, breeder of Ashley Nettle, whose interest was still strong after World War I; D. J. Thomson Gray, and others began to make the Scottish Terrier an individual breed apart from the other varieties of Scotch Terriers known and produced at the time. They were aided by many others, for example, Mr. B. McMillan of Abertay Kennels in Dundee, whose alliance continued for almost 60 years and went back to the days before breed recognition.

H. J. Ludlow, breeder of the famous Chs. Aisla II, Lorna Doone, Alister and others; M. L. McDonald, Dunolly's breeder, and William McCandlish; to these and many more we owe a great debt for establishing a new and officially recognized breed.

During the last decade of the 19th century another man came on the scene who, with his sons, left an indelible mark on the history and improvement of the breed. This was Robert Chapman of Glenboig, Scotland. He bred his first champion, Heather Queen, in 1896 and continued until his death, whereupon the Heather Kennels were carried on by his sons, one of the same name, until into the 1930's. Throughout its history, the kennel presented a strong stud force and was a major competitor in the show ring. Prior to World War I, it was not unusual to find 100 or more dogs in its pens. Of course during the conflict, operations were curtailed, as was the case with all other establishments, but when the war ended the younger Chapmans began to rebuild the stud force. From about 1927 to 1935, Heather gained its greatest prominence. Records show that through the years 1930, '31 and '32, dogs owned by Heather together with their progeny dominated the breed and captured 108 out of a possible 132 challenge certificates available to the breed at all recognized shows that offered them.

The Chapmans seldom failed to recognize promise and quality in a young dog. They bought many a likely looking youngster and waited until maturity before deciding whether or not the dog would do. One of their most important purchases was Ch. Albourne Barty from A. G. Cowley in 1927 before the dog had reached his full promise, but he was already a definite comer. In fact, in 1928 Barty was well recognized but overshadowed by his kennel mate, Ch. Merlewood Aristocrat, which held sway during 1928–29.

Chapman's other prize purchase was, of course, Snooker's Double in 1928, which proved to be a stroke of genius. Renamed Heather Necessity, the dog did well from the start but was not immediately included in Chapman's first line, as evidenced by the advertising statement made in late 1929 which read, "Another high class dog is Heather Necessity. He is a good winner and with ordinary luck should have a great future." Chapman did not know how prophetic this statement would become. As mentioned before, Barty bitches bred to Necessity were particularly productive and thus the whole formula was concentrated in one kennel.

40

Necessity turned out to be one of the all-time greats in the breed yet many owned him, and not until he was purchased by Chapman was he apparently wanted. Bred by Mr. Walker on September 14, 1927, he was sold to a Mr. Leslie who showed him as a youngster with a catalogue claiming price of 100 pounds. A. G. Cowley quickly picked him up and immediately resold him to Chapman for 200 pounds, a tidy profit. Cowley's name did not even appear in the transaction which, according to Kennel Club records, indicates that Leslie transferred the dog directly to Chapman.

Returning to the Heather Kennels, it is interesting to note the concentration of the stud force at Glenboig during the height of its success. In 1928 it included Ch. Merlewood Aristocrat, Ch. Albourne Barty and Heather Necessity, to say nothing of Albourne Brigand and Ornsay Hustler. By 1932 such dogs as Ch. Crich Certainty, Ch. Heather Ambition and the great Ch. Heather Fashion Hint had been added to this already potent group. Little wonder that the kennel was a standout.

The Chapmans' interests were not tied to Scotties alone. In their extensive operation they had many other breeds, which from time to time included Fox Terriers, Alsatians, Gordon Setters and even some Clydesdale horses. In addition, Heather was the starting location for many who have since made their mark in the breed. Chief among these is the Murphy family represented for many years by Tom Murphy, the kennel manager. He in turn employed the brothers Harry, Jimmy and Johnny Murphy, his nephews, as kennel help and it was in this environment that they obtained their training in the breed. Bob Gorman was another who acquired his experience at Heather. He, of course, was later engaged by Mrs. Winant to take over her Edgerstoune Kennels. Thus, Heather Kennels, in addition to being one of the great establishments in Scottish Terriers, was the training ground for many whose efforts have done so much to further the breed in this country.

It should be pointed out that the Chapmans would buy anything of quality which they believed would be useful to them. For this reason the breeding record of the kennel, while good, is not startling when compared with its longevity and the size of the establishment. Robert Chapman, Sr. bred some eight titleholders from 1896 to 1906 while his son Robert bred an additional six from 1929 to 1934. James Chapman, another son, took up the challenge in 1934

41

THE "HEATHER" SCOTTISH TERRIERS,

Belonging to
Mr. ROBERT CHAPMAN
Glenboig,
Scotland.

Telephone: Coatbridge 351.

CH. HEATHER AMBITION.

CH. HEATHER FASHION HINT.
Sire of three Champions.

CH. HEATHER NECESSITY

CH. HEATHER AMBITION.
Property of Mr. James Chapman.

CH. ALBOURNE BARTY.
Sire of seven Champions.

CH. HEATHER NECESSITY.
Winner of twenty Challenge Certificates and Sire of twelve Champions.

HEATHER EXCELLENCE.

CH. CRICH CERTAINTY.

HEATHER SPELLBINDER.

CH. U.S.A. ALBOURNE VINDICATED OF BENTLEY.

HEATHER RADIANT.

HEATHER ADELINE.

Heather Kennels' advertisement showing the strength of their stud force.

and bred seven more, so that by 1944 the Chapman family total of British champions was 21 during a period of 48 years.

This record does not compare with another great name in the breed, that of a contemporary, A. G. Cowley of Horley, Surrey, whose Albourne prefix is still a famous trademark in the breed. Cowley bred Albourne Beetle, his first champion, in 1915. Beetle was subsequently imported into the United States by R. M. Cadwalader's Fairwold Kennels and placed best Scottie at Westminster in 1921. Cowley's record from 1915 through 1934 totalled 23 champions. This was no mean accomplishment when working under the English Kennel Club rules, which limit the number of challenge certificates available. Of course, Cowley's greatest accomplishment was Ch. Albourne Barty, which was sold to Chapman, but many other Albourne dogs were famous both in Britain and America. One of these, Albourne Annie Laurie, rivals Barty in the records as a great one. Annie Laurie is considered by many as the top producing matron of all time, and her record supports this high regard. She was the dam of six champions including Chs. Albourne Brigand, Albourne Reveller and Albourne Braw Lass in a single litter. Ch. Albourne Reveller, considered one of the best Scots ever bred, proved his worth by siring the great Ch. Heather Reveller of Sporran when he was bred to Skerne Scotch Lass, Necessity's dam. Albourne Reveller, like so many of Cowley's dogs, eventually joined the stud force at Heather kennels.

Cowley was probably the most astute breeder in the history of the breed in Britain. He knew the formula for continued success and bred good ones by this formula consistently throughout his long and fruitful career. He offered some of his secrets to the fancy in an article carried by the 1931 Christmas issue of *Our Dogs*, which said:

> To breed champions and to continue to breed champions, one must have a strain and must stick to type by inbreeding. All of the best-known strains of livestock are inbred, and, in fact, we must inbreed to produce a type and to stick to that type. To mate bitches to dogs of different blood is, in 99 cases out of 100, to breed nothing but rubbish. It is because the general run of breeders do these stupid things—often after asking advice which they do not take—that it is left to the very few in each breed to attain success and to keep the high position they hold. [It is believed that the reference to "inbreeding" is directed more correctly to "line breeding" since Cowley was interested basically in breeding within the same bloodlines.]

This is certainly good advice which, as Cowley says, is asked for but seldom heeded by the average breeder. It is also the reason why some breeders advance and others do not. The concepts behind the success of Cowley's formula will be expanded upon in the chapter on breeding in this book. In any event, the Master of Albourne had the formula; he practiced what he preached and he sold many good ones both in Britain and in the United States for the best interests of the breed and the good name of "Albourne."

Many other names were prominent during the same era which embraced the years until the start of World War II, when breeding operations all but ceased in Britain. The Barlae Kennels of William Prentice at Haddington, Scotland was one of these. Prentice was not only an able breeder but a capable handler as well. His first titleholder was Barlae Proof bred in 1917. He was also widely known for his Cairn and West Highland White Terriers. Prentice later moved his kennels and family to America where the name Prentice became a legend through his accomplishments, followed by those of his son Phil and his daughter Florence, all great Scottish Terrier experts.

The Jhelum Kennels of G. D. Lyell of Brockenhurst, Hampshire, began in the early twenties with the purchase of Ch. Albourne Adonis, which headed a stud force including Littlebury Puck. Puck was a son of Ch. Laindon Luminary, which gained his title in 1920 and was one of a strong kennel owned by Mr. H. R. B. Tweed at Billericay, Essex. Laindon Kennels was active as early as 1906 when Mr. Tweed bred his first champion in Laindon Locket. Through more than 20 years of operations some six champions were bred, which included the aforementioned Luminary, Ch. Laindon Lumen, Ch. Laindon Lightsome and Ch. Laindon Lancelot, among others.

Other kennels of merit were Garnock, owned by Robert Houston of Kilburnie which, active for more than two decades, began operations around the turn of the century; Andrew H. Lister's Rothesay Kennels at Rothesay, Scotland; George Davidson's Merlewood Kennels at Hawick, Scotland, which bred such dandies as Ch. Merlewood Rose, Ch. Merlewood Cleopatra and Ch. Merlewood Hopeful, later exported to the U.S.; the Gaisgill Kennels of Mrs. C. M. Cross at Elstree in Hertfordshire, which was a strong establishment that exported many to the States; and the Sandheys Kennels of Mr. Richard Lloyd at Birkdale that once owned the aforementioned

Mrs. Dorothy Caspersz, long dean of the breed.

A group of famous champions.

Ch. Sandheys Sheriff, owned by Mrs. F. E. Fowler.

Ch. Ortley Angela.

Albourne Annie Laurie. Many Sandheys dogs, such as Ch. Sandheys Silvertip, are well known even today.

An establishment that made a quick success story was the Ortley Kennels of Conrad Bremer at Hull, Yorks. Beginning operations about 1930, its rapid rise to the top was due to sound breeding techniques that produced many good ones. Ch. Ortley Carmen, her dam Ch. Ortley Elegance, Ch. Ortley Patience, and Ch. Ortley Ambassador are a few. A number of Ortley dogs came to the U.S. and did well as will be noted later. Quite active into the early fifties Ortley bred about 14 English champions. Sam Bamford, owner of the Walnut Kennels, was widely known in both Britain and the U.S. Dogs bearing the Walnut prefix made their mark in both countries and some 16 Walnut Scotties that came to the kennels of Dr. F. W. Zimmerman at Youngstown, Ohio, made their U.S. titles. Glenisla Kennels, owned by Mr. and Mrs. A. M. Robb of Glenboig, neighbors of Chapman's, owned a well known bitch in Ch. Albourne Romance the dam of such greats as Chs. Heather Essential and Heather Ambition, while the Rookes Kennels of John Sharp of near Halifax owned Ch. Heather Fashion Queen, Grey Steel of Rookes and Ch. Masterpiece of Rookes.

A breeder still known and active is Mr. W. M. Singleton. He bred his first Eng. Champion, Walsing Wallet, in 1933. Thereafter, he had tremendous success and is still breeding toppers. In all some nine English titleholders have been produced at this kennel while many more bear its prefix. On September 23, 1946, Singleton bred his famous Scottie, Ch. Walsing Winning Trick, sold to Mrs. John G. Winant who added the suffix "of Edgerstoune" to his name. He made an unprecedented record climaxed by best in show at Westminster in 1950. One of the latest Walsing dogs to gain prominence in this country is Ch. Walsing Wild Winter of Barberry Knowe.

The War practically stopped dog breeding in England and Scotland. Food was scarce and thoughts of survival came first in most British minds. In spite of this condition, a few staunch breeders kept a bitch or two and shared their scant rations with them. They even enjoyed a few shows during the years when most sporting activities had ceased. To be sure they were not championship affairs but they were competitive, which helped the breed and kept interest alive while offering a diversion during a time when pleasures were few. The backbone of these "clandestine events" was the Scottish

47

Terrier Breeder's and Exhibitor's Association, a group made up of true supporters of the breed. Members of this group with other holdovers from pre-war years formed the small nucleus that was responsible for the rebirth of the breed when hostilities ceased. The success of the venture is apparent and the Scottish Terrier in Britain is once again strong. Ch. Desert Viscountess, bred by A. Brown, was the first post-war titleholder in 1946. Thereafter competition became extremely active for in 1947, 12 Scots claimed the coveted title. Imports from Britain again made their presence felt in the U.S. rings although there is no doubt that American stock had moved forward into full contention with the best Britain now had to offer.

In the late forties a number of new names became prominent on the British scene in addition to some who have been previously mentioned. W. M. Singleton was still active with Chs. Walsing Winning Trick, Walsing Watch Light and Walsing Winoway, as was C. Bremer with Chs. Ortley Monty, Ortley Simon· and others. The Rosehall prefix was also carried over with Chs. Rosehall Edward and Rosehall Toryglen Tam O'Shanter. Names that had not previously been noted included W. Berry's Wyrebury prefix with such dogs as Chs. Wyrebury Woodnymph, Wyrebury Wonder and Wyrebury Witching. The Westpark Scotties came along strong with a host of widely known winners including the great Ch. Westpark Derriford Baffie (a son of Ch. Westpark Romeo), which captured 35 CCs in England and then became a big winner and a great sire in the United States; H. Wright's Woodmansey Winetaster, a recent winner of 16 challenge certificates, together with the Gillsie dogs of Messrs. Gill and McShane that have included a host of good ones including Ch. Gillsie Principal Girl and Ch. Gillsie Starturn. Add the Desco Scots of Mrs. L. J. Dewar, Newcastle-upon-Tyne, and one gains a perspective of some of the many kennels that have been active over varying periods of time including the era since the war.

The Kennelgarth Kennels of Miss Betty Penn Bull of Streatham came into their own. Miss Penn Bull began her kennel in about 1935 with a bitch, Kennelgarth Greena by Ch. Albourne Admiration The establishment grew and the dog, Heather Herald (Heather Realisation ex Heather Louise), was purchased from Chapman. He proved to be a worthwhile investment for he sired many good ones including Kennelgarth Blacksmith, which is behind most of the

48

Eng. Ch. Kennelgarth Viking, a leading English stud.

Eng. and Am. Ch. Merlewood Hopeful.

The famous Ch. Albourne Scot, sire of Ch. Albourne Barty.

Ch. Albourne Admiration.

present stock. After the close of the war the kennel thrived and challenge certificates began to come its way. Many champions have been owned by this kennel including its first, Ch. Kennelgarth Mallich, a granddaughter of Herald's bred by Mrs. Owen. Some of the homebred titleholders include, Chs. Kennelgarth Great Scot, Kennelgarth Eros, Kennelgarth Sharon, Kennelgarth Venus and, of course, the present bellwether, Ch. Kennelgarth Viking (Ch. K. Eros out of Ch. K Gleam), linebred to Kennelgarth Blacksmith five times. Viking has already sired some 12 titleholders including Ch. Brackenscroft Rye and Dry, Ch. Gillsie Starturn and the great Ch. Gaywyn Viscountess. He is one of the leading English studs of the day, and time will undoubtedly make him one of the truly great sires. Kennelgarth is noted for its "blacks." Miss Penn Bull has specialized in the color and has bred a strain that for many years has been known for excellent coat texture, something often lacking in this attractive color.

Mr. A. W. Gee's Glenview Kennel at Swinford near Rugby is another that has shown to advantage during the post-war period, with Chs. Glenview Idealist, Glenview Grace and Glenview Gran Lass, and more recently Chs. Glenview Golden Disc, Glenview Silver Gilt and Glenview Merry Princess. The name is doubly important in the U.S. in view of several dogs imported into this country that have done quite well. Ch. Glenview Grand Duke is one of these.

The Glendoune Kennels of R. H. McGill has also exported some good ones to the U.S. Ch. Glendoune Gaytime, Ch. Glendoune Gaibonnie and Ch. Glendoune Gwenda have made enviable records in this country. In addition, the kennel's record in England includes many top winners, among them Chs. Glendoune Gypsy, Glendoune Gauntlet and Glendoune Enchantress.

Mrs. Muriel Owen of Hatfield, Herts has been interested in the breed for many years. Since the war her prefix "Gaywyn" has come forward remarkably well under strong competitive conditions. One of the ablest contenders in the establishment is the homebred bitch Ch. Gaywyn Viscountess, by K. Viking, that has won some 14 challenge certificates including Crufts in 1962 and 1965, going best of breed the last time. She has been a consistent winner throughout her career. As a brood she is equally good, having already produced English Chs. Gaywyn Emperor and Gaywyn Titania, and American

51

Ch. Gaywyn Baroness. In addition to Viscountess, Mrs. Owen has bred some seven other English titleholders including such recent winners as Chs. Gaywyn Matador and Gaywyn Castanet. We had the pleasure of visiting the kennel during the fall of 1964 and were surprised to see such a compact kennel so well stocked with toppers. Most amazing was the temperament of the dogs. After "going over" many of the inmates, Mr. Owen opened all of the stalls and crate doors and some 19 Scotties of all ages and both sexes came out in the very limited floor space to greet us en masse. There was no bickering, much less fighting, and all I could see was a forest of wagging tails indicating the temperaments bred at Gaywyn. Upon command, the dogs went back to their own quarters, but not without a bit of help to see that each went to the proper place.

Mrs. Elizabeth Meyer of Hatfield, Herts, has a very prominent post-war kennel at Reanda. Here a steady stream of good ones have been bred and many of these have also been sold in the U.S. Most will recall such dogs as Chs. Reanda Rheola and Reanda Rhee, which made their U.S. titles quite easily. Rhee was out of Reanda Rosita, which whelped nine titleholders, a record for the time. Rosita's granddam, Reanda Medwal Marchioness, was the foundation of this fine kennel and her name will be noted in the background of some 23 titleholders bred by Mrs. Meyer. In addition Mrs. Meyer has had a host of toppers in Britain headed by Ch. Reanda Roger Rough, which ruled the boards for several years beginning in about 1957–58 and ended his brilliant career with 25 challenge certificates and a best of breed at Crufts. Other widely known Reanda champions include Reanda Rio Rita, Reanda Rory, Reanda Rosalina and Reanda Raith, to name a few from this prolific breeding establishment. Ch. Reanda Ringold, a young dog with many challenge certificates and a best in show at Paignton to his credit, is the present kennel leader. He is by the redoubtable Ch. Bardene Bingo.

Last but not least is the Bardene Kennels of Mr. Walter Palethorpe in Derbyshire, which will go down in history since Mr. Palethorpe has the knack of breeding toppers. Ch. Bardene Boy Blue sent to the U.S. several years ago was not bred by Palethorpe, but he has made a name for Bardene by winning well all over the country and climaxing the run with best of breed at Westminster in 1964. To date, however, the greatest accomplishment of Mr. Palethorpe's is the breeding of that great Scot, Ch. Bardene Bingo. This dog burned up the shows in England and has been doing the same in the U.S. after his purchase by Carnation Farms in 1964. He has already won many best in shows, including Westminster in 1967.

We were fortunate to be present at the 1962 National Terrier show at Leicester when Bingo was but an 11-month-old puppy. He cleaned the boards in the breed and went on to best in show over the top Terriers of England. The dog was a sensation; he looked beautiful at that age, and maturity has done nothing to detract from his sterling appearance. To date Bingo has sired many top dogs both in England and in America. His son Bardene Bobby Dazzler is already a U.S. champion and is just one of many that will be seen. It takes no sage to predict that Bingo will go forward to become one of the Scottie greats in America, a place he already holds in Britain.

Many other British Kennels bear mention but space limits this short review and those that have been chosen are best known to me. It may be said that the Scottish Terrier had made an all-the-way comeback in Britain after the disastrous period of the war. From the line-up now offered, there will be no dearth of good stock from across the sea in future years.

Head study of Ch. Kennelgarth Viking.

Ashley Charley, a Scottie of 1884.

Tiree, the first American champion, 1898.

5

The Early Scottish
Terrier in America

THE advent of the Scottish Terrier in America was about coincidental with that of other early Terrier breeds. To John Naylor of Mount Forest (Chicago area), Illinois, goes the honor of introducing the Scot to this country. In the 1883 records show that he exhibited such dogs as Tam Glen, Heather and Bonnie Bell in classes for "Rough-haired Terriers." In 1885 Naylor registered the first Scottish Terrier in Volume 2 of the *National American Kennel Club Stud Book*, forerunner of the *American Kennel Club Stud Book*. The dog, named Prince Charlie, was assigned #3310. He was by Billy out of Lady, whelped in April 1881, and bred by D. O'Shea of London, Ontario, Canada, indicating that the breed was possibly established above the border before its entry into the United States. The English import, Queen Lilly, #3311, registered by Naylor at the same time as Prince Charlie, was whelped January 20, 1881, and was sired by King out of Lady Blossom.

The above information disagrees with some other authors who credit the first registration in this country to O. P. Chandler's Dake,

#3688 in the now defunct *American Kennel Register,* a competitive registry to the *National American Kennel Club Stud Book.* Dake was not registered until 1886, about one year after Prince Charlie. It is interesting to note, however, that Dake was sired by Naylor's Tam Glen out of Queen Lilly, which, as noted above, was imported and registered by Naylor. From these particulars there seems very little basis for dispute that Naylor should be credited with bringing the breed to this country.

While no great amount of information is available concerning Naylor's activities, we do know that he imported and showed extensively and that he bred a number of Scottish Terriers in the years following their introduction into this country. Such dogs as Glenlyon (a semi-erect eared one), whelped in 1879 and brought over some time thereafter, Glengarry and Rosie, followed by the home-bred litter of Dunbar, Fannie Fern and Gypsy Queen are all found in early records, with the last three exhibited extensively during the 1887 show season.

In spite of his activity, Naylor failed in his efforts to popularize the Scottie and interest in the breed was slight. In fact, the class for "Scotch and hard-coated Terriers" at New York in 1888 failed to secure a single entry. A great improvement came about when several new establishments entered the field shortly afterward. The most successful of these was the Wankie Kennels of Messrs. Henry Brooks and Oliver Ames of Boston, Massachusetts. These fanciers purchased a number of top dogs that made competition interesting for all. Among their acquisitions were Chs. Kilroy, Kilcree, Culblean, and later Tiree and Rhuduman. Of this group, Ch. Tiree proved to be the gem and was certainly worth every cent paid for him. It is said that he won the special for best dog in show at Philadelphia in 1893, although the show catalogue does not list the award. If this is true, Tiree was the first of the breed to capture a best in show in the United States. In 1898, at the age of nine, he completed his U.S. title and became the first U.S. Scottish Terrier champion. Bred by Capt. Wetherall and whelped on May 16, 1889, Tiree was sired by Eng. Ch. Alister out of Coll; these two were half-brother and sister. To Henry Brooks goes the honor of being the first American to breed a U.S. titleholder: Ch. Wankie Diana, whelped in 1892 and sired by Kildee ex Flegg Thistledown. She completed her championship in 1898. Her pedigree is of great interest since Eng. Ch.

56

Alister, by Rambler, was her double grandsire while her paternal grand-dam, Eng. Ch. Ailsa II, was also sired by Rambler. Thus three of her four great-grandsires were the same dog, indicating an early and successful use of intensive line breeding.

By 1895 the Scottish Terrier entry at New York had risen to an all time high of 39, and the breed's show classification that year included the *first* American-bred classes for any breed. Sixteen of the entries came from the Wankie Kennels while seven were from James L. Little's Newcastle Kennels of Brookline, Massachusetts. This was a new and large establishment that through the years registered hundreds of Scotties. Little's big winner of the day was Bellingham Baliff, which made his title in 1899 to become the fifth AKC titleholder in the breed. Baliff was by Whinstone out of a Dundee bitch. The efforts of Little's kennels contributed much to the fancy for many years to come. He imported the great Ch. Ashley Crack, which finished the same year as Baliff, in addition to many others, and he ran the kennel personally until about 1914 when his son, Dr. C. C. Little, took over.

In spite of the upsurge of interest caused by the advent of these newcomers, the fortunes of the Scottish Terrier once again began to wane and competition became difficult to find. Mr. Brooks retired from active participation followed by Mr. Ames in about 1899; this closed the once dominant Wankie Kennels. Some of the slack was taken up by Mrs. Jack Brazier (Craigdarroch Kennels), who owned such dogs as Ch. Heworth Merlin, Ch. Silverdale Queen and Ch. The Laird; Mrs. G. S. Thomas (Brandywine Kennels), who owned the imported half-brother–half-sister team of Chs. Brandywine Jock and Brandywine Jean; Mrs. E. S. Woodward (Sandown Kennels), with Chs. Sandown Garnett, a homebred, and Sandown Heather; and Mrs. H. T. Foote, all of whom showed along the line with Mrs. Brazier taking the lead. In fact, her great little dog Ch. The Laird, whelped in 1901 and imported by George Thomas, dominated the breed for four straight years at Westminster. He was said to have been a grand animal and the best exhibited in the breed until that time and had much to do with the public acceptance of the Scottie to prove an old adage:

Guid gear goes in mickle bundles.

Concurrent with the demise of the great Wankie Kennels, a new-comer was seen at the shows. He was Dr. Fayette Ewing of near St.

Louis (Kirkwood and Webster Groves), Missouri. Although his interest began in about 1897 when he imported Romany Ringlet, he did not come into big time competition until 1899 when he exhibited the aforementioned Ringlet and the import Loyne Ginger at New York. Ginger gave early evidence of Dr. Ewing's lifetime interest in wheatens and finished her title requirements the following year, to become the seventh American titleholder and the *first* American wheaten champion in the breed. In spite of Dr. Ewing's early efforts, the shows still suffered from small entries and apparent apathy among the fancy. However, Dr. Ewing became the "spark plug" needed to bring about a change for the better. The Scottish Terrier specialty club that had been formed in 1885 was revitalized and in 1900 became the Scottish Terrier Club of America with Ewing as its secretary. This brought together a wide cross-section of Scottie fanciers who now had the interest to work toward a common goal, the good of the breed. The club became a member of the American Kennel Club the same year.

Dr. Ewing was active until about 1947, when he retired from direct participation and ended a glorious half-century in the breed. The kennels, then located in Louisiana, were continued by the family with good success. In fact, the import, Ch. Wyrebury Wrangler made an excellent record in the ring and finished his title in 1955, while the imports Chs. Nosegay Napier and Nosegay Mistress Riverside, both by Eng. Ch. Wyrebury Wilwyn, a Wrangler son, made their titles in 1957 along with a homebred, Ch. Nosegay McDuff.

During his long and active association with the Scotsman, Dr. Ewing imported scores of English champions and was responsible for about as many homebreds. He wrote the first expansive American book on the breed in 1931 which still remains a classic. In addition, he advised fanciers regarding breed happenings through a monthly column carried by one of the leading magazines. As previously noted, Dr. Ewing always had a strong interest in the wheaten. After Loyne Ginger, his next widely publicized import was Glencannie Gingerbread. When exhibited in New York about 1931 he caused quite a stir but did not win. Through the years many others, such as Polhill Pilgrim, Nosegay Buckwheat and Nosegay Lemon Lily, etc., were brought out, and these with their get were used successfully in the breeding programs of Nosegay and other kennels interested in the wheaten. Dr. Ewing will always be remembered as a benefactor of the breed and a champion of the wheaten Scottie.

In 1906, a large kennel, destined to be highly successful, began operations at Bernardsville, New Jersey. It was the Walescott establishment of Francis G. Lloyd. A steady influx of top imports together with the application of sound breeding techniques provided a host of dogs capable of holding their own in any company. By 1910, Ch. Walescott Invader was a big winner for the kennel. He was an import known in Britain as Ch. Clonmel Invader.

The spotlight was taken from Walescott, for a time at least, when in 1911 a 3½ year-old Scot named Ch. Tickle 'Em Jock went best in show at Westminster. This first such triumph for the Scottish Terrier helped breed popularity immeasurably. Jock, owned by Andrew Albright, Jr. of Newark, New Jersey, had been purchased in London the year before for a paltry $500. Jock once sired three champions in a single litter but his accomplishment at Westminster was the feat for which he will always be remembered.

The following year, 1912, found Walescott regaining much of its prestige, and by 1914 the kennel frequently dominated important shows along the East coast. Its chief competition came from the aforementioned Newcastle Kennels, which still showed sporadically, the Earlybird Kennels of W. T. Stern, together with a host of individuals including Henry Bixby (Boglebrae) and Caswell Barrie (Ballantrae), both of the latter widely known in the breed. The Earlybird Kennels of W. T. Stern, New York housed a host of great Scots including Ch. Earlybird Romany Olivia, Ch. Earlybird Troubadour and Ch. Bapton Beryl, one of the great show bitches of the times. The success of the kennels was aided by Bert Hankinson, who was brought over around 1912 from the Bapton Kennels as kennel manager. He stayed with Earlybird until about 1917, when activity slacked off, and then went into Mr. Lloyd's employ.

It was not unusual for Walescott to bring from 10 to 25 entries to Westminster, no great problem with a kennel census of around 75. In 1918, for example, George Thomas was on the woolsack with some 40 entries to pass on, and 11 of them belonged to Walescott. The winning dog that year was Ch. Walescott Albourne Crow, a repeat from 1917, with Walescott Whim going reserve. Whim was one of a litter by Ch. Walescott Maister Wullie ex Merlewood Merle whelped September 1, 1916; it also included Walescott

59

Wag and Walescott Winkie, all three eventually becoming champions. Wullie himself was a homebred by Walescott Daredevil ex Ch. Walescott Shady Lady. Many other great ones came from the kennels with some 17 eventually claiming the title.

After Mr. Lloyd's sudden death in 1920, Walescott was disbanded and the breed lost a successful and constant supporter. Lloyd was at one time president of the Scottish Terrier Club of America, and a perpetual Memorial Trophy in his name is still the most important of all club offerings.

Three other fanciers who were active before 1920 deserve mention because of their substantial contribution to the breed: Miss Margaret Brigham, Sherwood Hall and R. M. Cadwalader, Jr., who operated the Fairwold Kennels at Fort Washington, Pennsylvania. The importation of Ch. Albourne Beetle from Cowley was a fortunate stroke, for Fairwold benefited from this dog's efforts and was a strong contender for many years.

Thus ends the early history of the breed and its supporters in the United States. Many other persons had their share in laying the foundation of sound breeding techniques and proper ethics, but those noted here surely deserve special mention for their efforts. Had it not been for them, the breed may well have fallen out of favor and into oblivion. That it became perennially more virile is evidence that their efforts were not in vain. We of today owe to those of yesterday a large vote of thanks for a job well done.

6

The Modern Scottish Terrier in America

THE preceding chapter delineates the early activi
ties of individuals and kennels that supported the Scotsman in
America from its introduction to about the year 1920. This chapter
will begin with happenings after that date until the present day.
There will be some overlap since the interest of a few fanciers
embraced parts of both periods. In any event this era is an important
span of years that has meant a great deal to the breed.

After World War I we find establishments that were active before
the War still breeding and exhibiting dogs. Some of these will be
scanned more thoroughly since they gained in stature as time went
on. Included among this select group were the strong contenders,
Caswell Barrie, Henry Bixby and R. M. Cadwalader, Jr. Mr.
Barrie's Ballantrae establishment had such Scots as Ch. Heather
Venture O'Ballantrae and Ch. Ballantrae Wendy in the ring, while
Bixby's Boglebrae Kennel was exhibiting Ch. Boglebrac Muskrat
and Ch. Ornsay Autocrat, to name two. Bixby will also be remembered because of his many years of association with the Ameri-

can Kennel Club as its Executive Vice President. Cadwalader's Fairwold complex was previously mentioned because of Ch. Albourne Beetle, but the years greatly improved its stature with such Scots as Ch. Fairwold Albourne Rocket, Ch. Fairwold Ornsay Bill, Ch. Fairwold Osmond Lily and Ch. Fairwold Plaid, a homebred by Beetle out of Clonmel Plaid. The kennels remained active well into the 1930's.

The modern Scottie has these and their predecessors to thank together with that knowledgeable breeder, Frank Spiekerman (Hitofa Kennels), who owned many toppers, including Ch. Heather Essential, Ch. Heather Aristocrat and Ch. Hitofa Chief, and Prentice Talmadge's Bentley Kennels, which imported many good ones including Ch. Albourne Adair, about 1922. Adair was, of course, the keystone of both the Necessity and the Barty lines through his two sons Chs. Albourne MacAdair and Albourne Scot, respectively. When this kennel was dispersed, Adair went to Robert McKinven's Ardmore Kennels near Detroit. Here he was used with great success on many of the Ardmore bitches to produce such get as Ch. Ardmore Wallace, the immortal Ch. Ardmore Skipper and the brood Ardmore Jewel. She was bred twice with great results. The first time when put to her half-brother Skipper, she produced a bitch named Ch. Ardmore Keepsake; the second time, bred to Ch. Ardmore Legacy, an Adair grandson, she produced Ch. Ardmore Toddler.

McKinven did not lose his advantage and bred Toddler to Keepsake, and the dog Ch. Ardmore Royalist resulted. He was a great winner and with a triple cross of Adair blood in his veins was another bit of proof, if proof be needed, that line breeding is the surest means of obtaining results. Bob McKinven retired from active participation about 1937 after breeding some 14 champions, and the kennel was carried on by his son Charles, who is still breeding Scotties with the Ardmore prefix, to make the establishment one of the oldest in the breed in this country.

Returning to other fanciers during the twenties we find Jock McOwen of Mine Brook; John Goudie of Cedar Pond, who always has been able to breed a good one; Ben Brown, the West Coast handler and long time Scottie impresario, who brought over Ch. Abertay Harry; the Balgay Kennels of Dr. and Mrs. Cecil Jelley, who bought many good ones from the Abertay Kennels in Scotland including Chs. Abertay Crag, Abertay Hawk, and Abertay Scot, and which also bred Chs. Balgay Barrister, Balgay Baroness and later Ch. Balgay Drummer Boy; Edward Danks, a long time breeder and judge and a lifetime fancier of the breed; Dr. and Mrs. Charles Lynch of Red Gauntlet fame; Bert Hankinson and his Scotsholme Kennels at Basking Ridge, New Jersey; Mr. and Mrs. H. Alvin McAleenan, who owned the Vigal Kennels with a topper in Ch. Goldfinder's Babe and still strongly interested in the breed; and of course, Mr. and Mrs. E. F. Maloney, who owned and operated the Goldfinder Kennels for so many years.

Maloney was one in a million when it came to breeding prowess. The list of good ones he owned and bred seems never ending. Always operating a small establishment, he repeatedly came up with toppers. He owned the great Ch. Heather Gold Finder, a sterling name in the breed and the sire of the aforementioned Goldfinder's Babe, together with some 18 other champions. Possibly his most successful show dog was a homebred, Ch. Goldfinder's Admiral, which was shown by Johnny Murphy during the early fifties and made a great name for himself. Maloney was active until his death and will always be remembered as an astute breeder and a staunch supporter of the breed.

This about ends the decade of the twenties, when the Scottie became of age and improvement was accomplished by a greater distribution of interest than ever before. The thirties opened without fanfare, but little did proponents of the breed know that the next ten years were to be the most productive in its history. In spite of the depression, which thwarted everything else, the Scottish Terrier enjoyed its greatest moments. The ten-year span was the spawning ground for more strong kennels than any other time in the long history of the breed. The period found the Scottie reaching its peak in representation. In 1933, 1936, 1937 and 1938 the breed placed third in numbers registered among all breeds of dogs on the American Kennel Club rolls. Numerically, too, the breed reached its pinnacle. In 1936, a total of 8,359 dogs were registered, the largest number in Scottie history. Compare this with the 1965 figure of 5,457; thus one can readily understand how the breed has slipped. Indeed, this was a golden era for the Scottish Terrier and one that will not soon be forgotten. Carlyle once said: "Popularity is as a blaze of illumination," and such was the case here.

So many fine kennels got their start in the thirties that it would be difficult to list them all. Few still remain, so these will be considered first, with those that have closed to be mentioned later.

At the start of the decade we find that the Barberry Knowe Kennel of Mr. and Mrs. Charles G. Stalter bears early mention, since it was begun in 1930 and is still one of the strongest show kennels in the breed in the United States. Situated in Hohokus, New Jersey for the past 37 years, it was started when Mrs. Stalter bought her husband a Scottie for Christmas. The dog, Diehard Robin, matured into a likely looking youngster. For a lark, the Stalters decided to show him at Englewood, New Jersey in 1930. He won his class, and as is the case with so many others, the Stalters were bitten by the show bug. Although Robin never quite made the grade, the Stalters were sufficiently interested to return to William McBain (Diehard Kennels) and purchase another male puppy, Diehard Reveller, sired by Ch. Heather Reveller of Sporran out of an imported bitch, Glenisla Grizelda. They brought him out in 1932 and by July of the following year the Stalters had their first champion. The next purchase was a bitch, Caenmohr Cora, which proved a worthy investment when, bred to Ch. Diehard Reveller, she produced Ch. Barberry Knowe Reveller, their first homebred titleholder.

Since that time Barberry Knowe has been a name with which to reckon at the shows all over the eastern section of the country. The Stalters had a host of good ones and more than their share of great ones. Their Ch. Barberry Knowe Barbican was one of the leading winners during the period of the early fifties when Scottie competition was extremely difficult. More lately, their Ch. Carmichael's Fanfare was one of the top Scots for the years 1963 and 1964, climaxing her already illustrious career with best in show at Westminster in 1965 to become the fourth of the breed to make this difficult and coveted win. She was wisely retired after the accomplishment.

From the beginning of their operations until early in 1965, the Stalters were fortunate in availing themselves of the knowledge, good counsel, and superlative handling ability of the Prentice family. William (Bill) Prentice, his son Phil, and his daughter Florence were all associated with Barberry Knowe at one time or another and in overlapping periods. The early handling and counsel was done by Bill Prentice, a Scot of great knowledge and good

64

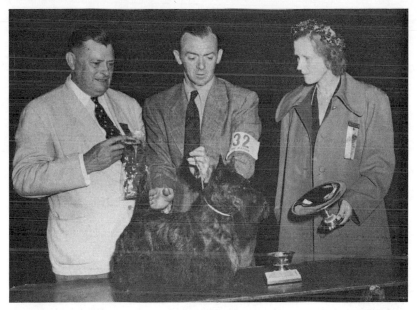

Ch. Barberry Knowe Barbican with Phil Prentice, Mrs. John G. Winant and George Hartman, judge, 1950.

Ch. Carmichael's Fanfare winning the Garden, 1965, with Johnny Murphy handling; Robert Kerns, judge, and William Rockefeller awarding the trophy.

judgment and the owner of Barlae Kennels. When Bill was unable to continue because of other commitments, Phil took over and did a remarkable job. Concurrently, Florence Prentice was kennel manager and private handler for the kennels, continuing in this capacity until her death in 1965. Her knowledge and ability to condition Scotties for show and to bring youngsters along to maturity, as well as her frank and pleasant personal approach, were major factors in the steady success of the establishment. It is difficult to realize that all three Prentices are now gone. All were top dog people; all were superlative Scottie conditioners and handlers. Their passing was a great loss to the breed.

Since about 1960, Johnny Murphy, who gained his early training at the Heather Kennels and who came to this country as a member of a Scottish soccer team, has handled the Barberry Knowe dogs in the ring, and a wonderful job he has done. The climax of his career was, of course, the 1965 best in show at the Garden with Fanfare.

The Stalters bred and/or owned more than 60 champions. In later years, some of their toppers, in addition to Barbican and Fanfare, included Ch. Barberry Knowe Merrymaker (Fanfare's sire), Ch. Barberry Knowe Revival, Ch. Barberry Knowe Wyndola, Ch. Walsing Wild Winter of Barberry Knowe, and Ch. Barberry Knowe Blizzard, to name a few. Considering the special abilities of its owners, Barberry Knowe should continue to be a power in the breed for many years to come.

Over the past 35 years another kennel of long standing that has shown to advantage is the Shieling establishment of Mr. and Mr. T. Howard Snethen. Getting its start in Wisconsin, the dogs were moved to Allison Park (Pittsburgh area), Pennsylvania soon after its beginning, where they remained for many years. Today, the Shieling scotties are housed at DeWittville, N.Y.

The most important fact about this group is the absence of professional help in the exhibition and grooming of its dogs. Mr. Snethen has always done the trimming and handling, and his artistry in doing up a Scot rivals that of the best professional. He is also a great ring competitor. The kennel, like many others, gained its start through a top brood bitch, Dark Maid. She whelped several of the early titleholders and got the show on the road. One of the first toppers bred by Shieling was the dog Ch. Shieling's Stylist. He was followed by Ch. Shieling's Designer, Ch. Shieling's Flash, Ch.

Bill Prentice of Barlae fame.

Eng. & Am. Ch. Bardene Bingo, bell-wether of Carnation Farms Kennels.

Ch. Carnation Girl, first wheaten Scot to go best in show all-breeds.

Ch. Shieling's Signature winning Westminster Best in Show, 1945.

```
                                                        Eng. Ch. Heather Ambition
                                    Ch. Heather Independence of E.
                                                        Heather Marina
                        Ch. Heather Criterion
                                                        Eng. Ch. Heather Realisation
                                    Heather Doris
                                                        Albourne Black Tulip
        Ch. Shieling's Salute
                                                        Ch. Drum Major of Docken
                                    Ch. Glencannie Crusader O'Briarcroft
                                                        Eng. Ch. Albourne Red Mary
                        Ch. Shieling's Winsome
                                                        Sandheys Simon of Wotan
                                    Dark Maid
                                                        Wotan's Frost Lassie
CH. SHIELING'S SIGNATURE
(Whelped 5/5/1942                                       Ch. Drum Major of Docken
Breeder: Mr. and Mrs. T. H. Snethen)
                                    Ch. Glencannie Crusader O'Briarcroft
                                                        Eng. Ch. Albourne Red Mary
                        Ch. Shieling's Stylist
                                                        Sandheys Simon of Wotan
                                    Dark Maid
                                                        Wotan's Frost Lassie
        Ch. Shieling's Symphony
                                                        Eng. Ch. Heather Fashion Hint
                                    Ch. Walnut Dandy O'Briarcroft
                                                        Eng. Ch. Albourne Braw Lassie
                        Ch. Shieling's Enterprise
                                                        Sandhey's Simon of Wotan
                                    Lucky Nancy
                                                        Wotan's Black Ruby
```

Shieling's Signature, Ch. Shieling's Masterkey and Ch. Shieling's Insignia, among many others. All of these were homebreds and all won best in show honors with Mr. Snethen on the other end of the lead. Signature had the added honor of topping all breeds at Westminster in 1945 to become the second Scotsman to turn the trick. This was a great achievement for man and dog, for seldom does this prize go to a dog handled by an amateur.

In more recent years, the kennel has imported some good ones including Ch. Reanda Rheola and Ch. Glenview Grand Duke; both have done extremely well. Today, more homebreds are making their appearance at the shows and are as competitive as ever. The kennel has bred more than 40 champions and has owned a host of others to make it one of the most successful in the breed.

Another kennel, and surely the most extensive on the West Coast, is the Carnation Farms establishment of E. H. Stuart, at Carnation, Washington. Mr. Stuart's interest in the breed began during the middle twenties while he resided in Wisconsin, through association with Mrs. Marie Stone, Charles Schott, and others. Not until about 1932, however, did a kennel evolve, and this was at its present location. Several top Scots were purchased during the thirties including an import, Ch. Gaisgill Daphne, and two outstanding American-breds in Ch. Goldfinger's Lady and Ch. Quince Hill Brick. The latter sired the kennel's first homebred titleholder in 1938, Ch. Carnation Classic.

Increased exhibition and success came with Bob Bartos, who became manager of the kennel in 1947. One of his first acts was to bring over Ch. Reimill Radiator, a son of Westpark Masterpiece. He was followed a few years later by a half-brother, Ch. Westpark Rio Grande, which sired 12 English and 21 American titleholders to place him high in the lists of great producers. Ch. Westpark Derriford Baffie was the next top import, purchased after he had won an unprecedented 35 challenge certificates in English rings. He proved equally successful in this country, as Bartos piloted him to 50 best of breeds at all-breed shows without a defeat; he went on to best dog in show at 22 of the outings, and he won four specialties as well. His siring ability was also highly commendable, with eight English and 19 American champions to his credit. Many other fine dogs have been inmates of this successful kennel, including particularly Ch. Dorel Black Nugget and Ch. Deephaven Red Seal. Carnation was also the first to have a wheaten good enough to go best in show, this honor won by homebred Ch. Carnation Golden Girl, which topped the Yakima, Washington show in 1951. She was strong in the blood of Heather Asset. Today Ch. Bardene Bingo, a titleholder in the United States, Canada and England, heads the show and stud force and is destined to carry on in big fashion for the kennel if present progress is any indication of things to come. Over the years, Carnation has owned many great champions and has bred a total of over 38 titleholders, a record of which they can be proud.

Among the many kennels that were successful in the thirties but no longer active we find the Quince Hill prefix of Dr. and Mrs. Morgan Steinmetz, William Prentice's Barlae Kennels, which began even earlier, and the Kinclaven Kennels of Mrs. Marie Stone of Milwaukee. This last establishment was begun in the late twenties but gained a large measure of its fame in the next two decades. It was closed by the death of its owner which was a great loss to the fancy. Kinclaven produced some three score champions which included the best in show winner Ch. Kinclaven The Stooge, together with Ch. Kinclaven Classic and Ch. Kinclaven Wild Oats, among others. Mrs. Stone handled her own dogs and was most successful. She also bred some of the country's great wheatens, exemplified by Wild Oats, which owned a beautiful golden wheat color without the usual heavy black pencilling and hair tipping so prevalent in dogs of this shade. Further, he was a refined animal with a clean skull and small dark eyes; all are factors difficult to obtain in the color. Mrs. Stone bred other wheatens and in all cases they excelled in these hard-to-get qualities.

When speaking of wheaten Scotties we cannot forget two other ladies who did much for the breed: Mrs. Ray Constable of Boston and Mrs. A. M. Henshaw of Cincinnati. The latter was a contemporary of Dr. Ewing and she had a great deal to do with popularizing the color, although her success in the ring was limited by lack of interest in this phase of activity. Mrs. Constable obtained stock from Mrs. Henshaw, among others, and continued the effort to put wheatens on an equal footing with blacks and brindles. However, neither fancier was able to breed consistently the type of the aforementioned Wild Oats and the dark tipped hairs; the tendency towards coarseness of head and apparent large eyes held down the winnings of the dogs that did make the ring. Mrs. Con-

Howard Snethen and his winning homebred, Ch. Shieling's Insignia, 1950.

Ch. Kinclaven Claudette.

Ch. Kinclaven Wild Oats, a classic wheaten Scottish Terrier.

stable's most famous wheaten, and the one with which she had the greatest success, was Ch. Murray Rag Doll.

Two kennels that showed to advantage in the Midwest during the era beginning in the thirties were Briarcroft at Youngstown, Ohio, and Deephaven at Minneapolis, Minnesota. Briarcroft was owned by Dr. F. W. Zimmerman. He, with Clint Schenck of Columbus, who was his inseparable companion at the shows, imported and exhibited a host of great ones. Most came from the aforementioned Sam Bamford's Walnut Kennels in England. He also bred some fine dogs and showed consistently for many years. He owned Ch. Hillcote Laddie during the period when the dog made history in both ring and breeding pen. Dr. Zimmerman's interests were also captivated by Welsh and Airedale Terriers, although Scots were his last effort before bowing out of competition in the late forties.

The Deephaven Kennels of Mr. T. W. Bennett was an amazingly successful establishment which began in the early thirties to climax an interest in the breed that extended several previous years. Mr. Bennett was fortunate in having Bob Bartos from the beginning until 1947, when he left to join Carnation Farms. The kennel closed its doors about 1950. Top dogs became the order of the day when the bitch Scotsward Romance was purchased at the Morris and Essex show from Mrs. C. B. Ward. She later became the first titleholder for Deephaven. Following closely was the great Ch. Crich Certainty, an import that proved to be a good sire. Thereafter more than 20 titleholders came from Deephaven, including Deephaven Fair Damsel, the first homebred champion, Deephaven Goldust, the Deephaven Honeysuckle, the great show dog, Ch. Deephaven Warspite, and finally Ch. Deephaven Red Seal, sold to Marlu Farms at a year old. This dog became one of the truly great sires of all time. The breeding record of Deephaven was surely exemplified by an inscription on the wall of the kennel lounge, which read, "The Best Is None Too Good."

In addition, some others who began serious efforts during this period include Dr. Flora Pedicord, whose dogs were shown by that old master, Dick Davis; John Hillman, a judge today and the breeder of Ch. Hillcote Laddie. Laddie and his litter brother, Mrs. Henshaw's Ch. Hillcote Essential Knight, were by Ch. Heather Essential out of Henshaw's Gloaming, a daughter of Ch. Heather Reveller of Sporran. Hillman also bred Ch. Hillcote Destiny which

72

Ch. Deephaven Red Seal.

```
                                            Eng. Ch. Heather Fashion Hint
                              Eng. Ch. Heather Realisation
                                            Gaisgill Sylvia
             Ch. Walsing Warrant
                                            Eng. Ch. Malgen Juggernaut
                              Eng. Ch. Walsing Wellborn
                                            Walsing Waitress
    Ch. Marlu Crusader
                                            Eng. Ch. Heather Fashion Hint
                              Eng. Ch. Dandy of Docken
                                            Brilliant of Docken
             Ch. Marlu Milady
                                            Scotshome Humorist
                              Roseneath Miss Muffett
                                            Sandridge Sabula
CH. DEEPHAVEN RED SEAL
(Whelped 6/26/1945
Breeder:  Deephaven Kennels)   Ch. Kinclaven Tobasco  Heather Asset
                                            Ch. Carioca
             Ch. Kinclaven Classic
                                            Eng. Ch. Heather Realisation
                              Ch. Gleniffer Leading Lady
                                            Gleniffer Gaiety
    Deephaven Mary
                                            Nosegay Buckwheat
                              Deephaven Sir Galahad
                                            Graochen Bittersweet
             Mac's Welton Gold Penny
                                            Faraway Sandy of Mt. Tuck
                              Mac's Welton Hope
                                            Clarksdale Anne
```

Marguerite Kirmse and some of her Scots.

Ch. Glenafton Tamara and Ch. Walsing Wag Tail.

proved to be a big winner. He was by Claddoch Necessity of Briar-croft, another producing son of the incomparable Necessity. Mr. and Mrs. Henry Israel's Paisley Hill Kennels at Dayton also brought out many good ones, including Fashion Favorite and Ch. Marlu Clincher which, guided by Johnny Murphy, made history in the early fifties, while John Kemp of Acton Hill fame with Ch. Acton Hill Interventionist, etc. was a widely known name during the same period.

In the West, the Bryce Gillespie's Bothkennar Kennels merit mention for their excellence and longevity. Begun around 1930 it flourished until its closing after the war, and during this span finished nearly two score champions. One of the most outstanding of these, Ch. Trevone Tartar of Bothkennar, an import, developed into one of the country's top sires. In later years such dogs as Ch. Bothkennar Typesetter and Ch. Bothkennar Kilroy kept the name in the headlines. Returning to Eastern climes, the Glenafton Kennels of Miss Elizabeth Hull flourished for a period of years beginning in the thirties. Jimmy Murphy, Johnny Murphy's brother, was the handler, and his charges included such Scots as Ch. Goldfinder's Lassie, Ch. Walsing Wagtail, Ch. Glenafton Tamara and Ch. Glenafton Goldseeker. The kennels were located at Binghamton, New York in the winter and were taken to the cool shores of Lake Lenape during the hot summer months to assure complete comfort for all inmates.

Another one active in the breed during the general period under consideration was Mrs. George Cole, better known to art lovers as Marguerite Kirmse. She owned the Tobermory Kennels at Bridge-water, Connecticut and showed and judged Scotties as well. Miss Kirmse was best known for her appealing etchings of dogs, Scotties in particular. Many homes have one or more of these fine pieces of art, whose execution reflects her knowledge of the dogs represented. Her work has done a great deal to further interest in the breed.

Frank Brumby is widely known today as an expert on the breed, but few realize that his background extends for over 40 years in active participation with the Scotsman. He managed, among other kennels, the Hillwood establishment of Mrs. Thomas W. Durant at Roslyn, Long Island during the early thirties, and no expense was spared to import the best as foundation stock. The great Ch. Merle-wood Hopeful, which gained her English title in 32 days and her

Ch. Bramble No Less.

Eng. Ch. Gaywyn Viscountess with Frank Butler Memorial Trophy.

American title in 27 days, was one of these. Others were Ch. Wilfield Necessity, a Heather Necessity son, Albourne Reveller's Lad, Ch. Laurieton Lorraine, Chs. Rookery Doon and Rookery Romance, and Ch. Bramble No Less. Upon reduction of activity at Hillwood Brumby went to the Braw Bricht Kennels of Mr. and Mrs. Donald Voorhees at Jericho, Long Island, another important establishment that enjoyed a rather brief tenure. The plan of Braw Bricht began in about 1932 when Rogue of Hillwood was purchased. The following year the kennel gained momentum through the purchase of the import, Gleniffer Ideal, from Brumby, who then handled the dogs and became its manager. Later the same year Ortley Angela was brought over and both made their titles, with Angela accomplishing the feat in sensational style at her first five shows.

Flornell Soundman, purchased from Percy Roberts, became the bellwether of the kennel with many best in show awards—eight in one year—while one of the most satisfying wins was the award of best team in show at Westminster in 1934, captured by the quartet of Chs. Gleniffer Ideal, Gleniffer Frivolity, Gleniffer Glad Eye and Ramoan Certainty. The last named did well in the groups and even gained a best in show but was always overshadowed by his more glamorous kennelmate, Soundman. Two other Braw Bricht Scotties that warrant mention in view of their sterling type and ability were Ch. Cedar Pond Chloe, bred by John Goudie, and Ch. Craigieburn Expectation of Sporran.

Most readers today will identify Mr. Voorhees with music rather than Scotties; he is one of the best known conductors frequently seen on television with his Bell Telephone Orchestra. Braw Bricht is only a memory today, but during the middle 1930's it cut a wide swath in competitive breed activity.

This brings us to three of the largest kennels of the era, two of which continued for many years and actually dominated the breed through long periods. The first was short-lived but nonetheless large and important. This was the Sporran Kennels of author S. S. Van Dine, who wrote many intriguing mystery stories, one of which, *The Kennel Murder Case,* immortalized the Scottie. He was always a dog lover and began to breed seriously as a diversion from his hectic literary life. Sporran was a busy place around 1930 with more than 100 Scotsmen romping around the pens as the owner tried to evolve a plan for breeding dogs in America as well as they did in England.

77

He once said, "We have in the United States, with one or two exceptions, all the best Scottish Terrier sires living," and he added, "A similar statement is true in regard to brood bitches. Yet our American-breds are beaten time after time by imported specimens." He concluded, and rightly so, "We have been breeding to champions, not bloodlines." These remarks are reminiscent of similar views expressed by many knowledgeable breeders who decry the novice's desire to breed to the top dog of the year, whether the bitch has the proper bloodlines or not. It also goes back to related advice made by E. G. Cowley and found in the chapter on British Breeders and Kennels.

Van Dine had William Prentice as his handler and manager, the best available. He brought over Ch. Heather Reveller, which gained the "of Sporran" suffix upon his naturalization. Sporran also owned Ornsay Hustler of Diehard, a widely known stud. Reveller made his English title in three consecutive shows at the age of 11 months. In America his accomplishments were just as sensational although more extensive. In three years of exhibition he won the breed 49 times, the group 21 times and best in show ten times. There were only two events at which he failed to place in the group. Only one champion was ever bred with the Sporran prefix, Ch. Sporran Roger, and he was not by the kennel's big dog, Reveller. After Van Dine decided to close his kennel in late 1934, Reveller went to Prentice.

The other two "big" kennels of the era were Edgerstoune and Relgalf. They will be taken up separately and in some detail because of their impact on the breed and the excellence of their activities. One of the largest and most successful kennels in the country began operations in the late twenties when Mrs. Marion Eppley, then Mrs. John G. Winant, started Edgerstoune. In the beginning the inmates were mostly West Highlanders, but in 1934 Scottish Terriers came into the picture. For the remainder of its long and glorious tenure these two Scottish breeds made history, with close to 100 champions being bred or owned from its inception in New Hampshire until its closing at Valley Cottage, New York in 1954.

Edgerstoune obtained the best from England, and these, with proper breeding, brought a host of top homebreds into the fold. Some of the better known imports were Ch. Gleniffer Tid Bit of Edgerstoune, Ch. Heather Resolution of Edgerstoune, Ch. Heather Commodore of Edgerstoune, and the incomparable Ch. Walsing

Ch. Trevone Tartar of Bothkennar.

Ch. Hillcote Essential Knight, owned by Mrs. A. M. Henshaw.

Ch. Marlu Milady's Beau.

Ch. Walsing Winning Trick of Edgerstoune going best in show at Westminster, 1950.
Left to right: Phil Prentice, John Cross, George Hartman and Ross Proctor.

Winning Trick of Edgerstoune. Homebreds were legion and Ch. Edgerstoune Troubadour, by Trick, stands out; he was sold as youngster, before he became a champion, to Dr. and Mrs. Stewart Carter. Additionally there was Ch. Edgerstoune Spitfire, Ch. Edgerstoune Orphan, and the great Ch. Edgerstoune Pepper, a fine dog that was overshadowed by his more spectacular kennelmate, Trick.

The kennels always had good young stock to replace the class dogs as they completed their titles. This was not happenstance, for Mrs. Eppley used an unusual method to raise her homebreds. Puppies were always an operation unto themselves. Mrs. Fred Leonard had charge of this phase of the work, and her efforts were certainly apparent. The older dogs and show stock were housed in a separate kennel with its own manager, who in most cases was also the show handler. Edgerstoune had the good fortune of having many fine handlers and managers in the persons of Harry Hardcastle, Bob Gorman, Jimmy Murphy, Joe Menary, and Cliff Hallmark. Phil Prentice also handled dogs for the kennel although he never managed its operations. In any event, Mrs. Leonard's concentrated efforts on puppies paid off because the youngsters received more attention, and their dispositions reflected this attention.

Much of the progress made by the kennel can also be attributed to Mrs. Eppley's ability to pick a winner at home or abroad. This was demonstrated by the way she acquired two of her best. When she judged in England, she placed a Westie bitch best in show. Immediately after the judging, she bought her and brought back to this country Ch. Wolvey Pattern of Edgerstoune, which went best in show at Westminster in 1942. Again in England, Mrs. Eppley placed a Scottish Terrier best in show, then bought the dog, Ch. Walsing Winning Trick. Of course, it is history now, but Trick subsequently emulated Pattern and won best in show at Westminster in 1950, when he carried the "of Edgerstoune" suffix to the top.

Before leaving Edgerstoune, a run-down of Winning Trick's record will be of interest, for it is an amazing one that has never been equalled. Shown sparingly with only 40 outings at large shows over a period of about three years, he was never defeated in the breed and only failed to win the group at three events where group competition was offered. At these he was second twice and out of the ribbons the other time. He won best in show 28 times including

S. S. Van Dine (left) with unidentified friends in the early thirties.

Ch. Flornell Sound Laddie.

such affairs as Morris and Essex (1949), Westchester (1949), Westbury (1948 and 1949), and Westminster, Eastern Dog Club and the International, all in 1950. In addition he captured all three specialty events in which he was entered.

The passing of the Edgerstoune Kennels was a great loss to the breed, since its fine stud dogs made available to the fancy the best of domestic and imported bloodlines.

The second of the pair began operations in about 1932 at Millbrook, New York when Miss Jean Flagler started her Relgalf establishment. Early operation was limited to Scottish Terriers, with Russell Openshaw as the manager and handler of the string. One of the initial purchases was a dog from England, Ch. Radical of Rookes, first champion for the kennel, which with Revealed of Hillwood and the bitches Sylvia of Hillwood and Reality of Hillwood formed the nucleus of the operation. Homebreds came rapidly and Relgalf was on its way.

A few years later the establishment was moved to Rye, New York where an entirely new and enlarged kennel complex became a model with everything for the comfort and development of dogs. Welsh, Airedales and Fox Terriers were added and the kennel population grew to around 60 dogs. Miss Flagler, then Mrs. Matthews, added Frank Ortalani to her staff, and the kennel soon provided stiff competition with a host of homebreds as well as its many fine imports, which now included such dogs as Ch. Flornell Soundfella, Ch. Flornell Sound Laddie, Ch. Silvertip of Gedling, Ch. Flornell Splendid and the great show bitches Ch. Rosehall Ideal, Ch. Broxton Battle, Ch. Ortley Angela, Ch. Cedar Pond Chloe (the last two from the now defunct Braw Bricht Kennels) and Ch. Grayling of Rookes.

The kennel had great success during the years 1940–1942 with two dogs: Ch. Bradthorn Bullion and Ch. Relgalf Ribbon Raider, a homebred. Between them they captured some 11 best in shows and were tops in the breed for the three-year period. Concurrently, Relgalf showed such Scots as Ch. Gillsie Dictator, Ch. Relgalf Rebel Leader and Ch. Relgalf Dictator to name a few.

During most of its activity, the kennel showed throughout the United States. It was not unusual to find Openshaw with his string in California or in the Southern States, and the name became a symbol of quality in the breed. While this mobility is not unusual

83

today, with air travel at hand, it was quite an innovation at the time and did much to popularize the breed.

The kennels were closed shortly after the war; the 1949 season was the last for this extremely successful establishment. Relgalf dogs are still found in many pedigrees and their contributions cannot be stressed too highly.

One other strong establishment begun during the golden era of the thirties warrants mention before we leave this fabulous decade: the Marlu Farm Kennels of Mr. and Mrs. Maurice Pollak at Long Branch, New Jersey. The dogs were handled by Bob Braithwaite and later by Johnny Murphy, and both had great success with the string. In addition to Scotties, Marlu had a strong force of Welsh that were highly successful in the ring. Mr. Pollak bred many good ones, including such dogs as Ch. Marlu Crusader and Ch. Marlu Clincher, and he bought others. Eng. Ch. Walsing Warrant, an early purchase, was used well at stud while Chs. Deephaven Warspite and Deephaven Red Seal both graced the kennel pens during their heyday; their successes are history now. The closing of Marlu Farm Kennels was a real loss to the fancy.

This brings the review of modern dogs to the period of World War II. While activities continued on an abbreviated scale in the United States during the conflict, many fanciers dropped out and others cut down, never to return. Some, as noted heretofore, continued with good success and a few are still active in a large way.

The period from about 1946 brought in a host of new names, many for the first time and others as a continued effort that proved more successful than before. The list is so long that it would be impossible to name all who deserve mention, so it will be limited to those who captured the larger plums and thus have enjoyed national prominence.

As mentioned, Stalters' Barberry Knowe and Snethen's Shieling establishments are still robust competition for the best. Added to these are a host of newer competitors whose accomplishments have been outstanding. Heading this list is Mrs. Blanche Reeg, owner of the Blanart Kennels. Her interest in dogs commenced in the early thirties, but not until she bred Ch. Blanart Barcarolle in 1947 did her fortunes begin to brighten. Actually, Barcarolle's great-grandsire was Blanart Bomber, a son of the incomparable Ch. Bradthorn Bullion, which indicates Mrs. Reeg's extended interest.

Ch. Blanart Bolero.

Mrs. Blanche Reeg with Ch. Blanart Bewitching.

Barcarolle was finished by Mrs. Reeg in 1949 and then retired from the ring to the breeding pen. She produced ten champion get and a host of other good Scots that have helped bring the breed along. To date, ten of her progeny have produced a total of 56 champions, and many of today's winners have Barcarolle blood in their veins. Two of her sons, Chs. Blanart Barrister and Blanart Bolero, are possibly best known since each has been a strong stud force. Her granddaughter, Ch. Blanart Bewitching, one of the all-time great show bitches, holds an enviable record of seven best in shows with 20 group firsts and 13 specialty bests in her limited show exposure. She twice won the group at Westminster and was best in show at the International, to pinpoint three of her greatest triumphs. Best of all, she was invariably shown and conditioned by her owner, a notable accomplishment. During the past 16 years Blanart has bred a total of 39 titleholders and has owned many more.

The kennel was located for years at Wantagh, Long Island but it is presently active at Boyds, Maryland. It has always been operated on a small scale which has permitted Mrs. Reeg to give personal attention to every dog, and this factor may have had a strong bearing upon its consistent success.

Todhill is another kennel that has done extremely well in the postwar era both with homebreds and imports. Owned by Mr. and Mrs. Robert Graham of Rome, New York, it gained additional fame as the home of the great Ch. Walsing Winning Trick of Edgerstoune from the closing of Edgerstoune in 1954 until his death in October 1960. Todhill has had other toppers, however; these have won well and were also important stud forces in the breed: Ch. Todhill Cinnamon Bear, sire of Ch. Gaidoune Great Bear and Ch. Gaidoune Grin and Bear It; Ch. Friendship Farm Diplomat, sire of Cinnamon Bear, Ch. Todhill's Honest John as well as four Gaidoune champions in a single litter out of Ch. Gaidoune Gorgeous Hussy; and Ch. Special Edition, sire of a host of great ones including the show winning bitch Ch. Scotvale Sunshine, Ch. Wychworth Wizard, etc., among others. In all, Cinnamon Bear, Diplomat and Special Edition have sired some 37 titleholders, indicating the strength of the kennel's stud.

Among others that have come to the fore are Mr. and Mrs. Al Ayres, whose Ayrescot Kennels bred many good ones. The Ayres have long since become successful handlers and have shown and conditioned many top Scotties. Colonel and Mrs. Weaver of the Washington area, too, have been quite active with the Scot's Guard dogs and with fine success, as has Ruth Johnson, whose "Carmichael" Scotties have done so well. Mrs. Johnson is of course the breeder of the great Ch. Carmichael's Fanfare. Mr. and Mrs. Frank Brumby's Rannoch Dune establishment is relatively new in years, but Frank's experience carries back to the great kennels of the past, and one can never forget his handling ability with the dogs of Hillwood and Braw Bricht nor his valuable advice which has been offered to newcomers without reservation.

In addition, Dr. and Mrs. Joseph Thomas' Highlander Scots included Ch. Wyrebury Worthwhile and Ch. Wychworth Heyday Hoagy. Mrs, Josten's Hampton Hill dogs included Ch. Walsing Wyndola of Hampton Hill and Cornelia Crissey, whose Ch. Crisscot Carnival did so well and whose puppy bitch, Blanart Betwixt, won the 1965 fall specialty of the S. T. C. A.

Still others: Mrs. William Worcester, with a good winner in Ch. Gillsie Wrockwardine Sirius; Mrs. Louise Benham and Ch. Glendoune Gondolier; Mr. and Mrs. Sheldon Winans, whose Fulluvit Wee Mousie caused a sensation at Morris and Essex in 1951 and whose other Fulluvit dogs did such good winning; Joseph Kelly whose great dog, Ch. Independent Ben, won the 1949 New York specialty under the redoubtable William Singleton with Jimmy Murphy on the lead; Mrs. William Constable (Murray) who has been mentioned before in connection with wheatens but whose interest and activity in the breed was a never-ending source of amazement to all who knew her; the McLoughlins of Lynnscot; Mr. and Mrs. Seth Malby (Rampart) interested vitally in the breed for more years than I care to remember and wonderful people; Charles Werber (Jepeca), who still loves a good Scot and who judges them that way; Merritt Pope of Philabeg; and so many more.

Passing to the West Coast, three fanciers that merit special mention are Mrs. Dorissa Barnes and the partnership of Martha Melekov and Lorraine Davis. Dorissa Barnes of Crescent Hill fame began breeding Scotties after the war with two English imports, Ch. Trevone Torquil and later Ch. Niddbanks His Nibbs. The first produced a bitch, Crescent Hill Ginger Blossom, which when bred to Ch. Wyrebury Wrangler produced the dog Ch. Crescent Hill Ace

O'Spades, while the second sired a bitch, Ch. Milpita Mia Merriment. Ace O'Spades joined with Merriment to produce two of the kennel's best in Ch. Crescent Hill Maverick and later, Ch. Crescent Hill Indian Scout. In this author's opinion, "Scout" was a great Scotsman, and his record supports this contention. In all, Mrs. Barnes has bred some ten titleholders and has owned many more. Her kennel has always placed quality over quantity and the results have been most gratifying.

Marlorain started in 1952 with two half-sisters, Mariglen Blithe Spirit and Glenby Lorna. Both were by Ch. Glenby Captain, a son of Ch. Deephaven Jeffrey. Blithe Spirit completed her title and was bred to Ch. Deephaven Red Seal; the result, Ch. Marlorain Dark Seal, a great stud in his own right with some eight titleholders to his credit. In 1955 the kennels purchased Wychworth Windfall, an English import, and quickly finished him. He in turn produced three champion daughters including Ch. Marlorain Silver Spoon, which when mated to her grandsire, Ch. Marlorain Dark Seal, whelped the present standard-bearer, Ch. Marlorain Proud Piper. To date, the partnership has ten champions to its credit with several others that have been purchased. Much of the early success of this kennel came from Mrs. Bertha Russell's efforts at the Glenby Kennels. Basic stock came through the Hillcote Laddie bloodlines by way of Ch. Glenby Bonnie, C. D., a double granddaughter of Laddie's.

Before leaving the West several others should be mentioned who have done well during the postwar period. Mrs. Edward Mansure of Merrie Oaks is one of these. Dr. and Mrs. Kenneth Grow had Ch. Garlu Haggis Baggis which under the tutelage of Daisy Austad did very well at the shows and attracted attention in New York in 1963, while Mildred and Robert Charves have been quite active, together with Mrs. Messinger (Medrick), Mrs. Richard Swatsley (Revran), and of course the aforementioned Lena Kardos, whose name has become synonymous with the breed in California. These and many more have had a hand in bringing the breed back on the West Coast where today specialty shows are teeming with good competition among West Coast fanciers.

In the South we find the breed not as well supported as in other sections. This condition is rapidly changing. Southern shows not only bring show dogs to the South but they interest people in the area in breeding and exhibiting.

The T. Allen Kirks of Roanoke, Virginia have been interested in the breed since they began about 1947, but they did not gain a champion until 1957. Their first was a wheaten bitch, Ch. Gran-Vue's Miss Manners. Once the ice was broken they began to achieve success rather rapidly with a long line of titleholders, some 30 to date. An import, Ch. Glendoune Gwenda, a great show bitch, was the starting point, along with Ch. Fran-Jean's Bridie Mollie. According to the Kirks, most of their present homebred stock goes back to one of these. This statement proves the adage that a good bitch is always the foundation of any successful kennel; in this case it was two. The present standard-bearers include Ch. Balachan Grenadier and the prolific stud, Ch. Balachan Agitator, which has already accounted for ten champion get.

The kennel is now an established threat at most shows in the South and East, and dogs bearing the Balachan prefix are often seen far from home. Besides being a breeder of stature, Dr. Kirk is a recognized authority on Scottish Terrier pedigrees, and his *Book of American Scottish Terrier Pedigrees* is a compilation that every person interested in the breed should own. It records the pedigrees of all champions from the start of competition until 1962.

In the South there are several other breeders that have contributed a great deal to the Scot's stature through the years. Mr. and Mrs. Heywood Hartley's Woodhart Kennels at Richmond, while small, has produced many toppers that have been owner-shown. Mr. Hartley is a highly respected multibreed judge and to him goes the honor of placing Ch. Carmichael's Fanfare at the head of the Terrier group at Westminster in the year she went on to best in show. The Hartleys' interest extends back many years. They bred their first breed champion, Woodhart Wendy, in 1943 to climax an effort that extended years before that. To date they have bred over a dozen titleholders including a good brindle dog, Ch. Woodhart Wingover, which represented some six generations of Woodhart breeding as well as strong line breeding to Edgerstoune Troubadour on both sides of his pedigree.

The Middlemount dogs bred by Bruce Webb are worthy of mention since he bred many fine ones in Florida, including about a dozen titleholders, among which were several wheatens. One of his big winners was Ch. Middlemount Juggernaut. Dr. and Mrs. Kater McInnes' Marymac prefix will also be found repeatedly in the records in view of their long-time interest. This leaves Dr. and Mrs. Stewart Carter of Louisville, whose Rebel Run establishment will long be remembered because of dogs owned and bred by them. Their first great dog, Ch. Edgerstoune Troubadour, bought from Edgerstoune, was purchased as a youngster of great promise and matured to that promise. Troubadour became one of the top show dogs as well as one of the top studs of all times. He captured many best in show awards; the two remembered best were Chicago International (1952), with Jake Terhune handling, and Westchester (1954), with Johnny Murphy on the end of the lead. The Carters also bred the litter brothers Ch. Rebel Invader and Ch. Rebel Raider in addition to their full sister, Ch. Rebel Rhythm, all top show specimens.

Although Troubadour will always be remembered, the Carters are best known for their wonderful hospitality that made the Scottish Terrier Club of Kentucky's annual show one of the biggest and most popular in the country. Starting on a small scale, the Carters built it into a "must" specialty for any Scot to win in hope of national recognition. It brought the best Eastern and Western dogs into competition for top officials of the country to judge. The show was indeed a tribute to the Carters, wonderful people whom the breed could ill-afford to lose.

As we move into the Midwest, a kennel that has become a threat at shows all over the country during the past ten years is the Anstamm establishment of Mr. and Mrs. Anthony Stamm of Kalamazoo, Michigan. Their first big nationally known winner was the import Ch. Bardene Boy Blue. He has won groups from coast to coast with Mrs. Lena Kardos as handler. In addition, the dog has proved useful as a stud and is producing well. The Stamms have bred a host of champions including Ch. Anstamm Dark Venture, a big winner. Prior to their marriage both were interested in Scots and were breeding and showing in competition against one another.

More lately the Stamms have a promising young import, Ch. Bardene Bobby Dazzler, which finished quickly and is expected to continue his winning ways. The Anstamms have bred and/or owned dozens of titleholders, and they show extensively, often having dogs on the circuit in the East and West simultaneously while exhibiting dogs in the Midwest themselves.

While in this area we should mention the Sandoone Kennels of

Ch. Marlorain Proud Piper, Daisy Austed handling; Heywood Hartley, judge.

Eng. & Am. Ch. Bardene Boy Blue.

Miss Betty Malinka of near Chicago—Ch. Sandoone Missy Lou was one of her standouts—and the Cantie establishment of Mary German of Elkhart, Indiana. Mrs. German bred many top dogs, and several did extremely well under the guidance of Lena Kardos, who showed them on the West Coast and in other sections. Ch. Cantie Captivator, Ch. Cantie's Ace and Ch. Cantie Confident are a few of these. Mrs. John Gilkey is another; she began in the Midwest but has since moved to New Mexico. Ch. Gilkey's Johnny Come Lately is one of her most successful homebreds.

Many other fanciers have had more than a modicum of success in the breed in the Midwest. For example: three Chicago area men who did their share to bring the breed along were P. K. Groves, Ernie Joresco and Bill Moore, known to many as Marie Stone's invaluable helper. Moving to Iowa, most will remember the Macauleys of Cedar Rapids, whose Mac's Welton dogs were known far and near. Also, the Misses Sanders and Portwood of Lansing, who own that grand import, Ch. Glendoune Gaytime, shown as a veteran in 1965 at the age of 13—she looked like a youngster, clear eyed and active; Math Rauen of Wisconsin, whose import Ch. Gillsie Roger Right and homebred Ch. Matscot Roger Ringleader have done so well on the circuits with Jack Funk. Richard Hensel, Allan Cartwright, Mr. and Mrs. Reason Krick, John Wright, Jr., Goldie Seagraves and a host of others own successful establishments that produce fine Scottish Terriers.

Before leaving the area, one of the largest and certainly one of the strongest kennels, as evidenced by its show and breeding record, is Gaidoune, owned by Miss Helen Gaither of Wheeling, West Virginia. Miss Gaither, together with Dr. Nancy Lenfestey, her manager and handler, has made terrific strides in the ten years of the kennel's existence. It all began with the purchase of a bitch, Glendoune Gaibonnie from England. She finished her American title in 1956 and was bred to Ch. Rebel Raider, a Troubadour son. Out of the litter came the incomparable Ch. Gaidoune Gorgeous Hussy, top producing bitch in the breed today. When Hussy was bred back to her grandsire, Ch. Edgerstoune Troubadour, the litter included three champions. The following year, 1959, bred to Ch. Friendship Farm Diplomat, she whelped four puppies that ultimately made their titles. In 1960 she was bred to Ch. Todhill's Cinnamon Bear and produced four more champions including Ch. Gaidoune Great

Ruth Johnson with Carmichael's Fanfare, best at the Scottish Terrier Club of America specialty, 1961, from the classes. Robert Graham, club president, left; and the author, judging.

Mrs. Dorissa Barnes with three of her champions, Crescent Hill Indian Scout, Crescent Hill Ace O'Spades, and Crescent Hill Maverick.

Bear, one of the present-day top winners (15 times best in show with 47 groups). Her last litter, in 1962 and again by Cinnamon Bear, brought the second top winner of the kennel, Ch. Gaidoune Grin and Bear It, presently being shown with great success.

Miss Gaither's rise as a breeder may be credited to a great brood bitch and to sound principles of line breeding, where the best possible studs have been chosen both as to bloodlines and individuals. From the steady stream of champions bred (more than 25 to date) and the many winners that are being shown it is evident that Gaidoune Scotties will make an indelible mark on the history of the breed.

Ch. Gaidoune Great Bear.

7

Interpretation
and Evaluation
of the Standard

THE Standard of Perfection for any breed is the specification set forth by breed proponents, generally the national specialty club that has been recognized and approved by the American Kennel Club. It prescribes the correct structure and temperament and is used as a guide by breeders and judges.

The standard is an important factor in the success of the breed. If it is sufficiently specific, it is relatively easy to understand; if it is too sketchy, it can confuse beginners and risk a wide variation of personal opinion among the more serious fanciers. Therefore a clear and concise standard is necessary if a breed is to progress. The Scottish Terrier Standard is an adequate specification. This chapter will examine its history and changes and attempt to clarify its more obscure points.

First, it should be remembered that every breed was produced for a definite purpose. In order to carry out its purpose, its basic factors did not necessarily contribute to the dog's beauty but were necessary for his usefulness and sometimes his very existence. The Scottish Terrier was originally a working Terrier, bred to outlast vermin of all kinds and under all conditions. For this reason, the characteristics required for work should be considered of utmost importance when breeding or judging. First, temperament. The Scottie has to be fearless, not quarrelsome but unafraid of man or beast. He must be armed with strong teeth set in powerful jaws so that he can defend himself. He must own a good double coat, profuse with soft undercoat and well thatched with a tough and harsh outer jacket that will shed rain or snow and protect against briars, teeth and cold. He has to have a strong back and adequate hindquarters so necessary to any Terrier to aid in holding his prey to the ground; above all, he must have good, strong legs and feet carrying thick, tough pads, because the Scottie is an earth dog, a digger. Without this equipment, he is useless for his life's purpose. In addition, a Terrier of any breed needs sharp eyes, small and dark and well protected against injury beneath a strong overhanging brow.

These are the fundamentals considered of great importance; without them no Scottie could do the work for which he was bred. Many will counter, "Why worry? We do not use them for work anymore." This has some validity, but if we forget the basic background we will eventually lose the very characteristics that have made the breed great. For this reason, basic factors should still be guarded jealously by every person who loves the breed and who wants it to progress.

Interpretation of the standard varies with different people and leaves rather wide latitude for breeder and judge. The type of a breed can become modified through breeders' caprice and judging trends, which is why winning dogs from different eras look different even though they have all been bred and judged by the same standard. The detailed discussion offered here will aid the novice and will illustrate the latitude that may be taken with certain measurable points.

The first recognized standard of the "Hard-Haired Scotch Terrier" was written by Vero Shaw about 1882–83 and is quoted verbatim in Chapter 2. It was a rather clear specification subscribed to by most of the leading breeders and judges of the day. It left few points of controversy and helped the breed to progress after several years of bickering sparked by personal likes and dislikes. This early breed specification was adopted without change by the first-formed Scottish Terrier Club in America in 1895. It continued to be the law until 1900, when the reorganized Scottish Terrier Club of America, with J. Steele MacKenzie and Fayette Ewing as a committee, added a paragraph on disqualification. It read as follows:

Disqualification

Evidences of the use of a knife or other instrument to correct any defects. (The removal of dew claws being excepted.)

It should be the spirit and purpose of the judge in deciding the relative merits of two or more dogs to consider the approximation of nature to the standard rather than the effect of artificiality.

Thereafter the standard remained the same until 1925, when a committee of Henry Bixby, Robert Sedgwick, Henry T. Fleitmann, S. Edwin Megargee and Richard Cadwalader were called upon to revise it. The "new" standard differed from the original in many respects and eliminated the "half prick ears" that were previously permissible. It also changed the neck to include the word "moderately" before short; but the most important change was in the body. Where the early standard specified a "moderately *long* body", the new one called for a body that was "moderately *short*." Many other minor changes were included, and this standard reads as follows:

SCOTTISH TERRIER CLUB STANDARD

As accepted by the Club, February 12, 1925
and approved by the American Kennel Club

Skull (5 points): Long, of medium width, slightly domed and covered with short hair. It should not be quite flat as there should be a slight stop or drop between the eyes.

Muzzle (5 points): In proportion to the length of the skull, with not too much taper toward the nose. Nose should be black and of good size. The jaws should be perfectly level and the teeth square, although the nose projects somewhat over the mouth giving the impression that the upper jaw is longer than the lower.

Eyes (5 points): Set wide apart, small and of almond shape, not round. Color to be dark brown or nearly black. To be bright, piercing and set well under the brow.

Ears (10 points): Small, prick, set well up on the skull, rather pointed but not cut. The hair on them should be short and velvety.

Neck (5 points): Moderately short, thick and muscular, strongly set on sloping shoulders, but not so short as to appear clumsy.

97

Chest (5 points): Broad and very deep, well let down between the forelegs.

Body (15 points): Moderately short and well ribbed up with strong loin, deep flanks and very muscular hindquarters.

Legs and Feet (10 points): Both fore and hind legs should be short and very heavy in bone in proportion to the size of the dog. Forelegs straight or slightly bent with elbows close to the body, as Scottish Terriers should not be out at the elbows. Stifles should be well bent and legs straight from hock to heel. Thighs very muscular. Feet round and thick with strong nails, forefeet larger than the hind feet.

Tail (2½ points): Never cut and about seven inches long, carried gaily with a slight curve but not over the back.

Coat (15 points): Rather short, about two inches, dense undercoat with outer coat intensely hard and wiry.

Size (10 points): About ten inches at the shoulder and weight about 18 or 20 pounds for both sexes. The correct size must take into consideration height fully as much as weight.

Color (2½ points): Steel or iron gray, brindled or grizzled, black, sandy, or wheaten. White markings are objectionable and can be allowed only on chest and that to a slight extent only.

General Appearance (10 points): The face should wear a keen, sharp and active expression. Both head and tail should be carried well up. The dog should look very compact, well muscled and powerful, giving the impression of immense power in a small size.

FAULTS

Eyes large, round or light colored. Light bone. Out at elbows. Ears round, drop, or too large. Coat soft, silky, or curly. Jaw over- or under-shot. Over- or under-size.

No further changes were made until 1947, when the Scottish Terrier Club of America believed additional revisions were necessary to keep up with breeding and judging trends. Again a committee was selected which was composed of S. Edwin Megargee, Theodore Bennett, John Kemps, and Maurice Pollak. The standard they proposed was adopted and is still the one by which the breed is judged. The main differences between the '47 specification and the '25 standard are an increased size which now reads: "19 to 22 pounds for dogs and 18 to 21 pounds for bitches," and the height for both sexes, which was set at about "10 inches" and was a far cry from the original 9 to 12 inches of the 1895 standard. The final important revision was inserted under "Penalties," where instructions were given to judges to turn down any dog for winners that does not have head and tail up. This last is a useful suggestion to improve showmanship and eliminate shy dogs, but it does not take into consideration the naturally dour temperament of the breed. Many judges who are not acquainted with the Scottie will turn

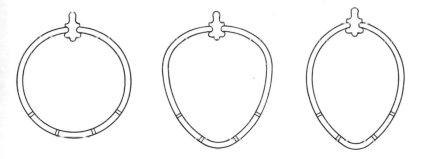

Rib structure. (Left) A round rib without depth, improper on a Scot. (Center)
A heart-shaped rib, well sprung and with good depth. (Right) A poorly sprung
rib not providing sufficient lung capacity.

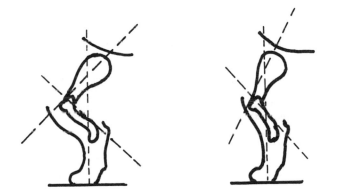

(Left) The shoulder with good layback provides overhang and
blends the neck into the back to shorten the latter. (Right) The
straighter or more upright shoulder lessens the degree of overhang
and lengthens the back.

down a better dog because the tail is not carried stiffly erect. This is not right for two reasons: first, the *Scotch* Terrier, as a basic breed from which all Scotch breeds were derived, did not carry a stiffly erect tail; rather, it was carried about three-quarters mast. Second, and more important, is the basic temperament of the Scottie. He is a dour dog that will not show if the urge is not there. This does not denote shyness, for which the requirement was incorporated, but rather a true Scotch temperament which refuses to do that which the dog does not want to do. It is believed that judges who know the breed can detect shyness in the dog's eye and that this should be the criterion rather than an inflexible turndown on showmanship.

A copy of the current Standard of Perfection for the breed is as follows:

Approved Standard of the
Scottish Terrier Club of America
Adopted 1947

Skull (5 points): Long, of medium width, slightly domed and covered with short hard hair. It should not be quite flat, as there should be a slight stop or drop between the eyes.

(1) *Muzzle* (5 points): In proportion to the length of skull, with not too much taper toward the nose. Nose should be black and of good size. The jaws should be level and square. The nose projects somewhat over the mouth, giving the impression that the upper jaw is longer than the lower. The teeth should be evenly placed, having a scissors or level bite, with the former being preferable.

Eyes (5 points): Set wide apart, small and of almond shape, not round. Color to be dark brown or nearly black. To be bright, piercing and set well under the brow.

Ears (10 points): Small, prick, set well up on the skull, rather pointed but not cut. The hair on them should be short and velvety.

Neck (5 points): Moderately short, thick and muscular, strongly set on sloping shoulders, but not so short as to appear clumsy.

Chest (5 points): Broad and very deep, well let down between the forelegs.

Body (15 points): Moderately short and well ribbed up with strong loin, deep flanks and very muscular hindquarters.

(2) *Legs and Feet* (10 points): Both fore and hind legs should be short and very heavy in bone in proportion to the size of the dog. Fore legs straight or slightly bent with elbows close to the body. Scottish Terriers should not be out at the elbows. Stifles should be well bent and legs straight from hock to heel. Thighs very muscular. Feet round and thick with strong nails, fore feet larger than the hind feet.

NOTE: The gait of the Scottish Terrier is peculiarly its own and is very characteristic of the breed. It is not the square trot or walk that is desirable in the long-legged breeds. The fore legs do not move in exact parallel planes—rather

100

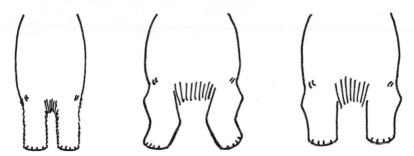

(Left) Narrow, pinched-in front suggesting a Fox Terrier build. (Center) Crooked forelegs out at elbows. (Right) Out at elbows.

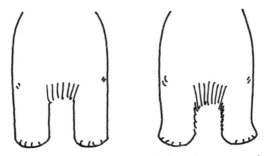

(Left) A good front with straight legs that seem to be acceptable to most judges. (Right) A proper front, the elbows close and the feet turning out slightly.

(Left) Proper hindquarters, the hocks turning neither in nor out, and spread apart to provide strength. (Right) Undesirable cow-hocks which, when turned in, tend to weaken the hindquarters.

in reaching out incline slightly inward. This is due to the shortness of leg and width of chest. The action of the rear legs should be square and true and at the trot both the hocks and stifles should be flexed with a vigorous motion.

Tail (2½ points): Never cut and about seven inches long, carried with a slight curve but not over the back.

Coat (15 points): Rather short, about two inches, dense undercoat with outer-coat intensely hard and wiry.

(3) *Size and Weight* (10 points): Equal consideration must be given to height, length of back and weight. Height at shoulder for either sex should be about 10″. Generally, a well balanced Scottish Terrier dog of correct size should weigh from 19 to 22 lbs. and a bitch from 18 to 21 lbs. The principal objective must be symmetry and balance.

Color (2½ points): Steel or iron grey, brindle or grizzled, black, sandy or wheaten. White markings are objectionable and can be allowed only on the chest and that to a slight extent only.

General Appearance (10 points): The face should wear a keen sharp and active expression. Both head and tail should be carried well up. The dog should look very compact, well muscled and powerful, giving the impression of immense power in a small size.

(4) *Penalties:* Soft coat, round or very light eye, over or undershot jaw, obviously over or under size, shyness, timidity or failure to show with head and tail up are faults to be penalized. No judge should put to Winners or Best of Breed any Scottish Terrier not showing real Terrier character in the ring.

SCALE OF POINTS

Skull	5	Neck	5	Tail	2½
Muzzle	5	Chest	5	Coat	15
Eyes	5	Body	15	Color	2½
Ears	10	Legs and Feet	10	Appearance	10
				Total	100 Pts.

Before leaving the written word of the standard it will be of interest to review the one presently used by the Scottish Terrier Club of England (1965). This differs in several respects from the American specification and suggests among other things, larger dogs having a shoulder height of 11 inches as a top limit together with heavier animals to go with the height. A copy of this standard is offered herewith to acquaint American fanciers with the English requirements:

Standard of the Scottish Terrier
Club of England—1965

General Appearance—A Scottish Terrier is a sturdy thick-set dog of a size to get to ground, placed on short legs, alert in carriage, and suggestive of great power and activity in small compass. The head gives the impression of being long for a dog of its size. The body is covered with a close-lying broken, rough-textured coat, and with keen intelligent eyes and sharp prick ears the dog

102

(Left) Ears should not be large. (Center) Ears well set and relatively small. (Right) Mule ears, set on sides of the head, are very undesirable.

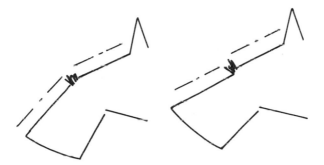

(Left) Muzzle and skull should be about equal in length from the stop. (Right) The top planes of the muzzle and skull should be parallel as shown by dot-dash lines, not down-faced as shown by the companion figure on the left.

(Left) Proper tail well set-up and carried correctly. (Center) Tail correctly set but not well carried. (Right) Tail poorly set.

looks willing to go anywhere and do anything. In spite of its short legs, the construction of the dog enables it to be very agile and active. The whole movement of the dog is smooth, easy and straightforward with free action at shoulder, stifle and hock.

Head and Skull—Without being out of proportion to the size of the dog it should be long, the length of skull enabling it to be fairly wide and yet retain a narrow appearance. The skull is nearly flat and the cheek bones do not protrude. There is a slight, but distinct drop between skull and foreface just in front of the eye. The nose is large, and in profile the line from the nose towards the chin appears to slope backwards.

Eyes—Should be almond-shaped, dark brown, fairly wide apart and set deeply under the eyebrows.

Ears—Neat, of fine texture, pointed and erect.

Mouth—Teeth large, the upper incisors closely overlapping the lower.

Neck—Muscular, of moderate length.

Forequarters—The head is carried on a muscular neck of moderate length showing quality, set into a long sloping shoulder, the brisket well in front of the forelegs, which are straight, well boned to straight pasterns. The chest fairly broad and hung between the forelegs, which must not be out at elbows nor placed under the body.

Body—The body has well-rounded ribs, which flatten to a deep chest and are carried well back. The back is proportionately short and very muscular. In general, the top line of the body should be straight; the loin muscular and deep, thus powerfully coupling the ribs to the hindquarters.

Hindquarters—Remarkably powerful for the size of the dog. Big and wide buttocks. Thighs deep and muscular, well bent at stifle. Hocks strong and well bent and neither turned inwards nor outwards.

Feet—Of good size and well-padded, toes well arched and closeknit.

Tail—Of moderate length to give a general balance to the dog, thick at the root and tapering towards the tip, is set on with an upright carriage or with a slight bend.

Coat—The dog has two coats, the undercoat short, dense and soft; the outer-coat harsh, dense and wiry; the two making a weather-resisting covering to the dog.

Colour—Black, wheaten, or brindle of any colour.

Weight and size—The ideally-made dog in hard show condition could weigh from 19 lbs. to 23 lbs.

Height at shoulder 10 to 11 inches.

A discussion of the several requirements in the present standard of the Scottish Terrier Club of America will be useful in its interpretation and to aid in evaluating the various points. The over-all appearance of any dog is of major importance. When judging a dog type, character and balance are important to consider. Any dog that lacks type, breed character and balance is not a good specimen even though his conformation is good, point by point. This is the reason that judging by the point system fails in many cases. Few standards give enough weight to type and character and overall balance (the Scottie standard is no exception), but stress various purely structural points. A dog may be perfect in each of these, but if the overall dog is not in balance, it is not a good specimen. Therefore, type, character, and balance should be considered, followed by specific structural factors. Holland Buckley said all of this in a few words when he remarked, "We must first strike for the true type of the breed, and bring our purely fancy points in afterwards."

Proceeding with a detailed discussion of the present standard we find that the skull should be long and of medium width, slightly domed and including a slight stop between the eyes where it joins the muzzle. In general, long-headed dogs prosper in the ring although today many Scotties are being shown that lack stop because emphasis has been placed upon extreme length. Lack of stop causes lack of brow or bone cover over the eyes and is a serious fault. Therefore, a stop should be present and when comparing two dogs of nearly identical quality, the one with stop and brow to go with it should prevail.

The muzzle of the Scot should be in proportion to the length of the skull. If the dog has a short skull, the muzzle should not be overly long since it unbalances the entire head. Actually, the skull and muzzle should be about equal in length, although it must be admitted that a muzzle *slightly* longer than the skull sets off the head and makes it more attractive, and dogs with this abnormality appear to be better in the ring.

The teeth of a Scotsman should be large and formidable. The upper incisors should meet squarely or slightly overlap the lower incisors, this being termed a level and a scissors bite, respectively. There should be six incisors between the canines (large tusk-like teeth) in *both* the upper and the lower set. This is important since some breeds are beginning to lose incisors and often only four are found. This is a fault that if permitted to continue will eventually lead to poor mouths. There is no leeway offered in the standard for "overshot" mouths, those where the lower incisors overlap the upper incisors.

The eyes, clearly described in the standard, should be relatively small, dark, almond-shaped and set wide apart. This means that the skull must be of *medium* width since a narrow skull will always cause the eyes to be set close together, which ruins the dog's expression. Round eyes are another bad fault, for here again, the outlook,

105

foreign to the breed, offers a vapid expression rather than the keen, sharp expression that is characteristic. The paragraph suggests also that the eyes should be set well *under* the brow. This goes back to previous remarks concerning the presence of stop. The ears are described as "small," yet many of today's Scots have what may be termed *large* ears which detract from general appearance and expression. Mule ears, another common fault, are caused by the ears being set on the sides of the skull and not "well up" as required. Mule ears spoil expression.

The dog's neck is of great importance to the overall appearance of the animal. A long neck is always out of proportion while a short one offers a generally cloddy appearance. The standard, which calls for a "moderately short, thick and muscular" neck, is believed to be misleading since it does not describe what is wanted today. The English standard states the desideratum much better by calling for a neck "of moderate length." This is what is wanted, not a short neck. Proper length with well laid back shoulders offers a balanced appearance without being cloddy.

The body of the Scottie is relatively short in back and deep with well sprung ribs. The English standard elaborates on the rib structure by saying the ribs "flatten to a deep chest." This indicates that the Scot should not have a round rib cage but rather a heart-shaped one with spring at the top and depth with a rather narrow structure adjacent the "keel." Many Scotties tend to be round-ribbed which robs them of depth. In all cases, the elbows should not be below the bottom of the rib cage and this may be gauged by trying to place a finger or pencil across the elbows. If it cannot be done, the brisket or bottom of the rib cage is properly placed; if it can be done, the body is shallow and probably quite round-ribbed. The chest, although taken separately in the standard, is certainly a portion of the body. It should be relatively broad whereby the front legs are set well apart. No Scotsman should ever have a narrow front of the order desired in the Fox Terrier. The brisket or "keel" should be well let down between the legs and should extend in front of the legs; in other words, the front legs should be set well under the dog. Too many Scots are being shown that have no "overhand," that is, the front legs are set forward and there is no body ahead of them. This generally indicates straight shoulders among other undesirable bone structures.

This brings us to the forelegs, which have already been placed properly with respect to the body of the dog. The legs may be relatively straight or bent with the elbows relatively close to the body. Short-legged Terriers never have as tight an elbow as the longer legged breeds since there is always some roominess between the elbow and the ribs. On the other hand, if the dog is "out at the elbow" this distance grows and is quite apparent upon moving the dog. The front feet are large in proportion to the dog since they were originally used for digging and for moving rocks and other impediments to the dog's progress in subterranean passages. The feet may point straight ahead; this generally indicates straight legs which are not natural so far as the basic structure of the dog is concerned. None of the early dogs of the breed had such legs since they would have been useless for the purpose for which they were bred. Dogs with slightly bent legs are more to the original type and these same animals have feet that turn out slightly. This is the proper structure.

Since the Scot is short-legged, it must, when digging, throw the dirt and debris sideways. This act is furthered by bent legs and turned-out feet. F. M. Ross commented upon this feature in her writings on the Cairn Terrier and stated: "No Cairn however deep or in what kind of soil he goes to ground, ever closes himself in. This may be attributed to the turned-out feet which help move the earth sideways instead of directly behind the digging dog. Cairns, Westies, *Scotties* that work should all have this type of foot, although accentuated turning out detracts from appearance and does not aid materially to the working character of the dog." This passage is a sound evaluation of the reason for the condition and also limits the toeing-out to a degree that does not detract from overall appearance. The standard is silent on this point, which often causes uninformed people to fault dogs when they have turned-out feet. The structure should only be faulted when the turn-out is excessive or when one foot is turned out more than the other.

The hind feet are smaller than the forefeet but are large in comparison with the dog. All feet should be well padded with thick, generous pads, and nothing approximating a thin pad or splayed foot can be tolerated. The breed is a digging breed and its feet are important.

The standard describes very well the characteristic Scottie gait. It is not like the gait of a Fox Terrier but rather a sort of roll, which causes a shift of the body so that the center of gravity remains over the vertical axis of the legs. This is required since the dog is short-legged.

The hind legs are much as those of other breeds. They require strong hindquarters with well bent stifles and the legs should move in generally parallel planes, neither cow-hocked nor bow-legged. The movement should be free and easy with the front legs reaching out and the hind legs driving with a decided push. Some dogs will move with hind legs underneath them at all times; such a dog does not have drive, and when moving with one that does, will take two steps to the other's one to cover the same ground. Reach with driving movement indicates well-laid-back shoulders and properly angulated rear equipment. A dog that does not cover ground is generally poorly angulated in front or in rear, or both.

The Scot should have a thick, relatively short tail, not more than about seven inches and tapering from its base to a point at its extremity. Indeed, it should be shaped like an inverted carrot of stubby variety. It should be carried stiffly erect, preferably with a slight bend towards the dog's head when he is at attention and never half-mast or between the hind legs. Early representations of the Scottish Terrier show the tail at less than the erect carriage and say that this is correct, but times have changed as has the standard. Today's Scotsman is required to have the proper shape, length and carriage of tail since nothing detracts more from the general appearance than,

"A gawkie tail, wi' upward curl."

The Scottie is a double-coated Terrier. This means that he should have a dense, soft undercoat and a hard, relatively long top coat. This should be about two inches in length when at its prime. The texture varies but should be as hard and wiry as possible. It will be found that blacks generally do not have as hard a texture as brindles, although there have been some that have owned exceptional coats. In all cases, coat texture can be improved by work but a poor coated dog can never be brought into a good coat. The color of the coat may vary through a wide range, including blacks, reds, grays, and wheatens together with brindle, and grizzle of any of these colors. Although there is no disqualification, white is not allowed and no more than a small patch or locket on the chest is tolerated. Dogs with excessive amounts of white should never be shown or bred, and although throw-backs of this nature may occur because of consanguinity with the West Highland White, they are rare today.

A few words on the wheaten may be helpful to prospective breeders of this attractive color. The wheaten color ranges from a light golden to a red, the color frequently accompanied by dark hairs around the eyes which gives the dog an expression foreign to the breed. It has the added drawback of making the eyes appear larger than they really are.

Wheatens, as a class, frequently suffer another penalty. Too often, the head is bumpy with a thick skull and prominent bones over the brow. Many oldtimers say that all of these faults come from an early mesalliance with the Cairn which was used to bring out the wheaten color. Whether or not this is true is a matter of opinion, but the fact remains that the above noted faults have harmed the color in the ring.

However, there have been a number of excellent wheatens without these problems, indicating that the faults can be overcome. The aforementioned Ch. Kinclaven Wild Oats owned the clear color of golden wheat and had no prominent bone structure to detract from his overall outstanding appearance. Neither was his coat shot with black hairs. In more recent times John Treleaven's bitch Ch. Yankee Pride Blushing Squaw II was a good one that could win over the best of the conventional colors. These and many more have overcome the usual drawbacks and anyone who wishes to attack the problem objectively can do it again. That the problem is generally universal and ever-present is apparent from Mrs. Caspersz' remarks concerning Glencannie Gingerbread (whelped in 1928), which she said was a "pale wheaten color without *any black hairs mixed in* which *one usually finds* with these very light ones."

In general, the Scottish Terrier should offer the keen, sharp appearance of an alert dog. He should appear compact and strong, never weedy or light. The standard says he should present an appearance of immense power in a small size and this is an adequate description of the dog.

Before leaving the subject of the breed standard, I would like to comment upon the extent of modification thereof during the 70 years since the first specification was adopted in 1895. If one reads this early standard and then the 1947 version there can be little doubt that today's Scottish Terrier is a greatly changed dog from the early breed representatives. He has increased in weight from a range of 13 to 18 pounds to the present-day figures of 19 to 22 pounds; his ears must be pricked or upright, whereas he could have half-dropped ears in the beginning; his neck has been lengthened from "thick and muscular" to "moderately short, but not so short as to appear clumsy"; his body has been remade from one "of moderate length, not so long as a Skye's" to "moderately short"; and his height has been modified from the 9 to 12 inches at the withers to a flat 10 inches. Further, while it is not mentioned in the present standard, a dog should have a level topline, in differentiation to the statement in the first specification that he "should appear higher on the hind legs than on the fore." This structure was still apparent in the early 30's, as noted in the photographs of dogs of that era. These changes have possibly made the dog of today a more attractive animal but they have not added to his working abilities. Be that as it may, today the Scottie is a popular breed and one with a host of followers. One point that has never been changed and the one that draws so many to this breed is the temperament of the Scot. No other dog is like him.

8

Raising, Training and Conditioning Show Stock

THE care, training and conditioning of good show stock require time and study. Show dogs do not "just grow" like Topsy; they are brought along carefully, and many a dog that would otherwise become an average specimen may be groomed and nurtured into a show prospect through intelligent care. I do not mean that a poorly conformed animal can be changed into a winner. I do mean, however, that many an average dog has done well in the ring through care and training, while many a good prospect has been ruined for exhibition purposes through lack of diligence in its rearing.

The average, well bred litter will include one or two youngsters worth working with for the first five or six months, when a more accurate estimate of their potentialities may be made. In choosing the most promising puppies in a litter, it is best to appraise coat, shortness of back and proportions of the head. The cutest puppies, those with the profuse and/or fuzzy coats, generally mature with soft coats requiring untold work to get into show shape, and then are on the poor side. Of course, if a puppy is otherwise outstanding, the balance may swing in his favor. A relatively short back, strong quarters, and well balanced head are necessities when choosing your future champion, so give these factors plenty of consideration before disposing of surplus puppies. It is a good idea to keep your first litter for at least six months in order to see how various points develop and retrogress. A little attention given the first litter will give you valuable experience that will pay off in subsequent litters.

It will aid in choosing promising puppies to watch the litter frequently at play at a sufficient distance so that your presence does not distract. In this way you can find out which puppy is the leader, the one that is "boss." Such an animal is generally an extrovert and will show well in the ring. You will also be able to observe tail carriage, ear set and general balance a great deal better than can be accomplished by having the puppies on a table where they are not at ease and are usually very tense. Added to these tests, find out which puppies like people the best, which ones come to strangers, and which keep their tails and ears up when being handled. When these characteristics have been determined, it will often be easier to decide which you want to keep. A well conformed dog that is not easily handled will be of little use in the ring. Of course, no irrevocable decision on the points should be made until after six months of age.

Feeding, first the dam and then the puppies, is important throughout the span of a dog's life, but of utmost importance during the formative stages. Feed plenty of animal protein food (meat) for substance, muscle and nerves, together with bone-building foods and a reasonable balance of carbohydrates, fats, etc. The diet should also contain calcium and vitamin supplements in the form of calcium salts, fish liver oils, preferably fortified, irradiated yeast, etc., although all supplements should be used with discretion since too much may be as harmful as too little.

The formation of strong bone and muscle is necessary if the dog is to develop properly. Weak, rickety puppies seldom grow properly, nor do their legs develop well. In fact, most weak puppies end up with bench legs, crooked and sorry looking. A poem found in Hugh Dalziel's book on *Diseases of the Dog* written in 1900 is apropos:

112

> There's some is born with their straight legs by natur,
> And some is born with bow legs from the fu'st—
> And some that should have growed a good deal straighter,
> But they was badly nu'ssed.

The moral is clear—nurse them well, that is, feed properly and let nature take its course.

Exercise, too, is required by dogs of all ages. It can best be given to puppies in a good sized run either indoors or outdoors according to the weather. As soon as the youngsters can safely be taken outside they should be given the benefit of the sun's rays during hours of healthful play. If you can arrange an enclosed run, sheltered with plastic-coated wire netting such as sold for chicken houses, etc., you will be able to give your puppies the benefit of the sun without exposing them to the weather. Such material does not filter out the ultraviolet rays as does ordinary glass.

At about eight weeks of age, strip off all flying, fluffy top coat. This will permit normal growth of healthy hair which will develop into a good tight, straight coat, a great benefit to the dog in later life. Daily grooming from eight weeks on in the form of brushing will aid immeasurably in improving its texture and bloom.

While working initially on the coat, it is a good idea to remove the hair from the ears. This will lighten the ears and make it possible for them to stand erect. As a rule, a puppy's ear will rise normally to a half-prick position and then to fully erect. This may occur simultaneously with both ears or one may go up followed by the other a few days later. Once up, the ears may drop several times before standing permanently. In general, the ears should go up at from eight to 12 weeks of age.

Puppies should be wormed at about six weeks for ascarids (stomach or round worms), preferably with the advice of a veterinarian with respect to the vermifuge used and the dosage. If no worms are expelled, do not worm again for about four weeks; if worms are apparent repeat the treatment in a week's time. Two important admonitions: first, over-worming is the worst thing you can do to a puppy or dog, and may cause arrested development in young stock and a highly nervous condition in a dog of any age; second, never worm a sick dog or puppy. If the animal is not healthy and full of pep *do not* worm without a veterinarian's advice. After a puppy has reached four or five months, no worming should be done unless you actually see evidence in the stool and can identify the type of parasite. If you cannot identify the type, or see no worms, do not dose without consulting a veterinarian. He can made a microscopic examination of the feces to determine the type of worms present and then prescribe the proper vermifuge and dosage, according to the dog's weight. A prominent veterianarian once said "promiscuous worming has killed more dogs than the worms" and any experienced dog breeder will bear out this statement.

All puppies should be protected against distemper at an early age, first, by isolating them from any dogs that have been in contact with dogs outside of the kennel, and second, by prophylaxsis and/or immunization administered by a competent veterinarian.

At approximately four months of age, the average puppy commences to lose his puppy teeth and acquire a permanent set. The teething period continues from one to two months according to the individual puppy. During this time, special attention should be given to the mouth. The puppy teeth do not always fall out. For this reason, if you see a permanent tooth crowding in alongside a puppy tooth, extract the offender and give the permanent tooth a chance to grow in straight. If you cannot remove the tooth yourself, enlist the aid of a veterinarian; milk teeth, however, usually come out easily since they have very little root. Many poor mouths can be attributed to failure to care for the teeth during teething, when in reality, the mouth was made poor by the owner's failure to aid nature. As a breed the Scottie has a good mouth, so keep watch over the teeth and there is little to cause further concern.

During the teething period, ears do funny things. Some ears will not stand erect before the puppy teethes, while others that have been up will drop. Personally, I prefer to help ears that are not erect at four months or which have dropped during teething. This may be done either by rolling them and taping them together at the desired distance, or by forming a tape backing for the ears and then taping them together. Either method is satisfactory. Another approach is to brush the ears with collodion. When it hardens, the film offers sufficient support to cause the ear to stand. In general, taping, etc., strengthens the weak ear cartilage and helps set the ears. Some ears may not stand for a long time and the taping must be repeated. The tape should be left on for a week or ten days and then removed before the ears become sore. Boric acid powder dusted around the base of the ears helps to prevent soreness.

At four to five months of age, the puppy is ready for preliminary show training. Lead breaking is the first step. This may be easily accomplished by first permitting the puppy to wear a light show collar for a day or two. The next step is to attach a lead to the collar and try gently to lead the dog. If he has a mind of his own, and most have, merely hold the lead and let the puppy balk and pull for about ten minutes. Repeat the lesson daily, for a few days, and you will notice that the dog's distrust of the lead lessens and that you can finally lead him around. In about a week's time, the puppy will permit leading for a walk. This should be short at first, as young dogs tire easily, then gradually increase in length until at eight months the puppy is walked about a mile a day in two periods.

This early lead training means much in later show experience. You will have a dog that does not fight the lead, moves easily and without fear, and is under complete control. Teach the pup to move on either a loose or a tight lead, at your left side, without pulling. Endeavor also to keep the ears and tail up by constant talking and periodic bribing with small pieces of liver or other choice tidbits. This makes the puppy a good showman—many an inferior dog has beaten a better specimen on showmanship alone! A good dog that does not make the best of himself is difficult to judge and a complete disappointment to his owner, while a good showman is always the "judge's friend."

Let the puppy run about the kennel or house while you are around and always keep tidbits in your pocket. Let the dog take a nibble occasionally, and before long you will have the youngster looking up at you even when being walked. This makes his exhibition a pleasure. During all walks with your puppy stop periodically and pose him as you would in the ring, make him stand with tail up and ears erect and with his neck well up. This gets him used to ring procedure and adds to his showmanship.

It is also useful to have someone not known to the puppy go over him now and then. This requires overall handling of the puppy and does not need any knowledge—anyone can do it. At the same time, have the lips lifted and gums and teeth examined. This will eliminate future antics when the judge wants to look at the teeth.

115

Lead breaking should be followed by walking your hopeful in congested areas where cars and people pass. This accustoms the puppy to the very atmosphere of a dog show with its excitement, noise and many strangers. A dog that does not shy at such things out-shows one that does.

It is also a good idea to train young dogs to ride in a car and in a crate for several weeks before starting to show them. In this manner, much of the excitement of their first few shows is eliminated as they ride like veterans and are comfortable and used to riding and crating. When first breaking a puppy to this experience, teach him to sleep in a crate by substituting it for his regular sleeping box. After a week of this, and when he is perfectly comfortable in the crate, take him for a short ride in it. Take him to the store or village several times for short rides. After a while he may be taken for longer rides until such time as he is perfectly broken to riding in a crate. By following this course of training, the puppy arrives at his first show fresh, not sick and scared, as would have been the case had he not been properly broken.

In the event he tends to be car-sick, you may administer a sedative prescribed by your veterinarian before you start out. This will calm his nerves and relieve car sickness to a marked degree. After several rides, you will probably not have to worry since most dogs are good travelers and like to ride.

The foregoing may seem like a great deal of trouble and work— and it is—but few, if any, dogs ever become top show animals without exhaustive training prior to reaching the ring. This is one of the reasons why professional handlers do so well. They spend time with their charges before they begin to show them.

Grooming your dog is the most important single item towards good show condition. This chapter will discuss general grooming techniques and requirements exclusive of show trimming, which will be expanded upon in the chapter to follow on "Trimming the Scottish Terrier." Grooming should begin at about two months of age and continue throughout the dog's life. Five to ten minutes' vigorous brushing every day will do more good for the texture and growth of the coat than any other treatment. It will also stimulate the skin and cause a flow of natural oils, thereby creating a healthy skin condition. At each grooming period, loose flying hairs should

116

be plucked out and very little combing should be done, since this tends to remove too much undercoat.

In order to stimulate the growth of hair at selected points, warm olive oil massaged into the skin is good. This is especially helpful around the muzzle and on the legs as it softens hard furnishings and thus prevents the whisker and feather from breaking off. Rain water lightly brushed into the hair may aid in bringing out the bloom.

Another frequent task concerns nails. These should be cut back with nail clippers and then filed a little each day or two to keep them very short. This is especially true on the front feet, since the nails on the rear feet wear off more readily than those in front. Short nails improve a dog's feet and make them more compact, while long nails tend to splay the foot and break down the pasterns. This task should start at about eight weeks and continue throughout the dog's life.

Teeth should also be cleaned periodically, and this may be paced by the time required for a noticeable build-up of tartar on the teeth. Tartar appears on the canines and molars near the gum line and is the reason why it is necessary to remove it before the build-up becomes sufficient to cause a receding of the gums. Periodic brushing of the teeth with a regular tooth brush dipped in bicarbonate of soda and/or salt will do a great deal towards maintaining healthy gums and clean teeth. If the tartar does not come off it may be necessary to scrape or chip it off with a dental pick using great care not to injure the gums. In this operation, if you are not proficient, let your veterinarian do the work.

Ears and eyes should also be carefully watched. Bloodshot eyes may be eased with an ophthalmic ointment if the condition is caused by local irritation such as dirt, or by wind. If the eyes do not clear up within a day, the aid of a veterinarian should be enlisted promptly. Ears generally do not require any attention other than a periodic superficial cleaning, but they should be watched carefully so that canker does not gain a foothold. If the dog scratches his ears constantly or continually shakes his head, the ears may be in trouble. Examine them carefully and give prompt remedial treatment if indicated.

These are the major items of care. Early training, conditioning and general care will become a habit after you have raised a few

117

litters. Knowledgeable dog people do the many things recommended in this chapter as a matter of course and if asked what to do, they would be hard pressed to tell you. In any event, following the suggestions here will help your puppy to grow into a better dog, physically and show-wise, and certainly will eliminate many of the difficulties that may arise.

Ch. Special Edition winning BOB at Montgomery County, Pa., specialty, with Johnny Murphy handling.

9

How to Trim
the Scottish Terrier

THE art of trimming a Scottish Terrier or any other double coated, hard-haired Terrier involves ability and knowledge. It is not impossible to learn the art, but it will take time and more than the usual tenacity of purpose. Trimming makes a dog look smarter and improves its general appearance just as a hair cut or "hair do" improves the appearance of a man or woman. This operation takes a little time each day and the best trim may be decided upon by observation and comparison.

In all cases, a dog's trim should be personalized, that is, trim to make the dog look *his* best by bringing out good points and hiding faults as much as possible; never use a stereotyped pattern. One dog may require heavier trimming than another, one may require thinning of the coat, where another may need more coat. In other words, trimming must be carried out to suit the specific dog. If a dog is too heavy in front, the hair should be thinned on the shoulders to give the appearance of a proper front. If the tail is low set, hair should be taken off the back and grown on the front of it, and additional coat should be cultivated behind the tail to give it the proper appearance. Large-eared dogs need more hair between and in front of the ears than small-eared ones. Short forefaced and short-headed dogs require longer and heavier whiskers to give the illusion that the head is longer than it really is. In other words, there can be no set trimming formula, since the actual work on any dog must be done to present *that* dog in the best light, to accentuate good points and minimize the known faults. As Carlyle said:

The greatest of faults I should say,
is to be concious of none.

Actually trimming is an art. There is no easy way to learn. Experience and knowledge are the only teachers. First, one must know how a good specimen of the breed should look, and second, he must be able to properly fault his dog. If you are not adept at using stripping combs, thinning scissors and other paraphernalia you cannot do the work. Thus, it is apparent that it requires background and knowledge tempered with more than average experience to do a really good job.

This is why professional handlers often do better in the ring than the less experienced. The professional's dog is generally put down properly while the novice-trimmed animal is often poorly presented. This should not be a discouraging condition but rather a challenge to learn and do better. There can be no set formula since Scotties should be trimmed to suit the particular dog. That all good dogs of the breed bear a resemblance to one another is a tribute to the trimmer's art, since these same dogs, if stripped bare, would not look alike. Faults would appear that are entirely hidden by expert trimming. A good judge can find these faults. He not only knows what he is looking for but he knows the devious ways used to hide faults, and by use of his hands can quickly discover them. Often one finds a straight-stifled animal, almost cow-hocked, that appears to have good angulation. Upon inspection, it will be found that much hair is trained to stand away from the hock. At the same time, hair has been grown on the thigh to round out an otherwise weak hindquarter. The overall picture is good but the bone structure is just as bad as before the expert went to work. So it goes, faults are minimized, good points are accentuated until the dog appears at his best.

120

The trimming charts offered here are about all the help anyone can give; the rest comes with experience, appreciation of conformation and a knowledge of what is wanted in the breed. The fine points of trimming can only be mastered by hard work, mistakes, observation of experts at work, and experience, the same formula that is applied to every other breed that requires trimming.

Some learn slowly while others have a capacity to learn more quickly. Trimming of feet in itself is an art seldom mastered. Yet neat feet do more to set off a dog than any other single factor. Much the same is true of tails and ears. These are all-important in the trimming of our breed and the ability to trim these parts of the body properly should be mastered first. The rest will come with experience, if you are patient and anxious to learn.

A good dog poorly presented has its chances of winning cut tremendously. This is not because the judge does not know faults of the dogs in competition, but rather because overall appearance generally has a strong bearing on the outcome of the placements. Type is of major importance and a dog poorly done often appears to lack type due to the faulty trim. On the other hand, a reasonably good dog properly put down exemplifies the proper type and even when hidden faults are found, it is difficult to beat him, for the most important act in judging is to pick dogs that look like Scotties. For this reason, faulty trimming often spoils the chances of an otherwise good dog.

This commentary on trimming does not answer the question of how a Scotsman should be trimmed because such a question cannot be answered by a general statement. However, any exhibitor who will pick up the challenge can learn through experience, study and intelligent observation. One comforting thought: you can never ruin a dog by trimming, for your mistakes will soon be obliterated by new growth of coat.

Tools used for trimming differ with different people but usually include combs, brushes and gloves, together with scissors, thinning scissors, clippers, and a stripping or plucking comb or knife. Scissors may be used for trimming around the ears and feet, although some adept individuals use the knife for all of these operations.

Thumb and forefinger plucking is nearly a lost art but the few experts who remain prove that it is still the best means for bringing along a coat. Using the plucking knife is the next best approach, since both methods eliminate dead hair while leaving live, strong hair in place, with the former being the more effective of the two. Clippers and thinning shears are probably the most often used for trimming; they are the poorest since they do not remove dead coat but cut it off along with the live coat, leaving the dead roots in the dog's skin. These tend to slow the growth of new hair and in some cases actually stop it, with the result that the dog's coat suffers badly. It is true that thinning a coat with thinning shears has its advantages but clipping has very little in its favor except speed. Yet clipping is generally used on heads and throats by most exhibitors both in America and in England.

The harmful part of clipping the body coat revolves around the double coat of the Scottie. Clipping cuts off all hair at the same length. This means that the undercoat as well as the harsh outer jacket is shortened. Since no hair is eliminated from its roots, the dog's coat is now shortened without proper conditioning. For this reason, if you do use clippers as a fast method of taking a dog down, be sure to grub out under coat and comb thoroughly before clipping, so that at least a portion of the dead hair is eliminated. After this, use the clippers.

Getting back to plucking by hand or with a comb or knife, take only a few hairs at a time. Grip the hair rather loosely and pull. Dead hair comes out readily and live hair draws through your fingers or finger according to the method used. This leaves the live hair in place, and it in turn can be shortened later, if desired, by means of a plucking knife held a bit tighter to cause some cutting of the live hair, or more appropriately, by singeing. This last seems to be a forgotten tool but it is very useful. A lighted barber's taper drawn across the dog's coat in the direction of the lie will singe off the unruly hairs and will also, if desired, burn or singe back the longer hairs to a more desirable length. Singeing should not be used until the coat is in condition as it is not a good means of trimming from the rough since, like clipping, it does not remove dead roots from the skin.

Many experts begin trimming a dog in the rough by the "spot" method. That is, they take off the hair at the spot or spots that it grows the slowest. A week or so later they take off another spot or spots and so on until at the end of about four weeks the entire dog is trimmed down, and the first trimmed areas are beginning to re-

122

Head study of Ch. Blanart Bewitching showing proper trimming of the head. Note that neither the whisker, eyebrows or tufts at the inner juncture of the ears are excessive.

Trim tail to the shape of an inverted carrot.
Trim topline to level any dips, and blend into shoulders.
Trim ears smooth, with tufts at inner juncture with head.
Leave eyebrows, but not too long.
Clean cheeks and top of head.

Clean off straggling hair on hindquarters so legs may be seen.
Trim underline to give shape to the body, but do not leave
too much drop. Trim furnishings on forelegs to make them
appear straight. Trim hair off elbows and around feet.

grow. Thereafter, the coat is worked frequently, thinning and shortening where required and grooming all the time to keep the coat at its peak. Once the dog is in show coat, periodic work may be done to keep him in show coat. This is best accomplished by "rolling the coat," that is, taking off some of the coat while leaving enough long hairs to maintain the coat's lying correctly. In time, three distinct coats will be carried by the dog, one coming, one prime and the other "going." When this is accomplished, the "going" coat is taken off at a time that another week's growth will cause the prime coat to pass over, bring the coming coat to prime, and permit new coat to "come." When this condition is attained, the dog may be kept "in coat" for months. True, there may be periods when the coat is not as good as at other times, but it will always be presentable and may be brought to its peak at any time with about two weeks' work.

The "spot" trimming technique may be all right for the expert but the novice is best served by overall trimming at the start. This means taking off all of the top coat and some of the undercoat on the body, head, neck and tail. The coat on the "drop" or "skirt" should never be taken off since it requires months to re-grow. The same is true of the leg feather and whiskers. This hair is best brought along by selectively trimming the ends to bring the same to a more or less uniform length and by brushing the hair to keep it lively and to remove dead hair. All the while the trimmed body and head coat is being "worked" to maintain proper lengths at various parts of the dog. See the charts for more detailed information concerning the trimming pattern which, as explained, should be varied for individual dogs to bring out good points and minimize faults.

A good trimming bench or table is an invaluable aid when working on your dog and also helps to train him for show. The table should be of the proper height so that you may stand comfortably while working and should not be too large in area. A table about 25 inches long by 18 wide is adequate. Mounted on the side of the table near the front should be an adjustable upright from which can be suspended a slip collar adjustable to the proper height for each dog. This aids you in your work, keeps the dog's head up, and teaches him to stand properly. Instead of an adjustable upright you may hang a collar from the ceiling directly over the table. This collar may be adjusted for proper height from the table. Either method is satisfactory.

When getting your dog ready for the ring it is best to wipe off the coat with a damp Turkish towel for cleaning purposes. The feather and whisker should also be cleaned or washed if need be. Thereafter, the coat should be thoroughly dried and, if it is overly long, towelled until show time. If the coat is the proper length or short, towelling is not required. Before entering the ring the dog should be thoroughly combed to remove all tangles and the coat rubbed over lightly with brilliantine or vaseline. This should be used sparingly and be well rubbed into the hands before application. The coat may again be combed and the dog is ready.

When the coat is overly long or when unruly hairs are present, a hair spray may be used—it is also useful on the feather and whisker. Lightly sprayed on, it will hold the coat in position. Some use "sugar-water" for holding the coat and in a few cases for stiffening the hair. This is a solution of sugar in water, boiled until dissolved. It may be of varying degrees of concentration according to the use. Rubbed onto the coat, it should be permitted to dry before combing. It will cause the individual hairs to adhere and in some cases, if not thoroughly combed out, will lend texture to the coat. Any judge who knows the breed can feel this and other coat stiffeners so the only benefit obtained is in holding the coat close.

An admonition on the use of sugar water that has a rather humorous twist concerns an exhibitor who was addicted to the stuff. He was in a rush to get into the ring one hot summer day and did not let the dog dry. The result was disastrous, since the dog was shown in a cloud of flies that enjoyed the sweetener and refused to leave the poor animal. Needless to say, the dog had a bad day—as did the exhibitor.

This is about all of the advice on trimming that can be offered. The rest is up to the exhibitor. Remember, however, you cannot help losing if your dog is inferior anatomically to another exhibit, but losing because of inferior condition or showmanship are conditions controlled by you and you alone.

Apropos is a remark accredited to the late George Steadman Thomas, well known Anglo-American Terrier expert, handler, and judge, who said, "The best looking dog will often beat a better dog put down indifferently," and truer words were never spoken.

10

Breeding Formulas, Rules and Axioms

WHENEVER a person becomes interested in breeding dogs the usual question is, "What is the best way to begin?" Such a query has a multitude of answers, many of which may be good counsel. However, I believe the soundest advice that can be given the tyro is to obtain a good, high quality, well bred bitch. With this start years of heartaches and disappointments can be avoided. The breeding of show dogs, show horses, and, in fact, any high quality livestock is never easy. Persistence is generally rewarded and to those who have tasted this reward, the work is worthy of the effort. To quote a successful English breeder—"To attain continued success needs patience and endurance and the optimistic temperament of never ending hope."

Disappointment over the failure to breed a winner quickly has caused many to drop out of the dog fancy. Thousands of fanciers breed their stock every year with the idea of getting a show dog. Many fall by the wayside when their efforts are not successful.

Most people begin seeking show honors in the wrong way and

Eng. Ch. Reanda Rutlin.

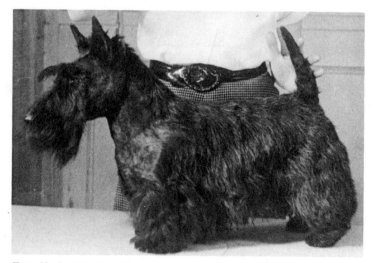

Eng. Ch. Reanda Rio Rita.

thus delay their ultimate goal many years. There is no short-cut to high quality and, therefore, the use of inferior stock prolongs the time required to produce a winner. Of course, there are instances where a fine dog has come from parents of mediocre type, but these cases are indeed rare and such dogs seldom reproduce their own quality.

The surest and quickest way to be successful, which is attested to by all leading breeders of any kind of livestock, is to acquire the best matron obtainable, of high quality and unquestioned pedigree, and then line or inbreed her to the best stud dog available. Offspring from this mating may not be the ultimate, but the choice of the litter will generally be good foundation stock. No successful kennel has ever perpetuated the breed without an abundance of top quality bitches. Good stud dogs are many and available to all, but a good bitch is a rare asset whose value cannot be overestimated.

Thus, sound advice to anyone endeavoring to begin breeding operations is to get a *good* bitch. This does not mean a puppy, but preferably a proven brood bitch, not over five years old, of success-ful bloodlines. Breed her well, and if only one litter is whelped she has done her part in the long-term program. From this litter, select the best one or two female puppies, if there is a choice, and breed them in the same family. The offspring of this second generation breeding will usually be of high quality and will stand a chance in the show ring if properly "put down," trained and shown.

Don't be "kennel blind." This affliction is defined as the in-ability, or lack of desire, to see faults in your own stock. No dog is perfect. Be critical, for to paraphrase Pope,

> Whoever thinks a faultless dog to see,
> Thinks what ne'er was, nor is, nor e'er shall be.

Look for and see the faults in your dog, for without knowing shortcomings, you can never overcome them by intelligent breeding. On the other hand, appreciate good points and use them objectively in the choice of young stock. Study the pedigree of your bitch and learn as much as possible about her forebears, their family good points and their family faults. With this information, you can breed away from these faults by proper selection of a stud dog.

Family failings are of great importance; they generally over-shadow individual faults. A dog from a family of poor-coated dogs, even though the coat is passable, will usually throw poor-coated dogs. Conversely, a poor-headed dog from a good-headed family will usually pass this fault to only a small minority of its offspring. Family faults are difficult to overcome, and intelligent breeding is the only means of rectifying the mistakes of previous breeders.

This does not mean that you should overemphasize families; at the same time, you should not overlook individual faults. For example, try to get for breeding purposes two individuals which do not exhibit family faults and are free from glaring individual faults. Endeavor to complement your breeding stock and try to use a stud that is strong in the weak points of the bitch, and vice versa. In this manner, you are combating faults from two or three different approaches. Never perpetuate a fault by breeding in a manner likely to strengthen that fault.

Character is all-important when selecting a stud dog. Bitchy dogs rarely produce well, nor do weedy, weak-boned dogs make good sires. A dog that is masculine, of good size and full of fire, with heavy bone and plenty of substance, has the best chance of passing on his good points. Such a dog is said to have "plenty to give."

Some stud dogs have the illusive quality of prepotency. Definition of this term is difficult; suffice it to say that it is the ability to reproduce good qualities. A prepotent stud, when used with the same bitches, will sire, on an average, more good puppies than an equally typey dog that does not possess this quality. Ch. Heather Necessity was certainly one of these as proved by his accomplishments. When choosing a stud, endeavor to find one that is prepotent as determined by his success as a sire. Champion dogs are not always the best studs; many fine dogs never enter the ring but produce as well or better than the popular studs of the day. Therefore, choose a dog that meets specific requirements, rather than the champion of the moment which may not be best for your bitch.

Age is another consideration. It is generally conceded that old bitches produce better when bred to young dogs, and vice versa. Animals within the range of two to five years old may be bred together but older animals are best bred to young, virile mates, while very young animals nick better with consorts of greater maturity.

The bitch's type and character are important. Astute breeders say that a bitchy or feminine bitch is best, but no less an authority than

A. G. Cowley (Albourne) allowed that a doggy bitch was the best producer. The argument could be enlarged upon but with little gain; so, to repeat, the bitch should be as good an individual as you can afford and can obtain. It is a fallacy to keep bitches for brood purposes that are not good enough to show. Wise breeders have long followed the course of using only the best. Somerville, more than 200 years ago, gave this counsel:

> Watch o'er the bitches with a cautious eye,
> And separate such as are going to be proud.

This is as good advice today as it was then, for seldom does a bitch amount to much that is not "proud" as exemplified by temperament, bearing and courage.

Certain breeding formulas yield the most satisfying results. Breeding in a line and inbreeding, as a rule, produce the quickest, best and surest results. Line breeding may be defined broadly as breeding within the same family. According to latest authorities, line breeding is concerned with the mating of two individuals, one of which is an ancestor of the other: for example, grandsire to granddaughter. Inbreeding, on the other hand, is defined as the breeding of two related individuals, neither of which is an ancestor of the other and, generally, not over two generations removed, for example, half-brother to half-sister, first cousin to first cousin, etc. Both inbreeding and line breeding bring out recessive as well as dominant factors, and it is for this reason that family background is so important. Line breeding accentuates recessives to a lesser degree than inbreeding. Both types may be practiced with great success if careful selection of the mating material is maintained, together with careful choice of the progeny for subsequent breeding operations.

A third type of breeding formula is known as out breeding. This is concerned with the mating of two unrelated, or distantly related individuals. The latter is generally the case, although in Scotties there are several outcross breedings available due to the geographical sovereignty of the breed. Even here, it will be found that most modern Scots are related in the sixth or seventh generation. All of these formulas have produced well, with the first two being the most successful for obvious reasons.

There is one other type of breeding formula used more fre-

131

Eng. Ch. Reanda Roger Rough, a big winner.

Eng. Ch. Reanda Ringold.

quently than any other; this may be termed "random breeding" for want of a more appropriate term. Unfortunately, this path is followed by the majority and may be why there are so many poor specimens of every breed seen on the streets. This is directed to the practice of breeding a bitch to the dog that is available at the lowest cost in spite of faults, bloodlines or what have you. The results are nearly always the same: poor stock, generally poorer than either of the parents, which downgrades the breed with each successive generation. It has another unhappy result. When a bitch of this kind falls into the hands of a sincere person who wants to breed properly, it will generally require generations to straighten out past mistakes. This is the reason why any person starting as a breeder should buy as good and as well-bred a bitch as possible. It will cut years off the otherwise tedious road to success.

When practicing line and inbreeding the breeder should keep close check on the size and virility of the stock produced. It has been found that when too close breeding of this nature is carried on for several generations, a tendency sometimes develops towards loss of size and virility. These tendencies have been proved by experiments conducted with mice and rats. For example, Weisman and Von Guaiti inbred mice for 35 generations and found that the average per litter dropped from an initial 6.1 to a final 2.9. Ritzma Bos, when experimenting with rats, found that inbreeding was also responsible for loss in size. Average figures showed a 20 percent decrease in weight of offspring at the end of six years of breeding. Of course, dog breeders would not repeat these techniques for as extended periods as did the researchers, but the trend has been proved, and when the evidence is apparent, it is best to breed out of the line. This does not mean a complete outcross, even if one is available, but the use of a rather distant relative. The progeny of this mating may be bred back into the original line.

This word of caution is to allay the fears of many concerning the alleged "evils" of line and inbreeding. Selective breeding close up has always been the surest and quickest way to "set" good points. Since no moral issues prevail in nature, breeders should take advantage of these methods, while tempering their zeal with a constructive and critical eye on the results of their efforts.

The reasons behind the success of line and inbreeding may be explained by the theories expressed in the laws of heredity. Study of these theories will help explain many factors which are otherwise

Ch. Marlorain Dark Seal.

Ch. Glendoune Gwenda with Lena Kardos and Percy Roberts.

difficult to understand. Heredity is, however, a very intricate study. Many excellent books are available that delve deeply into the subject. For this reason, only a very short resume of the theories will be stated here.

The hereditary influence may be broadly surveyed by the application of the Law of Ancestral Influence. This law may best be defined as the diminishing influence of each successive generation of ancestors upon the inherited traits of a given dog. The parents are said to contribute 50 percent (25 each), the grandparents 25 percent ($6\frac{1}{4}$ each), great-grandparents $12\frac{1}{2}$ percent ($1\frac{9}{16}$), and so on.

Arithmetically broken down as to the influence of each ancestor in pedigree form, we find the following chart to be illustrative:

Parents (50%)	Grandparents (25%)	Great Grandparents ($12\frac{1}{2}$%)
		G. G. Sire ($1\frac{9}{16}$%)
	Grand Sire ($6\frac{1}{4}$%)	
		G. G. Dam ($1\frac{9}{16}$%)
Sire (25%)		
		G. G. Sire ($1\frac{9}{16}$%)
	Grand Dam ($6\frac{1}{4}$%)	
		G. G. Dam ($1\frac{9}{16}$%)
		G. G. Sire ($1\frac{9}{16}$%)
	Grand Sire ($6\frac{1}{4}$%)	
		G. G. Dam ($1\frac{9}{16}$%)
Dam (25%)		
		G. G. Sire ($1\frac{9}{16}$%)
	Grand Dam ($6\frac{1}{4}$%)	
		G. G. Dam ($1\frac{9}{16}$%)

From this chart it will be seen that the more distant the ancestor, the less its influence on the dog. This also explains why line and inbreeding are useful. Either type of breeding reduces the number of individual relatives, increases their influence, and thereby cuts down the variables with which we must deal.

Mendelism is the specific application of the laws of heredity as applied to a given factor or factors. Dominant and recessive characteristics may be charted so that when breeding two individuals having known backgrounds, the results may be predetermined within limits. It is generally impossible to obtain the known background of many characteristics of a given dog, so that the application of the theory is sometimes difficult and often impossible to follow.

In color determination, however, it is very successful since the color of a dog is usually a known quantity and is noted on the registration certificate and thus may be traced back through generations of breeding. For this reason, the color of progeny from two individuals may be accurately foreseen.

Other breeding factors are not as easily predetermined by Mendelian formula due to unknown quantities in the backgrounds of the stock. The complexity of the problem is further increased by the fact that the same laws apply with equal force and effect to all characteristics. If an experimental breeding can be made, and if a breeder is patient and willing to sacrifice two or three breedings, he may predetermine certain factors which will be of benefit in future matings as well as in subsequent breeding operations. In general, however, the broad theory finds its greatest success in color determination. In this connection, breeders of the wheaten Scottie have found the rules most helpful.

Much of the foregoing advice is succinctly offered by a series of four axioms set forth by the late William McCandlish, author, judge and breeder of the Scottish Terrier. He proposed the following as rules to be followed to which I have added some explanatory remarks.

Like begets like—McCandlish says that this is more of a law than an axiom. The closer two animals are to one another in appearance and temperament, the greater the likelihood of the offspring being like the parents. Thus, if the parents are top specimens, the get should be good; if the parents are poor, the get may be poor or poorer.

Breed to breed—Meaning never breed with a mere litter in mind but, rather, with subsequent breedings from the offspring being of paramount consideration. Proceed with the view that the progeny will have improved breeding value over either of the parents.

Never breed from a second generation fault—Second generation faults are generally family faults that will continue to reproduce with increased emphasis. Conversely, second generation virtues indicate a dominant influence that is desirable.

No animal is well bred unless it is good in itself—The axiom points to the fallacy of breeding to pedigree alone. The majority of pedigreed animals are not show specimens, in fact only about one in ten is even a good specimen. The axiom stresses the necessity of using only animals with the best conformation and temperament for breeding purposes.

11

Value and Procedure
of Dog Shows

WHAT is the value of a dog show? This question is frequently asked when discussing the advisability of entering a dog in one of these events. The answer is simple, and the reasons for showing stock are logical and sound. The only true measuring stick of breeding progress and success is comparison of the best you have with the best of other breeders. If your dog or dogs win consistently, you can rest assured that the type of dog you breed is desirable and that you are progressing in your breeding program.

Furthermore, showing of dogs keeps you on your toes. The results of the shows are a constant challenge to your ability. If your dogs do not win, or win very seldom, do not be "kennel blind" but begin to look for failings, and when you find them, start to breed away from these faults to improve your stock. Dog shows provide an opportunity for comparison, and there you may obtain unprejudiced criticism, such as a judge's placement of your dog with reference to other dogs. If, after attending three or four shows, you find that all the judges have similar reactions towards your entries, rest assured that their opinions, good or bad, are correct, and be guided accordingly.

Dog shows, with their long and varied history, are conducted differently in different countries. In England, the first event of bench type was held for sporting dogs at Newcastle-on-Tyne in 1859. Sixty Pointers and Setters made up the entry. Judges for this historic affair included Messrs. J. Jobling, T. Robson, E. Foulger, R. Brailsford and J. H. Walsh ("Stonehenge"). Shows of varying success were held from that time until April, 1873, when the English Kennel Club was organized. It brought about a stabilization of the events and created their first real bid for prominence. S. E. Shirley, founder of the club, served as its first chairman and later as its first president.

In the United States, early history of shows is obscure, but honor for the first bench show here is credited to Hempstead, Long Island, near which place a show was held in 1874. Westminster was the first of the better organized clubs to hold a show and its initial event was staged May 7 to 11, 1877, in New York City, where it has been held continuously ever since. The following year, the Boston and Baltimore clubs held shows in addition to the New York fixture. The American Kennel Club was organized September 17, 1884, in Philadelphia, Pennsylvania.

Until that time, registration for dogs in the United States was with one of two early organizations. The National American Kennel Club, whose *Stud Book* was first published in 1878 in Chicago by Dr. W. Rowe, was the forerunner of the American Kennel Club *Stud Book* and the *American Kennel Register* (*Field and Stream*) published by E. C. Sterling in St. Louis. This last effort lasted only a few years. In any event, we may take the 1884 date as the real start of organized interest in bench-type dogs and their breeding. The American Kennel Club did in the United States what the English Kennel Club did in Great Britain. It systematized dog show practices. Uniform rules were provided by an impartial governing body operating for the best interests of purebred dogs and their owners.

Dog shows in different countries, as staged by various kennel clubs, operate in different ways and award their championships after certain requirements have been met. English shows are divided into several classifications, depending on their importance and scope. The only shows that have any bearing on championships are those events termed, "championship shows." The remaining fixtures, which are numerically superior, may be likened to our sanction matches. The English championship shows are analogous to our licensed or member shows, in that a dog, by winning in its sex, is awarded a challenge certificate. No relation exists between the number of entries and the certificate awards; this is taken care of by the fact that relatively few championship shows are held each year (24 shows in 1965), thereby assuring a good entry with worthy competition. It requires three such certificate awards under three different judges to qualify for the title of champion.

In the United States, a different system prevails. To become a champion of record a dog must win 15 championship points (including two major shows) under three different judges. The number of points awarded at any given show depends on the number of dogs of the sex actually shown in the breed for a given geographical division. For example, in 1917, when the point rating system went into effect, the Scottish Terrier's rating was as follows:

Dogs and Bitches

1 Point	4
2 Points	7
3 Points	11
4 Points	15
5 Points	20

The breed enjoyed its highest point rating in 1939, when breed popularity was at its greatest. The rating at that time for either dogs or bitches was:

Dogs and Bitches

1 Point	6
2 Points	10
3 Points	15
4 Points	10
5 Points	25

This schedule has since been changed many times, and today we find the 1965 schedule for the North and East Division offers a different rating for dogs and bitches.

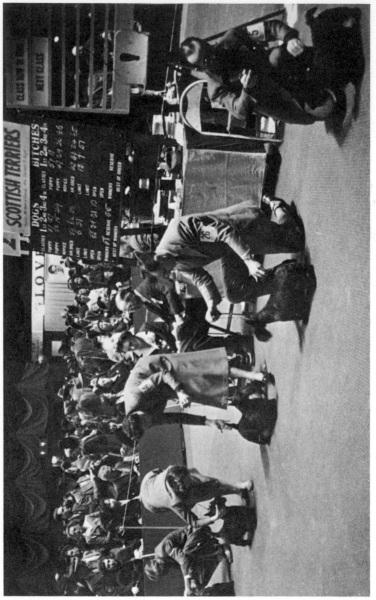

Informal study of Scottish Terrier class at Westminster.

	Dogs	*Bitches*
1 Point	2	2
2 Points	4	4
3 Points	6	7
4 Points	10	11
5 Points	16	21

These changes emphasize the constant fluctuations in point ratings that are being made by the American Kennel Club in an effort to keep competition strong and allow for changing conditions in breed popularity. In this manner no dog can become a champion easily; he must meet competition consistent with the number of dogs being shown.

In general, the American Kennel Club endeavors to keep the number of three, four and five-point shows to about 20 percent of the total shows in a given division. This means that major shows (three-point or better) will be available but will not be so numerous that the average exhibitor can finish a dog in three shows. It also means that in a small registration breed, where competition is hard to find, it will not be impossible to finish a champion, which would be the case were all breeds to have the same rating.

Prior to 1917, the American system was entirely different. At that time the point rating at any show depended upon the total number of dogs exhibited at the show. Thus, it was actually possible for a dog to win five points without any competition. The ratings for shows were as follows: 1000 dogs and over, 5 points; 750 to 1000 dogs, 4 points; 500 to 750 dogs, 3 points; 250 to 500 dogs, 2 points; and 250 dogs and under, only one point. The obvious unfairness of this system revolved around the fact that at a one-point rated show, a winning dog might beat more dogs of the breed than at some other show where a five-point rating prevailed. The present system eliminates these inequities and permits the maximum point rating at any show, regardless of size, providing the required number of dogs in the sex of the breed are present.

Canadian championships are acquired in much the same manner as American championships except that only ten points are needed. The other requirements are substantially the same, and ratings vary in accordance with the numbers being shown in each breed.

The method of procedure and ultimate goal of a dog show is relatively simple to comprehend and is analogous to any other sporting contest where many opponents vie for honors. It is an elimination contest where dogs compete in relatively small groups and classes for the purpose of eliminating certain unsuccessful contestants. The winner of each elimination round progresses to the next higher competition for further elimination until only one dog remains, and that dog is awarded the title of best dog in show.

Every dog show consists of breed competitions usually subdivided by sex, with at least five regular classes being provided in each sex. These classes, together with their official definitions, may be found in Chapter 7, Sections 3 to 8 inclusive, of *Rules Applying to Registration and Dog Shows* (American Kennel Club), the context of which is briefly:

Puppy Class—for dogs six months of age and not exceeding 12 months. This class is open only to puppies whelped in the United States or Canada and entry must include date and place of birth, breeder's name and sire and dam.

Novice Class—for dogs six months of age and over that have not acquired championship points and have not won three first prizes in novice classes or a first prize in any regular class, puppy class wins excepted. Entry form must state place and date of birth, and name of breeder. Only dogs whelped in the United States or Canada are eligible.

Bred-by-Exhibitor Class—for AKC registered dogs six months of age or over (except champions) which are owned wholly or in part by the person or spouse of the person who was the breeder or one of the breeders. Dogs entered in this class must be handled in the ring by the owner or by one of his immediate family. Entry must state name of breeder and sire and dam and place and date of birth of dog, together with the registered name and registration number.

American-bred Class—open to any dog six months of age or over (champions excepted) whelped in the United States by reason of mating which took place in the United States. Entry must state date and place of birth and name of breeder.

Open Class—open to any dog six months of age or over, except at specialty shows for American-bred dogs only, at which time the Open Class shall be for American-bred dogs only.

Winners Class—open to the first-prize winners of each of the above five classes.

The above explanations are in their simplest form. Technicalities regarding calculation of age, eligibility to entry in the Novice and Bred-by-Exhibitor Classes, etc., will be found in detail in the definition of classes accompaning entry forms and also in the American Kennel Club booklet.

Entry may be made in any of these classes except the winners class, where entry is automatic upon qualification. All class entries, except in the Open Class, require careful study of the dog's eligibility. In general, young dogs over six months and under a year old that were whelped in the U.S. or Canada should be entered in the puppy classes for experience. After they pass one year of age, they are eligible for three wins in novice. They should then be sufficiently seasoned for entry in the upper classes. Before making an entry for any show, be sure to check the requirements of the class in which you are entering, since if the dog is ineligible your entry will be disqualified after the wins are checked by the AKC.

The championship points in each sex of each breed are contested for by the winners of the above mentioned five blue ribbon winners. These dogs compete in the winners class, and the ultimate winner is designated winners dog or winners bitch (purple ribbon), as the case may be. The two winners are the only dogs in the breed to receive championship points. A reserve winner (purple and white) is designated in each sex and may be any dog that has not been previously defeated except by the winner. The reserve winner is the recipient of the championship points in the event the winner is later disqualified. In some shows where there are insufficient entries to make points, if the sexes are divided, dogs and bitches may compete together. In this case, only one winner is chosen and it may be a dog or a bitch; this contingency is rare and is always noted in the entry information, i.e., the premium list, for the particular show.

The next step in the process of elimination is for the winners dog and winners bitch to meet for best of winners (blue and white ribbon). The one so designated may gain extra points if the other sex carries a higher rating. The best of winners gets the highest point rating available in either sex of the breed at that particular show. This dog then meets any dogs entered for specials-only in the breed—champions of record—competing for the honor of best of breed (purple and gold ribbon), and the winner of the class is so named.

In the United States, champions are seldom entered in the classes in competition for the championship points even though they may be entered in the puppy class (if they meet the qualifications) or in the open class. This is not true in England, where champions are frequently entered in the open class for challenge certificate competition. Many arguments have been made pro and con, and it is apparent that if the practice were the same in the U.S. as it is in England, fewer champions would be made and possibly the urge to show dogs would be dulled among the less ardent exhibitors.

All-breed shows are further subdivided by the AKC into six variety groups which consist of arbitrary classifications of breeds that have some relation from point of use. Thus, Sporting dogs (Group 1) includes such breeds as Spaniels, Setters, Pointers, and Retrievers. Hounds (Group 2) includes Beagles, Greyhounds, Dachshunds, etc. Working dogs (Group 3) are represented by Doberman Pinschers, Great Danes, Boxers, Collies, etc. Terriers (Group 4) are all dogs that go to ground and include the Scottie. Toy dogs (Group 5) are self-explanatory, with Pekingese, Pomeranians, Chihuahuas, Toy Spaniels and Pugs being representative breeds. The sixth and final group is known as the Non-sporting group and includes a more heterogeneous collection of breeds than in any of the other five groups. Bulldogs, Boston Terriers, Dalmatians, Poodles, and Chow Chows are some of the members of this group.

The final judging at any all-breed show revolves around the variety group judging, and it is this phase in which the best of breed winner of every breed within each group competes for the honor of best in that group. In this manner, the show has been finally narrowed down to the six group winning contestants for the judge to go over for the best dog in show. The ultimate winner has eliminated every dog in the show to gain the coveted position.

Incidentally, if a class dog wins a group or best in show award, that dog becomes the recipient of the highest number of points available in the group or show, as the case may be. In this manner, if only one point is available in its breed and a dog ultimately wins a group or best in show including a five-point entry breed, that dog acquires five points instead of the original one. This applies only to dogs that have come up from the classes.

The foregoing is a brief explanation of show procedure. The

144

same general plan is followed at specialty shows (shows for one breed only) except that group judging is eliminated.

Sanction matches are shows held for experience, and no championship points are awarded. These matches may be of the specialty or all-breed variety, for puppies only or for all-age dogs. They are a great deal of fun and excellent training ground for dogs and exhibitors, since they are conducted in substantially the same manner as point shows.

All-breed shows, specialty shows and sanction matches may be held indoors or outdoors and may be benched or unbenched. New rules make it mandatory for a club to state on its premium list (for point shows) whether or not the show is benched. If benched, it is required that the dogs remain on their benches throughout the show except when being exercised, readied or shown. This does not apply to puppies, which need not be benched until after they have been judged.

Premium lists are the prospectus of the show issued by each show-giving club. They list the approved judges and their assignments, show hours, and include prizes, entry forms, etc. Having exhibited at a show or two you will automatically be placed on the exhibitors mailing list and will receive subsequent lists for shows in your locality. If you are not on these lists, the show dates and super-intendents' addresses are carried by all dog magazines and by the *American Kennel Gazette* months in advance. A letter to the proper official will bring a list promptly.

If you plan to exhibit dogs, endeavor to join a local dog club. Most cities have such organizations and they generally include a majority of the active exhibitors in the vicinity. Contact with these fanciers will help you over many rough spots and you can also learn through this association.

In general, dog shows are wonderful places to gain knowledge of your breed and of dogs in general. Professional handlers and experienced exhibitors should be watched as they prepare their dogs, and their actions in the ring should be noted. Most of them are willing to assist the novice if asked courteously when they are not rushed to show or prepare another dog. They were all novices at one time, since there is no means yet devised of skipping this phase. Intelligent observation and courteous questioning will help more than anything else to acquire the knack of showing dogs.

One more word on the subject of dog shows. While awesome the first time, they get under your skin. There is no more fascinating hobby than showing dogs. The bustle of the shows, the rush to get your dog ready and the thrill of winning cannot be equalled. To all this add lasting friendships built up through association with congenial companions met everywhere you exhibit, and you will appreciate why so many people follow the shows with interest, year after year.

Eng. & Am. Ch. Bardene Bingo, shown winning Best in Show at Westminster, 1967. Bob Bartos, handler; owned by E. H. Stuart, Carnation Farms Kennels.

12

Helpful Facts
and Figures

THIS chapter, more or less statistical in nature, will offer the reader a collection of unrelated data and interesting facts concerning the Scottish Terrier. It will give registration figures for the breed, both in England and in America, for the ten-year period from 1956 through 1965. It will list the number of champions of record by years for the same period in both countries and will give a tabulation of the English champions together with their sires, dams and breeders over the same period. Similar information for American champions is available in this country.

In addition, there is a tabulation of all Scottish Terriers that have won best in show at any all breed event in the United States during the period, and in this manner many quality dogs not previously mentioned will be given credit for their excellence.

As an added feature, a list of fanciers together with their kennel names covers many of the more prominent breed devotees in America and Britain. The above facts will aid in rounding out a knowledge of the breed that may be helpful to tyros and useful to old-timers.

Registration Figures for Scottish Terriers
1956–1965 inclusive

Year	Number Reg. American Kennel Club	Placement among all Registered Breeds U.S. Only	Number Reg. English Kennel Club
1956	3255	25	1587
1957	3128	25	1418
1958	3083	25	1483
1959	3173	24	1482
1960	3098	24	1488
1961	3346	24	1395
1962	3671	22	1485
1963	3847	23	1338
1964	4677	23	1523
1965	5457	24	1449

These figures indicate that the Scottish Terrier is gaining in popularity in the United States while merely holding his own in Great Britain. Yet the steady influx of imports continues to bring across many top Scotsmen that more than hold their own among the American-breds. This condition will be noted in the following statistics regarding best in show wins in the United States, where the status of each winner is offered after the dog's name. From these figures over the past ten years we find that 41 different Scottish Terriers have accounted for a total of 139 best in show awards and that 56 of these have been made by the 16 imports.

Best in Show Winning Scottish Terriers for the Years 1956–1965
(AKC All-Breed Shows only)

1956 Total—20

Ch. Westpark Derriford Baffie* 9
Ch. Wyrebury Wrangler* 3
Ch. Cantie Captivator 2
Ch. Cantie Confident 2
Ch. Glad Mac's Show Girl 2
Ch. Carnation Dark Sentry 1
Ch. Rebel Raider 1

1957 Total—5

Ch. Judy Lee III 1
Ch. Nosegay Nakin* 1
Ch. Glad Mac's Show Girl 1
Ch. Westpark Derriford Baffie* 1
Ch. Wyrebury Water Gypsy* 1

1958 Total—14

Ch. Westpark Derriford Baffie* 9

Eng. & Am. Ch. Westpark Derriford Baffie.

Charles Stalter, Florence Prentice with best brace at 1956 Scottish Terrier Club of America being awarded ribbon by the author.

Ch. Glenview Grand Duke* 3
Ch. Jo Lee Lucky Seal 1
Ch. Wyrebury Water Gypsy* 1

1959 Total—8

Ch. Blanart Bewitching 4
Ch. Reanda Rheola* 2
Ch. Glendoune Gwenda* 1
Ch. Highlander Red Knight 1

1960 Total—9

Ch. Blanart Bewitching 3
Ch. Kentwelle Kadet* 2
Ch. Canties Ace 1
Ch. Firebrands Fury 1
Ch. Scotsvale Sunshine* 1
Ch. Special Edition* 1

1961 Total—9

Ch. Penvale Plutocrat* 3
Ch. Scotsvale Sunshine* 2
Ch. Firebrand's Fascinator 1
Ch. Scotsguard/Follower Camp 1
Ch. Special Edition* 1
Ch. Walsing Wild Winter of Barberry Knowe* 1

1962 Total—11

Ch. Gaidoune Great Bear 3
Bardene Black Jewel* 1
Ch. Carmichael's Fanfare 1
Ch. Gillsie Roger Right* 1
Ch. Rebel Edition 1
Ch. Scotsvale Sunshine* 1
Ch. Todhill's Bear Necessity 1
Ch. Walsing Wild Winter of Barberry Knowe* 1
Ch. Bardene Boy Blue* 1

1963 Total—23

Ch. Carmichael's Fanfare 8
Ch. Gaidoune Great Bear 7
Ch. Matscot Roger Ringleader 1
Ch. Scotsvale Sunshine* 2
Ch. Bardene Boy Blue* 1
Ch. Carnation Cynthia 1
Ch. Garlu Haggis Baggis 1
Ch. Wychworth Heydey Hoagy 1

1964 Total—29

Ch. Carmichael's Fanfare 21
Ch. Gaidoune Great Bear 5
Ch. Matscot Roger Ringleader 2
Ch. Bardene Bingo* 1

150

Ch. Anstamm Dark Venture.

Ch. Bardene Bobby Dazzler with Lena Kardos handling.

1965 Total—11
```
Ch. Bardene Bingo*  ........................................  4
Ch. Gaidoune Grin and Bear It  ...........................  4
Ch. Anstamm Dark Dennis  .................................  1
Ch. Barberry Knowe Blizzard  .............................  1
Ch. Carmichael's Fanfare  .................................  1
```
* indicates an import

Top Scotties during the period were Ch. Carmichael's Fanfare with 30 best in shows, followed by Ch. Westpark Derriford Baffie with 19 and Ch. Gaidoune Great Bear with 15.

The Champion Count in the U.S. and Britain

Every year a number of Scottish Terriers gain the required 15 points, including two major shows, to qualify for the title of American champion. These champions are listed each month in the *American Kennel Gazette* together with their sires and dams, and for this reason there will be no additional listing here. Interested persons may obtain copies of the Gazettes from local libraries or from breeders, most of whom maintain a file of these important magazines. It will be of interest, however, to list the number of titleholders made each year under American Kennel Club rules and to compare these figures with like figures established under the English Kennel Club. The tabulation will embrace a ten-year span from 1956 through 1965.

Year	American Champions	English Champions
1956	57	11
1957	66	12
1958	74	11
1959	69	16
1960	72	10
1961	65	12
1962	69	12
1963	65	7
1964	79	11
1965	77	12

These figures indicate that many more champions are made in the U.S. than in Britain. Even though Americans register from two to four times as many dogs each year, the relation between registrations and number of champions made each year is inordinately high when compared with English Kennel Club figures. This is because of the large number of shows in the U.S. that offer championship points—generally between five and 600, while in Britain it is generally about 24. Add to this the English practice of showing champions in the open class and one realizes how difficult it is to gain the title.

Since English Kennel Club records are not readily available to the average American, a listing of the English champions made each year from 1957 through 1965 is offered here. This listing includes the sire and dam and the breeder in each instance.

English Champions
(1956–1965 inc.)

1956

Ch. Happy Kimbo (Hargate Happy Boy ex Bardene Barley Sugar) Br. Mrs. M. A. Buxton

Ch. Reanda Ria Bella (Ch. Westpark Derriford Baffie ex Ch. Reanda Rio Rita) Br. Mrs. E. Meyer

Ch. Wyrebury Wilwyn (Ch. Wyrebury Wrangler ex Wyrebury Wildjig) Br. A. Lomas

Ch. Cumnoch Sonnet (Cumnoch Cheerful Comrade ex Kennelgarth Lyrical) Br. Miss B. Penn Bull

Ch. Cool of Conett (Ch. Westpark Derriford Baffie ex Candy of Conett) Br. A. R. Hanson

Ch. Reanda Raith (Ch. Westpark Derriford Baffie ex Reanda Silberjinn) Br. Mrs. E. Meyer

Ch. Walsing Winoway (Ch. Wyrebury Wrangler ex Walsing Winter Rose) Br. W. M. Singleton

Ch. Cumnoch Caper (Cumnoch Cheerful Comrade ex Kennelgarth Lyrical) Br. Miss B. Penn Bull

Ch. Percivalown Pandora (Ch. Medwal Wild Oats ex Medwal Miss Marcheta) Br. R. Aherne

Ch. Nerebrook Nicosia (Nerebrook Nearula ex Nerebrook Nightingale) Br. H. Greenhalgh

Ch. Eckersley Wee Mon (Eckersley Grandee ex Eckersley Eleanor) Br. Mrs. D. Law

1957

Ch. Rutherland Cherry (Shortwood Slogan ex Duart Feocodan) Br. Mrs. A. Magill

Ch. Reanda Roger Rough (Reanda Roderic ex Reanda Rosita) Br. Mrs. E. Meyer

Ch. Allascot Belinda (Glenview Grand Gesture ex Prelude of Kale) Br. Major J. Howard

Ch. Niddbank Princess (Niddbank Chip ex Niddbank Queen) Br. Mrs. K. M. Ross

Ch. Nerebrook Nonchalance (Nerebrook Nearlu ex Nerebrook Nightingale) Br. H. Greenhalgh

Ch. Kennelgarth Gleam (Kennelgarth King Fox ex Ch. Cumnoch Musical Comedy) Br. Miss B. Sedorski

153

Ch. Cedar Pond Charmer, winner of best
of breed at Westminster, 1938.

Ch. Bothkennar Kilroy.

Eng. Ch. Westpark Rio Grande owned by Carnation
Farms.

Eng. & Am. Ch. Reimill Radiator.

Ch. Wilfield Necessity.

Ch. Reanda Silver Belle (Ch. Reanda Raith ex Nicotine Happy Laughter) Br. J. Ashdown

Ch. Viewpark Vincent (Ch. Viewpark Pilot ex Viewpark Eleanor) Br. A. N. Maclaren

Ch. Wilburn Essential (Ch. Wyrebury Wilwyn ex Baldinny Brandycandy) Br. Mrs. S. Grieve

Ch. Glenview Princess Pat (Ch. Glenview Sir Galahad ex Glenview Hazel) Br. A. H. Gee

Ch. Wenbury Joel (Ch. Wenbury Sandson ex Wenbury Bernice) Br. Mrs. D. M. Randall

Ch. Reanda Rosalina (Ch. Reanda Raith ex Reanda Rashenna) Br. Mrs. E. Meyer

1958

Ch. Eckersley Wee McGregor (Ch. Eckersley Wee Mon ex Chesterton Caprice) Br. Miss Jenkins

Ch. Desco Doreen (Ch. Happy Kimbo ex Cesco Daylight) Br. Mrs. L. J. Dewar

Ch. Mullacre Matador (Maigarth Moonlighter ex Penvale Persistent) Br. J. M. McKim

Ch. Glenview Lady Grace of Hadlow (Ch. Glenview Sir Galahad ex Glenview Hazel) Br. A. H. Gee

Ch. Brimstane Rab (Glendoune Gayboy ex Ch. Glendoune Gaytime) Br. H. Tennant

Ch. Greeba Hawesgarth Robin (Ch. Viewpark Pilot ex Ch. Wyrebury Watercress) Br. L. Jackson

Ch. Reanda Rheola (Ch. Viewpark Vincent ex Reanda Rioletta) Br. Mrs. E. Meyer

Ch. Reanda Roystar (Ch. Reanda Raith ex Reanda Rosita) Br. Mrs. E. Meyer

Ch. Mullacre Mantilla (Ch. Mullacre Matador ex Mountcrag Merrygirl) Br. R. Mallinson

Ch. Lady Meg of Hadlow (Glenview Grand Master ex Ch. Glenview Lady Grace of Hadlow) Br. Miss S. V. Pollock

Ch. Linda May of Hadlow (Glenview Grand Master ex Ch. Glenview Lady Grace of Hadlow) Br. Miss S. V. Pollock

1959

Ch. Happygate Carefree (Ch. Happy Kimbo ex Bardene Beau Peep) Br. S. Betteridge

Ch. Kentwelle Kirk (Ch. Reanda Rohan ex Kentwelle Kami) Br. Mrs. R. Upex

Ch. Penvale Peter So Gay (Ch. Con of Conett ex Ch. Penvale Prunella) Br. J. Jeffs

Ch. Bardene Boy Blue (Ch. Happy Kimbo ex Bardene Beau Peep) Br. S. Betteridge

Ch. Reanda Rutlin (Caesar of Conett ex Reanda Rosita) Br. Mrs. E. Meyer

Ch. Triermain Gayscott (Glendoune Geordie ex Desco Dorable) Br. Mrs. M. E. Bousfield

Ch. Cumnoch Musical Comedy (Cumnoch Cheerful Comrade ex Kennelgarth Melody) Br. Miss B. Sedorski

Ch. Rob of Hadlow (Ch. Reanda Rohan ex Baffielena of Hadlow) Br. Miss S. V. Pollock

Ch. Walsing Wild Winter (Ch. Reanda Roger Rough ex Walsing Winter Rose) Br. W. M. Singleton

Ch. Penvale Plutocrat (Ch. Viewpark Vincent ex Penvale Prunella) Br. J. Jeffs

156

Mr. & Mrs. Henry D. Israel's Ch. Marlu Clincher.

Howard Snethen's best in show homebred, Ch. Shieling's Masterkey.

Ch. Rutherland Reanda Rixy (Reanda Roderic ex Ch. Reanda Ria Bella) Br. Mrs. E. Meyer
Ch. Penebruge Reanda Rouge (Ch. Reanda Raith ex Reanda Rosita) Br. Mrs. E. Meyer
Ch. Secombe Satisfaction (Glendoune Galcador ex Avenue Pride) Br. W. Badnage
Ch. Reanda Ribot (Ch. Reanda Roger Rough ex Kentwelle Kamelia) Br. Mrs. R. Upex
Ch. Roberta of Hadlow (Ch. Reanda Rohan ex Baffielena of Hadlow) Br. Miss S. V. Pollack
Ch. Balgownie Buttercup (Balgownie Bix ex Penhall Selkirk Tartan) Br. A. Black

1960

Ch. Allascot Clover (Ch. Glenview Sir Galahad ex Allascot Amber) Br. Major J. Howard
Ch. Broadeaves Briar Rose (Glengordon Greensleeves ex Reanda Rochelle of Broadeaves) Br. Miss D. M. White
Ch. Caldicot Meg O'Marine (Ammanview Alistair ex Brema Bonnie) Br. Mr. G. Kavanagh
Ch. Darmar Will I Do (Ch. Bardene Boy Blue ex Darmar About Time) Brs. Major & Mrs. F. P. Darroch & Mr. H. Wright
Ch. Desco Daphne (Ch. Happy Kimbo ex Desco Daylight) Br. Mrs. L. J. Dewar
Ch. Grand Revel of Hadlow (Ch. Greeba Hawesgarth Robin ex Lady Guinevere of Hadlow) Br. Miss S. V. Pollock
Ch. Jokyl Here We Go (Ch. Reanda Rohan ex Eilburn Elwyn) Br. Mr. M. Punton
Ch. Kennelgarth Great Scot (Kennelgarth Tweedledee ex Ch. Kennelgarth Gleam) Br. Miss B. Penn Bull
Ch. Penvale Persuader (Balgownie Bix ex Brienbry Butterkisk) Br. J. Jeffs
Ch. Reanda Luna Rossa (Ch. Greeba Hawesgarth Robin ex Ch. Reanda Ria Bella) Br. Mrs. E. Meyer

1961

Ch. Bardene Black Jewel (Ryeland Regal Scot ex Bardene Blue Cap) Br. Mr. G. Young
Ch. Glenview Merry Princess (Glenview Rocket ex Ch. Glenview Princess) Br. Mr. A. H. Gee
Ch. Hardlyn Rufus (Ch. Reanda Rohan ex Hardlyn Rosita) Mrs. V. G. Hardy
Ch. Kennelgarth Eros (Ch. Viewpark Vincent ex Ch. Kennelgarth Venus) Br. Miss B. Penn Bull
Ch. Kennelgarth Viking (Ch. Kennelgarth Eros ex Ch. Kennelgarth Gleam) Br. Miss B. Penn Bull
Ch. Kentwelle Krocus (Ch. Greeba Hawesgarth Robin ex Kentwelle Kristie) Br. Mrs. Y. M. Upex
Ch. Niddbank Kirsty (Niddbank Headline ex Niddbank Prudence) Br. Mrs. K. M. Ross
Ch. Niddbank Ladybird (Ch. Wyrebury Wrangler ex Niddbank Lady) Br. Mrs. K. M. Ross
Ch. Reanda Gloxinia of Hadlow (Ch. Glenview Sir Galahad ex Ch. Lady Meg of Hadlow) Br. Miss S. V. Pollock
Ch. Reanda Reeba (Reanda Blackamoor ex Reanda Ruta) Br. Mrs. E. Meyer
Ch. Reanda Rexis (Ch. Reanda Ribot ex Ch. Reanda Silver Belle) Br. Mrs. E. Meyer

158

Ch. Ladysman, owned by Mr. and Mrs. Stuart Erwin, 1936.

Ch. Ardoch Souvenir, owned by John Deardorf, 1936.

Ch. Viewpark Dictator (Ch. Greeba Hawesgarth Robin ex Valencia Queen) Br. Mr. A. N. Maclaren

1962

Ch. Bardene Bartelo (Ryeland Raffie ex Bardene Breezandi) Br. Mr. W. Palethorpe

Ch. Bardene Bingo (Bardene Blue Starlite ex Bardene Blue Cap) Br. Mr. G. Young

Ch. Cumnoch Clansman (Ch. Kennelgarth Eros ex Ch. Cumnoch Sonnet) Br. Miss S. D. Sedorski

Ch. Gaywyn Viscountess (Ch. Kennelgarth Viking ex Gaywyn Countess) Br. Mrs. M. Owen.

Ch. Glenview Golden Disc (Glenview Guardian ex Glenview Cindy) Br. Mr. A. H. Gee

Ch. Redwar Balgownie Betula (Maigarth Marantic ex Balgownie Bairn) Br. Mr. A. Black

Ch. Reanda Cellan of Conett (Ch. Cool of Conett ex Curtis of Conett) Br. Mr. A. R. Hanson

Ch. Reanda Kentwelle Kingpin (Ch. Reanda Roger Rough ex Kentwelle Kamelia) Br. Mrs. Y. M. Upex

Ch. Reanda Rexana (Ch. Reanda Rexis ex Ch. Reanda Luna Rossa) Br. Mrs. E. Meyer

Ch. Reanda Roumelia (Ch. Reanda Rohan ex Ch. Reanda Runic Regal) Br. Mrs. E. Meyer

Ch. Scotvale Soroya (Wyrebury Worthy ex Scotvale Sandra) Br. Mr. H. Heaton

Ch. Woodmansey Winetaster (Wyrebury Worthy ex Woodmansey Wanderlust) Br. H. Wright

1963

Ch. Eskside Dainty Lady (Maigarth Mahfhappen ex Eilburn Rohanna) Br. Mrs. M. Punton

Ch. Gaywyn Bonnilass (Ch. Kennelgarth Viking ex Gaywyn Bonigen) Br. Mrs. M. Owen

Ch. Gillsie Principal Girl (Ch. Bardene Bingo ex Balgownie Butterfluff) Br. Messrs. W. Gill & J. McShane

Ch. Glenview Silver Gilt (Turfield Buckwheat ex Glenview Silvernob) Br. A. H. Gee

Ch. Kennelgarth Minerva (Kennelgarth Jupiter ex Ravensden Rizzio) Br. Mrs. M. E. Lowden

Ch. Kennelgarth Sharon (Kennelgarth Lance ex Kennelgarth Sheena) Br. Miss B. Penn Bull

Ch. Wirescot Penny (Ch. Kennelgarth Eros ex Manorcourt May Sonnet) Br. A. C. Penny

1964

Ch. Bardene Bemine (Ch. Bardene Bingo ex Bardene Barefoot Contessa) Br. W. Palethorpe

Ch. Brackenscroft Rye and Dry (Ch. Kennelgarth Viking ex Brackenscroft Hazel Honey) Br. Mr. C. E. Brackstone

Ch. Brunnoch Rapid Riser of Hadlow (Ch. Reanda Roger Rough ex Ch. Glenview Lady Grace of Hadlow) Br. Miss S. V. Pollock

Ch. Caldicot Arabis (Caldicot Pennant ex Ch. Caldicot Meg O' Marine) Br. Mr. L. Burston

Ch. Gaywyn Matador (Cunmoch Kilts-A-Swinging ex Gaywyn Cresta) Br. Mrs. M. Owen

Ch. Glenellen Clan-Crest (Ch. Reanda Kentwelle Kingpin ex Reanda Rhodanthe) Br. Messrs. J. Chapman & H. McCormack
Ch. Inverdruie Scorchin (Ch. Kennelgarth Viking ex Inverdruie Sparkler) Br. Miss L. Vassilopulo
Ch. Milward Meadowmist (Eckersley Yellowhammer ex Milward Meadowsweet) Br. Mrs. G. D. Yates
Ch. Penvale Prolific (Balgownie Bix ex Brienbry Butterkisk) Br. J. Jeffs
Ch. Reanda the Rock (Ch. Reanda Kentwelle Kingpin ex Ch. Reanda Gloxinia of Hadlow) Br. Mrs. E. Meyer
Ch. Walsing Winter Weather (Ch. Walsing Wild Winter ex St. Quivox Quality Street) Br. Mr. W. M. Singleton

1965
Ch. Gillsie Starturn (Ch. Kennelgarth Viking ex Ch. Gillsie Principal Girl) Br. Messrs. W. Gill and J. McShane
Ch. Gillsie Highland Lass (Ch. Kennelgarth Viking ex Ch. Gillsie Principal Girl) Br. Messrs. W. Gill & J. McShane
Ch. Gosmore Gillsie Scotch Mist (Ch. Kennelgarth Viking ex Ch. Gillsie Principal Girl) Br. Messrs. W. Gill & J. McShane
Ch. Brio Wishbone (Ch. Kennelgarth Viking ex Brio Chorus Girl) Br. Miss Jane Miller
Ch. Brio Cabin Boy (Ch. Kennelgarth Viking ex Brio Chorus Girl) Br. Miss Jane Miller
Ch. Gaywyn Castanet (Ch. Kennelgarth Viking ex. Gaywyn Conchita) Br. Mrs. M. Owen
Ch. Kennelgarth Valorous (Ch. Kennelgarth Viking ex Kennelgarth Dairymaid) Br. Miss Betty Penn Bull
Ch. Gaywyn Emperor (Ch. Bardene Bingo ex Ch. Gaywyn Viscountess) Br. Mrs. M. Owen
Ch. Viewpark Viking (Viewpark Red Hackle ex Viewpark Vanity Fair) Br. A. Maclaren
Ch. Reanda Ringold (Ch. Bardene Bingo ex Stedplane Reanda Rainette) Br. Mrs. E. Plane
Ch. Reanda Renita (Ch. Reanda Kentvelle Kingpin ex Ch. Reanda Rosalina) Br. Mrs. E. Meyer
Ch. Gregorach Glorious Twelfth (Ch. Woodmansey Whietaster ex. Gregorach Chequers) Br. Miss P. Drummond

Kennel Names and Their Owners

Because of the difficulty of tracing the ownership of kennel names when applied to dogs, the following lists a large number of kennel prefixes and suffixes together with names of their owner or owners. The first lists American Kennels, the second British Kennels. No attempt has been made to have these listings complete since many more kennels have existed than are listed here. However, the names given are believed to be representative of the breed and include a large number of the more successful kennels through the years. In many cases the kennels listed are no longer in operation.

161

Acton Hill	Mr. and Mrs. John Kemps
Anstamm	Mr. and Mrs. Anthony Stamm
Ardmore	Robert McKinven
Ayerscott	Mr. and Mrs. Albert C. Ayres
Balachan	Dr. and Mrs. T. Allen Kirk
Balgay	Dr. and Mrs. Cecil Jelley
Ballantrae	Caswell Barrie
Barberry Knowe	Mr. and Mrs. Charles C. Stalter
Barlae	William Prentice (Also used in Britain)
Bentley	Prentice Talmadge
Blanart	Mrs. Blanche Reeg
Boglebrae	Henry D. Bixby
Bothkennar	Mr. and Mrs. Bryce Gillespie, later by Mr. and Mrs. Gordon D. Campbell
Brandywine	Mrs. George Thomas
Braw Bricht	Mr. and Mrs. Donald D. Voorhees
Brawyn	Mr. and Mrs. Turk Humphrey
Briarcroft	Dr. F. W. Zimmerman
Camydnas	A. E. Cartwright
Carmichael's	Mrs. Ruth C. Johnson
Carnation	E. H. Stuart
Cedar Pond	John Goudie
Craigdarroch	Mrs. Jack Brazier
Crescent Hill	Mrs. Dorissa Barnes
Crisscot	Miss Cornelia M. Crissey
Cy Ann	Cyrus K. Rickel
Deephaven	Theodore W. Bennett
Diehard	William McBain
Dunbar	Richard Hensel
Earlybird	W. T. Stern
Edgerstoune	Mrs. Marion Eppley (formerly Mrs. John G. Winant)
Fairwold	R. M. Cadwalader
Frangan	Mrs. Frances Gannon
Friendship Farm	Mr. and Mrs. William Sheiburn
Fulluvit	Mr. and Mrs. W. Sheldon Winans
Graecroft	Mrs. Charles Gray
Gaidoune	Miss Helen B. Gaither
Glenafton	Elizabeth Hull
Glenby	Mrs. F. J. Russell
Glen Shiel	Mr. and Mrs. Bernard P. Howes
Goldfinder	Edward F. Maloney
Hampton Hill	Mr. and Mrs. Werner Josten
Haycliff	Mr. and Mrs. Harry Haylor
Hibank	Mr. and Mrs. F. R. Newton
Highlander	Dr. and Mrs. Joseph A. Thomas
Hillcote	John Hillman
Hillwood	Mrs. Thomas W. Durant
Hitofa	Frank Spierkerman
Jepeca	Mr. and Mrs. Charles H. Werber, Jr.
Kelti	Mrs. John V. Kelly

162

Ch. Todhill Cinnamon Bear with Johnny Murphy handling.

Ch. Friendship Farm Diplomat.

Kelscot	Mr. and Mrs. Joseph W. Kelly
Kenbrick	Mr. and Mrs. Kenneth Halloran
Kinclaven	Mrs. Marie A. Stone
Lealscot	Mrs. John McGilvray
Lochearn	Mr. and Mrs. Charles J. Costabell
Lynnscot	Mr. and Mrs. R. J. McLoughlin
Mac-Bur	Marguerite J. Fuller
Mac R	Mr. and Mrs. Keith P. Rogers
Mac's Welton	Mr. and Mrs. William Macauley
Marlorain	Miss Lorraine Davis and Miss Martha Melekov
Marlu	Mr. and Mrs. Maurice Pollak
Marymac	Dr. and Mrs. B. Kater McInnes
Medrick	Mrs. Medora Messinger
Merrie Oaks	Mrs. Edmund Mansure
Middlemount	Bruce Webb
Mine Brook	Jock McOwan
Newcastle	James and Dr. C. C. Little
Nosegay	Dr. Fayette Ewing
'of Seaglen	R. C. E. Sharp (Canada)
Paisley Hill	Mr. and Mrs. Henry D. Israel
Philabeg	Dr. and Mrs. Merritt N. Pope
Poverty Hill	John F. Wright, Jr.
Rampant	Mr. and Mrs. Seth Malby
Rannoch Dune	Mr. and Mrs. Frank Brumby
Rebel Run	Dr. and Mrs. W. Stewart Carter
Red Gauntlet	Dr. and Mrs. Charles Lynch
Relgalf	Mrs. Flagler Matthews
Revran	Mrs. Richard Swatsley
Sandbark	Miss Evelyn Sanders
Sandoone	Miss Betty Malinka
Sandown	Mrs. E. S. Woodward
Scots Guard	Mrs. Richard Weaver
Scotsholme	Bert Hankinson
Sharonlane	Mr. and Mrs. Reason A. Krick
Shenscot	Mr. and Mrs. L. Bradford Branner
Shieling	Mr. and Mrs. T. Howard Snethen
Sporran	S. S. Van Dine
Tavviscot	Mr. and Mrs. S. Valdes
Tobermory	Mrs. George Cole (Marguerite Kirmse)
Todhill	Mr. and Mrs. Robert C. Graham
Vigal	Mr. and Mrs. H. Alvin McAleenan
Walescot	Francis G. Lloyd
Wankie	Henry Brooks and Oliver Ames
Wishing Well	Mrs. Florence Worcester
Woodhart	Mr. and Mrs. Heywood Hartley

British Kennels

Abertay	B. McMillam
Albourne	A. G. Cowley
Allascot	Miss D. Blackstone
Baldinny	Mrs. S. Grieve

Balgownie	A. Black
Bapton	J. Deane Willis
Bardene	W. Palethorpe
Barlae	William Prentice (also in the U.S.)
Bidfield	Miss R. Payne and Miss S. M. Harrold
Broadeaves	Miss D. M. White
Craig	Miss P. Drummond
Cumnoch	Miss B. Sedorski
Darmar	Mrs. M. Darroch
Desco	Mrs. L. J. Dewar
Desert	R. J. Gadsden
Eckersley	Miss M. Law
Elbury	Mrs. Rees
Ems	W. L. McCandlish
Farnock	Robert Houston
Gaisgill	Mrs. C. M. Cross
Gaywyn	Mr. and Mrs. H. F. Owen
Gillsie	W. Gill and J. McShane
Glendoune	R. H. McGill
Glenisla	Mr. and Mrs. A. M. Robb
Glenview	Mr. and Mrs. A. H. Gee
Gourock	Messrs. Mackie and McColl
Heather	Robert Chapman and sons
Heyday	Miss M. H. Morrison
Inverdruie	Miss L. Vassilopulo
Jhelum	G. D. Lyell
Kennelgarth	Miss Betty Penn Bull
Laindon	H. R. B. Tweed
Merlewood	George Davidson
Niddbank	J. R. and Mrs. K. M. Ross
Ortley	Dr. C. Bremer
'of Ralc	Miss D. I. Thorpe
Reanda	Mrs. E. Meyer
'of Rookes	John Sharpe
Rothesay	Andrew H. Lister
Ryeland	Mrs. S. A. Collins
Sandheys	Richard Lloyd
Scotia	Mrs. W. Barber
Stedplane	Mrs. E. Plane
Triermain	Mrs. M. E. Bousfield
Turfield	T. W. L. Caspersz
Viewpark	Mr. and Mrs. A. Maclaren
Walnut	Sam Bamford
Walsing	Mr. and Mrs. W. M. Singleton
Wenbury	T. W. and Mrs. D. M. Randall
Woodmansey	H. Wright
Wychworth	H. Knowles
Wyrebury	W. Berry

Ch. Heather Reveller of Sporran.

Ch. Heather Gold Finder.

Left to right: Ed Johnson, Edward Maloney and Johnny Murphy.

Scottish Terrier Bibliography

The following lists books and articles that deal with the breed in whole or in part.

Ash, E. C.—*The Scottish Terrier*, 1936.

Barrie, Caswell—The New Scottish Terrier Standard, *American Kennel Gazette*, March 1925 pp 20–22, 151.

Barton, F. T.—*Terriers, Their Points and Management*, 1907.

Bruette, Dr. William—*The Scottish Terrier*, 1934.

Buckley, Holland—*The Scottish Terrier*, 1913.

Caspersz, D. S.—*Scottish Terrier Pedigrees*, 1934, with supplements.
What the Scottie Will Become, *American Kennel Gazette*, July 1931 pp 25–27, 119.
The Scottish Terrier, 1938.
The Scottish Terrier (Foyles), 1958.
The Popular Scottish Terrier, 1962.

Davies, C. J.—*The Scottish Terrier*, 1906.

Deu, Edna et al.—*Stars in the Doghouse* (Deephaven Kennels) *Country Life In America*, April 1939 pp 55, 109–110.

Ewing, Dr. Fayette—*The Book of the Scottish Terrier*, 1932 and subsequent ed.

Gabriel, Dorothy—*The Scottish Terrier*, no date.

Gray, D. J. Thomson—*The Dogs of Scotland*, 1887 and 1893 (Whinstone).

Green, James E.—*The Scottish Terrier and the Irish Terrier*, 1894.

Haynes, William—*Scottish and Irish Terriers*, 1925.

Johns, Rowland—*Our Friend the Scottish Terrier*, 1933.

Jones, A. F.—*American Kennel Gazette*, Ballantrae's Reasons for Success, March 1927 pp 13–17, 71; Hillwood Turns to the Scottie, Feb. 1932 pp 9–13; Bred by Science and Humanity (Sporran Kennels), July 1932 pp 7–11, 124; Vigal is Building Slowly, Dec. 1932 pp 24–28, 157; A Kennel without a Fault (Relgalf Kennels) July 1934 pp 7–11, 173; Why Braw Bricht's Aim is to Breed Scotties of Highest Quality, Feb. 1936 pp 12–15, 99; Championship, the Standard for

Scotties of Miss Hull, March 1936 pp 11–14, 79; Raising Scotties that Win is Greatest Enjoyment to Owners of Barberry Knowe, July 1936 pp 13–16, 152; Scotties Started Relgalf on the Way to Fame, Aug. 1938 pp 27–31.

Kirk, Dr. Alan—*American Scottish Terrier Champions' Pedigrees*, 1962.

Marvin, John T.—*The Book of All Terriers*, 1964, includes breed chapter.

Matheson, Darley—*Terriers, 1962*, includes breed chapter.

Mason, Charles H.—*Our Prize Dogs*, 1888.

Maxtee, J.—*British Terriers*, 1909; *Scotch and Irish Terriers*, 1923.

McCandlish, W. L.—Chapter on the breed in *Dogs by Well Known Authorities*, 1906—*The Scottish Terrier*, 1909.

Megargee, Edwin S.—The Ideal Scottish Terrier, *American Kennel Gazette*, Jan. 1933 pp 17–20, 136.

Penn Bull, Betty—*Scottish Terrier Coats*, Re trimming the breed. n.d.

Robertson, James—*Historical Sketches of the Scottish Terrier*, 1899.

Scottish Terrier Club of America Yearbooks, 1948, 1959, 1961, 1965.

Scottish Terrier Club of England Yearbooks, various issues.

Smith, Croxton—*Terriers, Their Training, Working and Management*, 1937. Includes chapters on the breed by McCandlish.

Shields, G. O.—*The American Book on the Dog*, 1891. Includes chapter on the breed by John H. Naylor.

Van Dine, S. S.—Crashing the Dog-Breeding Gate, *American Kennel Gazette*, Dec. 1930 pp 29–32, 166.

Watson, James—*The Dog Book*, 1906, 2 vol. includes much early comment on the breed in America.

There are many more books that contain chapters on the breed. Most are useful but the ones mentioned will offer the reader a complete resume of the important literature on the breed.

Part II

GENERAL CARE AND TRAINING OF YOUR DOG

by

Elsworth S. Howell
Milo G. Denlinger
A. C. Merrick, D.V.M.

Introduction

THE normal care and training of dogs involve no great mysteries. The application of common sense and good judgment is required, however. The pages that follow distill the combined experience and knowledge of three authorities who have devoted most of their lives to dogs.

Milo Denlinger wrote many books out of his rich and varied experience as a breeder, exhibitor and owner of a commercial kennel. Elsworth Howell has been a fancier since young boyhood and claims intimate knowledge of 25 different breeds; he is an American Kennel Club delegate and judge of the sporting breeds. Dr. A. C. Merrick is a leading veterinarian with a wide practice.

The chapter on "Training and Simple Obedience" covers the basic behavior and performance every dog should have to be accepted by your friends, relatives, neighbors and strangers. The good manners and exercises described will avoid costly bills for damage to the owner's or neighbor's property and will prevent heartbreaking accidents to the dog and to the people he meets. The instructions are given in simple, clear language so that a child may easily follow them.

"The Exhibition of Dogs" describes the kinds of dog shows, their classes and how an owner may enter his dog and show it. If one practices good sportsmanship, shows can be enjoyable.

The chapter on feeding offers sound advice on feeding puppies, adult dogs, the stud dog and the brood bitch. The values of proteins, carbohydrates, fats, minerals and vitamins in the dog's diet are thoroughly covered. Specific diets and quantities are not given because of the many variations among dogs, even of the same breed or size, in their individual needs, likes, dislikes, allergies, etc.

"The Breeding of Dogs" contains the fundamental precepts everyone who wishes to raise puppies should know. Suggestions for choosing a stud dog are given. The differences among outcrossing, inbreeding and line breeding are clearly explained. Care tips for the pregnant and whelping bitch will be found most helpful.

The material on "External Vermin and Parasites" gives specific treatments for removing and preventing fleas, lice, ticks and flies. With today's wonder insecticides and with proper management there is no excuse for a dog to be infested with any of these pests which often cause secondary problems.

"Intestinal Parasites and Their Control" supplies the knowledge dog owners must have of the kinds of worms that invade dogs and the symptoms they cause. While drugs used for the removal of these debilitating dog enemies are discussed, dosages are not given because it is the authors' and publisher's belief that such treatment is best left in the hands of the veterinarian. These drugs are powerful and dangerous in inexperienced hands.

The chapter on "Skin Troubles" supplies the information and treatments needed to recognize and cure these diseases. The hints appearing on coat care will do much to prevent skin problems.

One of the most valuable sections in this book is the "instant" advice on "FIRST AID" appearing on pages 95-98. The publisher strongly urges the reader to commit this section to memory. It may save a pet's life.

The information on diseases will help the dog owner to diagnose symptoms. Some dog owners rush their dogs to the veterinarian for the slightest, transitory upsets.

Finally, the chapters on "Housing for Dogs" and "Care of the Old Dog" round out this highly useful guide for all dog lovers.

4

Training and Simple Obedience

E VERY DOG that is mentally and physically sound can be taught good manners and simple obedience by any normal man, woman, or child over eight years old.

Certain requirements must be met by the dog, trainer and the environment if the training is to be enjoyable and effective. The dog must be rested and calm. The trainer must be rested, calm, gentle, firm, patient and persistent. The training site should be dry, comfortable and, except for certain exercises, devoid of distractions.

Proper techniques can achieve quick and sure results. Always use short, strong words for commands and always use the *same* word or words for the same command. Speak with authority; never scream or yell. Teach one command or exercise at a time and make sure the dog understands it and performs it perfectly before you proceed to the next step. Demand the dog's undivided attention; if he wavers or wanders, speak his name or pat him smartly or jerk his leash. Use pats and praise plentifully; avoid tidbit training if at all possible because tidbits may not always be available in an emergency and the dog will learn better without them. Keep lessons short; when the dog begins to show boredom, stop and do not resume in less than two hours. One or two ten-minute lessons a day should be ample, especially for a young puppy. Dogs have their good and bad days; if your well dog seems unduly lazy,

5

tired, bored or off-color, put off the lesson until tomorrow. Try to make lessons a joy, a happy time both for you and the dog, but do demand and get the desired action. Whenever correction or punishment is needed, use ways and devices that the dog does not connect with you; some of these means are given in the following instructions. Use painful punishment only as a last resort.

"NO!"

The most useful and easily understood command is "NO!" spoken in a sharp, disapproving tone and accompanied with a shaking finger. At first, speak the dog's name following with "NO!" until the meaning of the word—your displeasure—is clear.

"COME!"

Indoors or out, let the dog go ten or more feet away from you. Speak his name following at once with "COME!" Crouch, clap your hands, pick up a stick, throw a ball up and catch it, or create any other diversion which will lure the dog to you. When he comes, praise and pat effusively. As with all commands and exercises repeat the lesson, until the dog *always* comes to you.

THE FIRST NIGHTS

Puppies left alone will bark, moan and whine. If your dog is not to have the run of the house, put him in a room where he can do the least damage. Give him a Nylabone and a strip of beef hide (both available in supermarkets or pet shops and excellent as teething pacifiers). A very young puppy may appreciate a loud-ticking clock which, some dog trainers say, simulates the heart-beat of his former litter mates. Beyond providing these diversions, grit your teeth and steel your heart. If in pity you go to the howling puppy, he will howl every time you leave him. Suffer one night, two nights or possibly three, and you'll have it made.

The greatest boon to dog training and management is the wooden or wire crate. Any two-handed man can make a ⅜" plywood crate. It needs only four sides, a top, a bottom, a door on hinges and

6

with a strong hasp, and a fitting burlap bag stuffed with shredded newspaper, cedar shavings or 2" foam rubber. Feed dealers or seed stores should give you burlap bags; be sure to wash them thoroughly to remove any chemical or allergy-causing material. The crate should be as long, as high and three times as wide as the dog will be full grown. The crate will become as much a sanctuary to your dog as a cave was to his prehistoric ancestor; it will also help immeasurably in housebreaking.

HOUSEBREAKING

The secret to housebreaking a healthy normal dog is simple: take him out every hour if he is from two to six months old when you get him; or the first thing in the morning, immediately after every meal, and the last thing at night if he is over six months.

For very young puppies, the paper break is indicated. Lay eight or ten layers of newspapers in a room corner most remote from the puppy's bed. By four months of age or after two weeks in a new home if older, a healthy puppy should not need the paper *IF* it is exercised outdoors often and *IF* no liquid (including milk) is given after 5 P.M. and *IF* it is taken out not earlier than 10 P.M. at night and not later than 7 A.M. the next morning.

When the dog does what it should when and where it should, praise, praise and praise some more. Be patient outdoors: keep the dog out until action occurs. Take the dog to the same general area always; its own traces and those of other dogs thus drawn to the spot will help to inspire the desired action.

In extreme cases where frequent exercising outdoors fails, try to catch the dog in the act and throw a chain or a closed tin can with pebbles in it near the dog but not on him; say "NO!" loudly as the chain or can lands. In the most extreme case, a full 30-second spanking with a light strap may be indicated but be sure you catch the miscreant *in the act*. Dog memories are short.

Remember the crate discussed under "THE FIRST NIGHTS." If you give the dog a fair chance, he will NOT soil his crate.

Do not rub his nose in "it." Dogs have dignity and pride. It is permissible to lead him to his error as soon as he commits it and to remonstrate forcefully with "NO!"

7

COLLAR AND LEASH TRAINING

Put on a collar tight enough not to slip over the head. Leave it on for lengthening periods from a few minutes to a few hours over several days. A flat collar for shorthaired breeds; a round or rolled collar for longhairs. For collar breaking, do NOT use a choke collar; it may catch on a branch or other jutting object and strangle the dog.

After a few days' lessons with the collar, attach a heavy cord or rope to it without a loop or knot at the end (to avoid snagging or catching on a stump or other object). Allow the dog to run free with collar and cord attached a few moments at a time for several days. Do not allow dog to chew cord!

When the dog appears to be accustomed to the free-riding cord, pick up end of the cord, loop it around your hand and take your dog for a walk (not the other way around!). DON'T STOP WALKING if the dog pulls, balks or screams bloody murder. Keep going and make encouraging noises. If dog leaps ahead of you, turn sharply left or right whichever is *away* from dog's direction— AND KEEP MOVING! The biggest mistake in leash training is stopping when the dog stops, or going the way the dog goes when the dog goes wrong. You're the leader; make the dog aware of it. This is one lesson you should continue until the dog realizes who is boss. If the dog gets the upper leg now, you will find it difficult to resume your rightful position as master. Brutality, no; firmness, yes!

If the dog pulls ahead, jerk the cord—or by now, the leash— backward. Do not pull. Jerk or snap the leash only!

JUMPING ON PEOPLE

Nip this annoying habit at once by bumping the dog with your knee on his chest or stepping with authority on his rear feet. A sharp "NO!" at the same time helps. Don't permit this action when you're in your work clothes and ban it only when dressed in glad rags. The dog is not Beau Brummel, and it is cruel to expect him to distinguish between denim and silk.

8

THE "PROBLEM" DOG

The following corrections are indicated when softer methods fail. Remember that it's better to rehabilitate than to destroy.

Biting. For the puppy habit of mouthing or teething on the owner's hand, a sharp rap with a folded newspaper on the nose, or snapping the middle finger off the thumb against the dog's nose, will usually discourage nibbling tactics. For the biter that means it, truly drastic corrections may be preferable to destroying the dog. If your dog is approaching one year of age and is biting in earnest, take him to a professional dog trainer and don't quibble with his methods unless you would rather see the dog dead.

Chewing. For teething puppies, provide a Nylabone (trade mark) and beef hide strips (see "THE FIRST NIGHTS" above). Every time the puppy attacks a chair, a rug, your hand, or any other chewable object, snap your finger or rap a newspaper on his nose, or throw the chain or a covered pebble-laden tin can near him, say "NO!" and hand him the bone or beef hide. If he persists, put him in his crate with the bone and hide. For incorrigible chewers, check diet for deficiencies first. William Koehler, trainer of many movie dogs including *The Thin Man's* Asta, recommends in his book, *The Koehler Method of Dog Training,* that the chewed object or part of it be taped crosswise in the dog's mouth until he develops a hearty distaste for it.

Digging. While he is in the act, throw the chain or noisy tin can and call out "NO!" For the real delinquent Koehler recommends filling the dug hole with water, forcing the dog's nose into it until the dog thinks he's drowning—and he'll never dig again. Drastic perhaps, but better than the bullet from an angry neighbor's gun, or a surreptitious poisoning.

The Runaway. If your dog wanders while walking with you, throw the chain or tin can and call "COME!" to him. If he persists, have a friend or neighbor cooperate in chasing him home. A very long line, perhaps 25 feet or more, can be effective if you permit the dog to run its length and then snap it sharply to remind him not to get too far from you.

Car Chasing. Your dog will certainly live longer if you make him car-wise; in fact, deathly afraid of anything on wheels. Ask a friend or neighbor to drive you in *his* car. Lie below the windows and as your dog chases the car throw the chain or tin can while your neighbor or friend says "GO HOME!" sharply. Another method is to shoot a water pistol filled with highly diluted ammonia at the dog. If your dog runs after children on bicycles, the latter device is especially effective but may turn the dog against children.

The Possessive Dog. If a dog displays overly protective habits, berate him in no uncertain terms. The chain, the noisy can, the rolled newspaper, or light strap sharply applied, may convince him that, while he loves you, there's no percentage in overdoing it.

The Cat Chaser. Again, the chain, the can, the newspaper, the strap—or the cat's claws if all else fails, but only as the last resort.

The Defiant, or Revengeful, Wetter. Some dogs seem to resent being left alone. Some are jealous when their owners play with another dog or animal. Get a friend or neighbor in this case to heave the chain or noisy tin can when the dog relieves himself in sheer spite.

For other canine delinquencies, you will find *The Koehler Method of Dog Training* effective. William Koehler's techniques have been certified as extremely successful by directors of motion pictures featuring dogs and by officers of dog obedience clubs.

OBEDIENCE EXERCISES

A well-mannered dog saves its owner money, embarrassment and possible heartbreak. The destruction of property by canine delinquents, avoidable accidents to dogs and children, and other unnecessary disadvantages to dog ownership can be eliminated by simple obedience training. The elementary exercises of heeling, sitting, staying and lying down can keep the dog out of trouble in most situations.

The only tools needed for basic obedience training are a slip collar made of chain link, leather or nylon and a strong six-foot leather leash with a good spring snap. Reviewing the requirements and basic techniques given earlier, let's proceed with the dog's schooling.

Heeling. Keep your dog on your left side, with the leash in your left hand. Start straight ahead in a brisk walk. If your dog pulls ahead, jerk (do not pull) the leash and say "Heel" firmly. If the dog persists in pulling ahead, stop, turn right or left and go on for several yards, saying "Heel" each time you change direction.

If your dog balks, fix leash *under* his throat and coax him forward by repeating his name and tapping your hip.

Whatever you do, don't stop walking! If the dog jumps up or "fights" the leash, just keep moving briskly. Sooner than later he will catch on and with the repetition of "Heel" on every correction, you will have him trotting by your side with style and respect.

Sit. Keeping your dog on leash, hold his neck up and push his rump down while repeating "Sit." If he resists, "spank" him lightly several times on his rump. Be firm, but not cruel. Repeat this lesson often until it is learned perfectly. When the dog knows the command, test him at a distance without the leash. Return to him every time he fails to sit and repeat the exercise.

Stay. If you have properly trained your dog to "Sit," the "Stay" is simple. Take his leash off and repeat "Stay" holding your hand up, palm toward dog, and move away. If dog moves toward you, you must repeat the "sit" lesson until properly learned. After your

11

dog "stays" while you are in sight, move out of his sight and keep repeating "Stay." Once he has learned to "stay" even while you are out of his sight, you can test him under various conditions, such as when another dog is near, a child is playing close to him, or a car appears on the road. (Warning: do not tax your dog's patience on the "stay" until he has learned the performance perfectly.)

Down. For this lesson, keep your dog on leash. First tell him to "sit." When he has sat for a minute, place your shoe over his leash between the heel and sole. Slowly pull on the leash and repeat "Down" while you push his head down with your other hand. Do this exercise very quietly so that dog does not become excited and uncontrollable. In fact, this performance is best trained when the dog is rather quiet. Later, after the dog has learned the voice signal perfectly, you can command the "Down" with a hand signal, sweeping your hand from an upright position to a downward motion with your palm toward the dog. Be sure to say "Down" with the hand signal.

For more advanced obedience the following guides by Blanche Saunders are recommended:

The Complete Novice Obedience Course
The Complete Open Obedience Course
The Complete Utility Obedience Course (with Tracking)
Dog Training for Boys and Girls (includes simple tricks.)
All are published by Howell Book House at $3.00 each.

OBEDIENCE TRIALS

Booklets covering the rules and regulations of Obedience Trials may be obtained from The American Kennel Club, 51 Madison Avenue, New York, N.Y. 10010. In Canada, write The Canadian Kennel Club, 667 Yonge Street, Toronto, Ontario.

Both these national clubs can give you the names and locations of local and regional dog clubs that conduct training classes in obedience and run Obedience Trials in which trained dogs compete for degrees as follow: CD (Companion Dog), CDX (Companion Dog Excellent), UD (Utility Dog), TD (Tracking Dog) and UDT (Utility Dog, Tracking.)

The Exhibition
of Dogs

NOBODY should exhibit a dog in the shows unless he can win without gloating and can lose without rancor. The showing of dogs is first of all a sport, and it is to be approached in a sportsmanlike spirit. It is not always so approached. That there are so many wretched losers and so many supercilious winners among the exhibitors in dog shows is the reason for this warning.

The confidence that one's dog is of exhibition excellence is all that prompts one to enter him in the show, but, if he fails in comparison with his competitors, nobody is harmed. It is no personal disgrace to have a dog beaten. It may be due to the dog's fundamental faults, to its condition, or to inexpert handling. One way to avoid such hazards is to turn the dog over to a good professional handler. Such a man with a flourishing established business will not accept an inferior dog, one that is not worth exhibiting. He will put the dog in the best possible condition before he goes into the ring with him, and he knows all the tricks of getting out of a dog all he has to give. Good handlers come high, however. Fees for taking a dog into the ring will range from ten to twenty-five dollars, plus any cash prizes the dog may win, and plus a bonus for wins made in the group.

Handlers do not win all the prizes, despite the gossip that they do, but good handlers choose only good dogs and they usually finish at or near the top of their classes. It is a mistake to assume that this is due to any favoritism or any connivance with the judges; the handlers have simply chosen the best dogs, conditioned them well, and so maneuvered them in the ring as to bring out their best points.

The services of a professional handler are not essential, however. Many an amateur shows his dogs as well, but the exhibitor without previous experience is ordinarily at something of a disadvantage. If the dog is good enough, he may be expected to win.

The premium list of the show, setting forth the prizes to be offered, giving the names of the judges, containing the entry form, and describing the conditions under which the show is to be held, are usually mailed out to prospective exhibitors about a month before the show is scheduled to be held. Any show superintendent is glad to add names of interested persons to the mailing list.

Entries for a Licensed show close at a stated date, usually about two weeks before the show opens, and under the rules no entry may be accepted after the advertised date of closing. It behooves the exhibitor to make his entries promptly. The exhibitor is responsible for all errors he may make on the entry form of his dog; such errors cannot be rectified and may result in the disqualification of the exhibit. It therefore is wise for the owner to double check all data submitted with an entry. The cost of making an entry, which is stated in the premium list, is usually from six to eight dollars. An unregistered dog may be shown at three shows, after which he must be registered or a statement must be made to the American Kennel Club that he is ineligible for registry and why, with a request for permission to continue to exhibit the dog. Such permission is seldom denied. The listing fee for an unregistered dog is twenty-five cents, which must be added to the entry fee.

Match or Sanctioned shows are excellent training and experience for regular bench shows. Entry fees are low, usually ranging from fifty cents to a dollar, and are made at the show instead of in advance. Sanctioned shows are unbenched, informal affairs where the puppy may follow his owner about on the leash and become accustomed to strange dogs, to behaving himself in the ring, and to being handled by a judge. For the novice exhibitor, too, Sanctioned shows will provide valuable experience, for ring procedure is similar to that at regular bench shows.

14

The classes open at most shows and usually divided by sex are as follows: Puppy Class (often Junior Puppy for dogs 6 to 9 months old, and Senior Puppy for dogs 9 to 12 months); Novice Class, for dogs that have never won first in any except the Puppy Class; Bred-by-Exhibitor Class, for dogs of which the breeder and owner are the same person or persons; the American-bred Class, for dogs whose parents were mated in America; and the Open Class, which is open to all comers. The respective first prize winners of these various classes compete in what is known as the Winners Class for points toward championship. No entry can be made in the Winners Class, which is open without additional charge to the winners of the earlier classes, all of which are obligated to compete.

A dog eligible to more than one class can be entered in each of them, but it is usually wiser to enter him in only one. A puppy should, unless unusually precocious and mature, be placed in the Puppy Class, and it is unfair to so young a dog to expect him to defeat older dogs, although an exceptional puppy may receive an award in the Winners Class. The exhibitor who is satisfied merely that his dog may win the class in which he is entered is advised to place him in the lowest class to which he is eligible, but the exhibitor with confidence in his dog and shooting for high honors should enter the dog in the Open Class, where the competition is usually the toughest. The winner of the Open Class usually (but by no means always) is also the top of the Winners Class; the runner-up to this dog is named Reserve Winners.

The winner of the Winners Class for dogs competes with the Winners Bitch for Best of Winners, which in turn competes for Best of Breed or Best of Variety with any Champions of Record which may be entered for Specials Only. In the closing hours of the show, the Best of Breed or Best of Variety is eligible to compete in the respective Variety Group to which his breed belongs. And if, perchance, he should win his Variety Group, he is obligated to compete for Best Dog in Show. This is a major honor which few inexperienced exhibitors attain and to which they seldom aspire.

Duly entered, the dog should be brought into the best possible condition for his exhibition in the show and taught to move and to pose at his best. He should be equipped with a neat, strong collar without ornaments or spikes, a show lead of the proper length, width and material for his size and coat, and a nickel bench chain

15

of strong links with which to fasten him to his bench. Food such as the dog is used to, a bottle of the water he is accustomed to drink, and all grooming equipment should be assembled in a bag the night before departure for the show. The exhibitor's pass, on which the dog is assigned a stall number, is sent by mail by the show superintendent and should not be left behind, since it is difficult to have the pass duplicated and it enables the dog's caretaker to leave and return to the show at will.

The time of the opening of the show is stated in the premium list, and it is wise to have one's dog at the show promptly. Late arrivals are subject to disqualification if they are protested.

Sometimes examination is made by the veterinarian at the entrance of the show, and healthy dogs are quickly passed along. Once admitted to the show, if it is a "benched" show, it is wise to find one's bench, the number of which is on the exhibitor's ticket, to affix one's dog to the bench, and not to remove him from it except for exercising or until he is to be taken into the ring to be judged. A familiar blanket or cushion for the bench makes a dog feel at home there. It is contrary to the rules to remove dogs from their benches and to keep them in crates during show hours, and these rules are strictly enforced. Many outdoor shows are not "benched," and you provide your own crate or place for your dog.

At bench shows some exhibitors choose to sit by their dog's bench, but if he is securely chained he is likely to be safe in his owner's absence. Dogs have been stolen from their benches and others allegedly poisoned in the shows, but such incidents are rare indeed. The greater danger is that the dog may grow nervous and insecure, and it is best that the owner return now and again to the bench to reassure the dog of his security.

The advertised program of the show permits exhibitors to know the approximate hour of the judging of their respective breeds. Although that time may be somewhat delayed, it may be depended upon that judging will not begin before the stated hour. The dog should have been groomed and made ready for his appearance in the show ring. When his class is called the dog should be taken unhurriedly to the entrance of the ring, where the handler will receive an arm band with the dog's number.

When the class is assembled and the judge asks that the dogs be paraded before him, the handler should fall into the counter-clock-

16

wise line and walk his dog until the signal to stop is given. In moving in a circle, the dog should be kept on the inside so that he may be readily seen by the judge, who stands in the center of the ring. In stopping the line, there is no advantage to be gained in maneuvering one's dog to the premier position, since the judge will change the position of the dogs as he sees fit.

Keep the dog alert and facing toward the judge at all times. When summoned to the center of the ring for examination, go briskly but not brashly. It is unwise to enter into conversation with the judge, except briefly to reply to any questions he may ask. Do not call his attention to any excellences the dog may possess or excuse any shortcomings; the judge is presumed to evaluate the exhibit's merits as he sees them.

If asked to move the dog, he should be led directly away from the judge and again toward the judge. A brisk but not too rapid trot is the gait the judge wishes to see, unless he declares otherwise. He may ask that the movement be repeated, with which request the handler should respond with alacrity. It is best not to choke a dog in moving him, but rather to move him on a loose lead. The judge will assign or signal a dog to his position, which should be assumed without quibble.

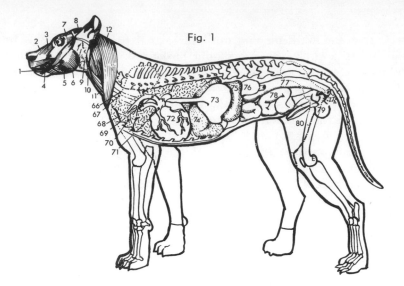

Fig. 1

Fig. 2

Fig. 1

1 Orbicularis oris.
2 Levator nasolabialis.
3 Levator labii superioris proprius (levator of upper lip).
4 Dilator naris lateralis.
5 Zygomaticus.
6 Masseter (large and well developed in the dog).
7 Scutularis.
8 Parotid Gland.
9 Submaxillary Gland.
10 Parotido-auricularis.
11 Sterno-hyoideus.
12 Brachio-cephalicus.

(Between figures 8 and 12 on top the Elevator and Depressor muscles of the ear are to be seen.)

66 Œsophagus (gullet).
67 Trachea (wind pipe).
68 Left Carotid Artery.
69 Anterior Aorta.
70 Lungs.
71 Posterior Aorta.
72 Heart.
73 Stomach.

74 Liver. (The line in front of Liver shows the Diaphragm separating Thoracic from Abdominal cavity.)
75 Spleen.
76 Kidney (left).
77 Rectum.
77A Anal Glands (position) just inside rectum.
78 Intestine.
79 Testicle.
80 Penis.
(Midway between 76 and 79 is the seat of the Bladder and behind this the seat of the Prostate gland in males, uterus in females.)

Fig. 2

Section of Head and Neck.
1 Nasal septum.
2 Tongue.
3 Cerebrum.
4 Cerebellum.
5 Medulla oblongata.
6 Spinal Cord.
7 Œsophagus (gullet).
8 Trachea (wind pipe).
9 Hard palate.
10 Soft palate.
11 Larynx, containing vocal cords.

18

The Feeding of Dogs, Constitutional Vigor

IN selecting a new dog, it is quite as essential that he shall be of sound constitution as that he shall be of the correct type of his own particular breed. The animal that is thoroughly typical of his breed is likely to be vigorous, with a will and a body to surmount diseases and ill treatment, but the converse of this statement is not always true. A dog may have constitutional vigor without breed type. We want both.

Half of the care and effort of rearing a dog is saved by choosing at the outset a puppy of sound constitution, one with a will and an ability to survive and flourish in spite of such adversity and neglect as he may encounter in life. This does not mean that the reader has any intention of obtaining a healthy dog and ill treating it, trusting its good constitution to bring it through whatever crises may beset it. It only means that he will save himself work, expense, and disappointment if only he will exercise care in the first place to obtain a healthy dog, one bred from sound and vigorous parents and one which has received adequate care and good food.

The first warning is not to economize too much in buying a dog. Never accept a cull of the litter at any price. The difference in first cost between a fragile, ill nourished, weedy, and unhealthy puppy and a sound, vigorous one, with adequate substance and the will to survive, may be ten dollars or it may be fifty dollars. But whatever it may be, it is worthwhile. A dog is an investment and it

19

is not the cost but the upkeep that makes the difference. We may save fifty dollars on the first price of a dog, only to lay out twice or five times that sum for veterinary fees over and above what it would cost to rear a dog of sound fundamental constitution and structure.

The vital, desirable dog, the one that is easy to rear and worth the care bestowed upon him, is active, inquisitive, and happy. He is sleek, his eyes free from pus or tears, his coat shining and alive, his flesh adequate and firm. He is not necessarily fat, but a small amount of surplus flesh, especially in puppyhood, is not undesirable. He is free from rachitic knobs on his joints or from crooked bones resultant from rickets. His teeth are firm and white and even. His breath is sweet to the smell. Above all, he is playful and responsive. Puppies, like babies, are much given to sleep, but when they are awake the sturdy ones do not mope lethargically around.

An adult dog that is too thin may often be fattened; if he is too fat he may be reduced. But it is essential that he shall be sound and healthy with a good normal appetite and that he be active and full of the joy of being alive. He must have had the benefit of a good heredity and a good start in life.

A dog without a fundamental inheritance of good vitality, or one that has been neglected throughout his growing period is seldom worth his feed. We must face these facts at the very beginning. Buy only from an owner who is willing to guarantee the soundness of his stock, and before consummating the purchase, have the dog, whether puppy or adult, examined by a veterinarian in order to determine the state of the dog's health.

If the dog to be cared for has been already acquired, there is nothing to do but to make the best of whatever weaknesses or frailties he may possess. But, when it is decided to replace him with another, let us make sure that he has constitutional vigor.

THE FEEDING AND NUTRITION OF
THE ADULT DOG

The dog is a carnivore, an eater of meat. This is a truism that cannot be repeated too often. Dog keepers know it but are prone to disregard it, although they do so at their peril and the peril of their dogs. Despite all the old-wives' tales to the contrary, meat does not cause a dog to be vicious, it does not give him worms nor cause him to have fits. It is his food. This is by no means all that is needed to know about food for the dog, but it is the essential knowledge. Give a dog enough sound meat and he will not be ill fed.

The dog is believed to have been the first of the animals that was brought under domestication. In his feral state he was almost exclusively an eater of meat. In his long association with man, however, his metabolism has adjusted itself somewhat to the consumption of human diet until he now can eat, even if he cannot flourish upon, whatever his master chooses to share with him, be it caviar or corn pone. It is not to be denied that a mature dog can survive without ill effects upon an exclusive diet of rice for a considerable period, but it is not to be recommended that he should be forced to do so.

Even if we had no empirical evidence that dogs thrive best upon foods of animal origin, and we possess conclusive proof of that fact, the anatomy and physiology of the dog would convince us of it. An observation of the structure of the dog's alimentary canal, superimposed upon many trial and error methods of feeding, leads us to the conclusion that a diet with meat predominating is the best food we can give a dog.

To begin with, the dental formation of the dog is typical of the carnivores. His teeth are designed for tearing rather than for mastication. He bolts his food and swallows it with a minimum of chewing. It is harmless that he should do this. No digestion takes place in the dog's mouth.

The capacity of the dog's stomach is great in comparison with the size of his body and with the capacity of his intestines. The amounts of carbohydrates and of fats digested in the stomach are minimal. The chief function of the dog's stomach is the digestion of proteins. In the dog as in the other carnivores, carbohydrates

21

and fats are digested for the most part in the small intestine, and absorption of food materials is largely from the small intestine. The enzymes necessary for the completion of the digestion of proteins which have not been fully digested in the stomach and for the digestion of sugars, starches, and fats are present in the pancreatic and intestinal juices. The capacity of the small intestine in the dog is not great and for that reason digestion that takes place there must be rapid.

The so-called large intestine (although in the dog it is really not "large" at all) is short and of small capacity in comparison with that of animals adapted by nature to subsist wholly or largely upon plant foods. In the dog, the large gut is designed to serve chiefly for storage of a limited and compact bulk of waste materials, which are later to be discharged as feces. Some absorption of water occurs there, but there is little if any absorption there of the products of digestion.

It will be readily seen that the short digestive tract of the dog is best adapted to a concentrated diet, which can be quickly digested and which leaves a small residue. Foods of animal origin (flesh, fish, milk, and eggs) are therefore suited to the digestive physiology of the dog because of the ease and completeness with which they are digested as compared with plant foods, which contain considerable amounts of indigestible structural material. The dog is best fed with a concentrated diet with a minimum of roughage.

This means meat. Flesh, milk, and eggs are, in effect, vegetation partly predigested. The steer or horse eats grain and herbage, from which its long digestive tract enables it to extract the food value and eliminate the indigestible material. The carnivore eats the flesh of the herbivore, thus obtaining his grain and grass in a concentrated form suitable for digestion in his short alimentary tract. Thus it is seen that meat is the ideal as a chief ingredient of the dog's ration.

Like that of all other animals, the dog's diet must be made up of proteins, carbohydrates, fats, minerals, vitamins, and water. None of these substances may be excluded if the dog is to survive. If he fails to obtain any of them from one source, it must come from another. It may be argued that before minerals were artificially supplied in the dog's diet and before we were aware of the existence of the various vitamins, we had dogs and they (some of them) appeared to thrive. However, they obtained such substances in their foods, although we were not aware of it. It is very likely that few dogs obtained much more than their very minimum of requirements of the minerals and vitamins. It is known that rickets were more prevalent before we learned to supply our dogs with ample calcium, and black tongue, now almost unknown, was a common canine disease before we supplied in the dog's diet that fraction of the vitamin B complex known as nicotinic acid. There is no way for us to know how large a portion of our dogs died for want of some particular food element before we learned to supply all the necessary ones. The dogs that survived received somewhere in their diet some of all of these compounds.

PROTEIN

The various proteins are the nitrogenous part of the food. They are composed of the amino acids, singly or in combination. There are at least twenty-two of these amino acids known to the nutritional scientists, ten of which are regarded as dietary essentials, the others of which, if not supplied in the diet, can be compounded in the body, which requires an adequate supply of all twenty-two. When any one of the essential ten amino acids is withdrawn from the diet of any animal, growth ceases or is greatly retarded. Thus, a high protein content in any food is not an assurance of its food value if taken alone; it may be lacking in one or more of the essential ten amino acids. When the absent essential amino acids are added to it in sufficient quantities or included separately in the diet, the protein may be complete and fully assimilated.

Proteins, as such, are ingested and in the digestive tract are broken down into the separate amino acids of which they are composed. These amino acids have been likened to building stones, since they are taken up by the blood stream and conveyed to the various parts of the animal as they may be required, where they are deposited and re-united with other complementary amino acids again to form bone and muscles in the resumed form of protein.

To correct amino acid deficiencies in the diet, it is not necessary to add the required units in pure form. The same object may be accomplished more efficiently by employing proteins which contain the required amino acids.

Foods of animal origin—meat, fish, eggs, and milk—supply proteins of high nutritive value, both from the standpoint of digestibility and amino acid content. Gelatin is an exception to that statement, since gelatin is very incomplete.

Even foods of animal origin vary among themselves in their protein content and amino acid balance. The protein of muscle meat does not rank quite as high as that of eggs or milk. The glandular tissues—such as liver, kidneys, sweetbreads or pancreas—contain proteins of exceptionally high nutritive value, and these organs should be added to the dog's diet whenever it is possible to do so. Each pint of milk contains two-thirds of an ounce (dry weight) of particularly high class protein, in addition to minerals, vitamins, carbohydrates, and fats. (The only dietary necessity absent

24

from milk is iron.) Animal proteins have a high content of dietary-essential amino acids, which makes them very effective in supplementing many proteins of vegetable origin. The whites of eggs, while somewhat inferior to the yolks, contain excellent proteins. The lysine of milk can be destroyed by excessive heat and the growth promoting value of its protein so destroyed. Evaporated tinned milk has not been subjected to enough heat to injure its proteins.

Thus we can readily see why meat with its concentrated, balanced, and easily assimilated proteins should form the major part of dry weight of a dog's ration.

It has never been determined how much protein the dog requires in his diet. It may be assumed to vary as to the size, age, and breed of the dog under consideration; as to the individual dog, some assimilating protein better, or utilizing more of it than others; as to the activity or inactivity of the subject; and as to the amino acid content of the protein employed. When wheat protein gliadin is fed as the sole protein, three times as much of it is required as of the milk protein, lactalbumin. It has been estimated that approximately twenty to twenty-five percent of animal protein (dry weight) in a dog's diet is adequate for maintenance in good health, although no final conclusion has been reached and probably never can be.

Our purpose, however, is not to feed the dog the minimum ration with which he can survive or even the minimum ration with which he can flourish. It is rather to give him the maximum food in quantity and balance which he can digest and enjoy without developing a paunch. Who wants to live on the minimum diet necessary for adequate sustenance? We all enjoy a full belly of good food, and so do our dogs.

Roy G. Daggs found from experimentation that milk production in the dog was influenced by the different kinds of proteins fed to it. He has pointed out that relatively high protein diets stimulate lactation and that, in the bitch, animal proteins are better suited to the synthesis of milk than plant proteins. He concluded that liver was a better source of protein for lactation than eggs or round steak.

THE CARBOHYDRATES

The carbohydrates include all the starches, the sugars, and the cellulose and hemicellulose, which last two, known as fiber, are the chief constituents of wood, of the stalks and leaves of plants, and of the coverings of seeds. There remains considerable controversy as to the amount of carbohydrates required or desirable in canine nutrition. It has been shown experimentally that the dog is able to digest large quantities of cornstarch, either raw or cooked. Rice fed to mature dogs in amounts sufficient to satisfy total energy requirements has been found to be 95 percent digested. We know that the various commercial biscuits and meals which are marketed as food for dogs are well tolerated, especially if they are supplemented by the addition of fresh meat. There seems to be no reason why they should not be included in the dog's ration.

Carbohydrates are a cheap source of energy for the dog, both in their initial cost and in the work required of the organism for their metabolism. Since there exists ample evidence that the dog has no difficulty in digesting and utilizing considerable amounts of starches and sugars for the production of energy, there is no reason why they should be excluded from his diet. Some carbohydrate is necessary for the metabolism of fats. The only danger from the employment of carbohydrates is that, being cheap, they may be employed to the exclusion of proteins and other essential elements of the dog's diet. It should be noted that meat and milk contain a measure of carbohydrates as well as of proteins.

Thoroughly cooked rice or oatmeal in moderate quantities may well be used to supplement and cheapen a meat diet for a dog without harm to him, as may crushed dog biscuit or shredded wheat waste or the waste from manufacture of other cereal foods. They are not required but may be used without harm.

Sugar and candy, of which dogs are inordinately fond, used also to be *verboten*. They are an excellent source of energy—and harmless. They should be fed in only moderate quantities.

FATS

In the dog as in man, body fat is found in largest amounts under the skin, between the muscles and around the internal organs. The fat so stored serves as a reserve source of heat and energy when the caloric value of the food is insufficient, or for temporary periods when no food is eaten. The accumulation of a certain amount of fat around vital organs provides considerable protection against cold and injury.

Before fats can be carried to the body cells by means of the circulating blood, it is necessary for them to be digested in the intestines with the aid of enzymes. Fats require a longer time for digestion than carbohydrates or proteins. For this reason, they are of special importance in delaying the sensations of hunger. This property of fats is frequently referred to as "staying power."

It is easily possible for some dogs to accumulate too much fat, making them unattractive, ungainly, and vaguely uncomfortable. This should be avoided by withholding an excess of fats and carbohydrates from the diets of such dogs whenever obesity threatens them. There is greater danger, however, that dogs may through inadequacy of their diets be permitted to become too thin.

Carbohydrates can in part be transformed to fats within the animal body. The ratio between fats and carbohydrates can therefore be varied within wide limits in the dog's ration so long as the requirements for proteins, vitamins, and minerals are adequately met. Some dogs have been known to tolerate as much as forty percent of fat in their diets over prolonged periods, but so much is not to be recommended as a general practice. Perhaps fifteen to twenty percent of fat is adequate without being too much.

Fat is a heat producing food, and the amount given a dog should be stepped up in the colder parts of the year and reduced in the summer months. In a ration low in fat it is particularly important that a good source of the fat-soluble vitamins be included or that such vitamins be artificially supplied. Weight for weight, fat has more than twice the food value of the other organic food groups—carbohydrates and proteins. The use of fat tends to decrease the amount of food required to supply caloric needs. The fats offer a means of increasing or decreasing the total sum of energy in the diet with the least change in the volume of food intake.

27

It is far less important that the dog receive more than a minimum amount of fats, however, than that his ration contain an adequate amount and quality balance of proteins. Lean meat in adequate quantities will provide him with such proteins, and fats may be added to it in the form of fat meat, suet, or lard. Small quantities of dog biscuits, cooked rice, or other cereals in the diet will supply the needed carbohydrates. However, cellulose or other roughage is not required in the diet of the carnivore. It serves only to engorge the dog's colon, which is not capacious, and to increase the volume of feces, which is supererogatory.

MINERALS

At least eleven minerals are present in the normal dog, and there are probably others occurring in quantities so minute that they have not as yet been discovered. The eleven are as follows: Calcium (lime), sodium chloride (table salt), copper, iron, magnesium, manganese, phosphorus, zinc, potassium, and iodine.

Of many of these only a trace in the daily ration is required and that trace is adequately found in meat or in almost any other normal diet. There are a few that we should be at pains to add to the diet. The others we shall ignore.

Sodium chloride (salt) is present in sufficient quantities in most meats, although, more to improve the flavor of the food than to contribute to the animal's nutrition, a small amount of salt may be added to the ration. The exact amount makes no material difference, since the unutilized portions are eliminated, largely in the urine. If the brand of salt used is iodized, it will meet the iodine requirements, which are very small. Iodine deficiency in dogs is rare, but food crops and meats grown in certain areas contain little or no iodine, and it is well to be safe by using iodized salt.

Sufficient iron is usually found in meat and milk, but if the dog appears anemic or listless the trace of iron needed can be supplied with one of the iron salts—ferric sulphate, or oxide, or ferrous gluconate. Iron is utilized in the bone marrow in the synthesis of hemoglobin in the blood corpuscles. It is used over and over; when a corpuscle is worn out and is to be replaced, it surrenders its iron before being eliminated.

When more iron is ingested than can be utilized, some is stored in the liver, after which further surplus is excreted. The liver of the newborn puppy contains enough iron to supply the organism up until weaning time. No iron is present in milk, which otherwise provides a completely balanced ration.

A diet with a reasonable content of red meat, especially of liver or kidney, is likely to be adequate in respect to its iron. However, bitches in whelp require more iron than a dog on mere maintenance. It is recommended that the liver content of bitches' diets be increased for the duration of pregnancy.

Iron requires the presence of a minute trace of copper for its utilization, but there is enough copper in well nigh any diet to supply the requirements.

Calcium and phosphorous are the only minerals of which an insufficiency is a warranted source of anxiety. This statement may not be true of adult dogs not employed for breeding purposes, but it does apply to brood bitches and to growing puppies. The entire skeleton and teeth are made largely from calcium and phosphorus, and it is essential that the organism have enough of those minerals.

If additional calcium is not supplied to a bitch in her diet, her own bone structure is depleted to provide her puppies with their share of calcium. Moreover, in giving birth to her puppies or shortly afterward she is likely to go into eclampsia as a result of calcium depletion.

The situation, however, is easily avoided. The addition of a small amount of calcium phosphate diabasic to the ration precludes any possible calcium deficiency. Calcium phosphate diabasic is an inexpensive substance and quite tasteless. It may be sprinkled in or over the food, especially that given to brood bitches and puppies. It is the source of strong bones and vigorous teeth of ivory whiteness.

But it must be mentioned that calcium cannot be assimilated into the bone structure, no matter how much of it is fed or otherwise administered, except in the presence of vitamin D. That is D's function, to facilitate the absorption of calcium and phosphorus. This will be elaborated upon in the following discussion of the vitamins and their functions.

VITAMINS

Vitamins have in the past been largely described by diseases resulting from their absence. It is recognized more and more that many of the subacute symptoms of general unfitness of dogs may be attributable to an inadequate supply in the diet of one or more of these essential food factors. It is to be emphasized that vitamins are to be considered a part of the dog's food, essential to his health and well being. They are not to be considered as medication. Often the morbid conditions resultant from their absence in the diet may be remedied by the addition of the particular needed vitamin.

The requirements of vitamins, as food, not as medication, in the diet cannot be too strongly emphasized. These vitamins may be in the food itself, or they may better be added to it as a supplement to insure an adequate supply. Except for vitamin D, of which it is remotely possible (though unlikely) to supply too much, a surplus of the vitamin substances in the ration is harmless. They are somewhat expensive and we have no disposition to waste them, but if too much of them are fed they are simply eliminated with no subsequent ill effect.

It must be realized that vitamins are various substances, each of which has a separate function. It is definitely not safe to add to a dog's (or a child's) diet something out of a bottle or box indefinitely labeled "Vitamins," as is the practice of so many persons. We must know which vitamins we are giving, what purpose each is designed to serve, and the potency of the preparation of the brand of each one we are using.

Any one of the "shotgun" vitamin preparations is probably adequate if administered in large enough dosages. Such a method may be wasteful, however; to be sure of enough of one substance, the surplus of the others is wasted. It is much better to buy a product that contains an adequate amount of each of the needed vitamins and a wasteful surplus of none. Such a procedure is cheaper in the long run.

There follows a brief description of each of the various vitamins so far discovered and a statement of what purpose in the diet they are respectively intended to serve:

Vitamin A—This vitamin in some form is an absolute requisite for good health, even for enduring life itself. Symptoms of advanced deficiency of vitamin A in dogs are an eye disease with resulting impaired vision, inflammation of the conjunctiva or mucous membranes which line the eyelid, and injury to the mucous membranes of the body. Less easily recognized symptoms are an apparent lowered resistance to bacterial infection, especially of the upper respiratory tract, retarded growth, and loss of weight. Diseases due to vitamin A deficiency may be well established while the dog is still gaining in weight. Lack of muscular coordination and paralysis have been observed in dogs and degeneration of the nervous system. Some young dogs deprived of vitamin A become wholly or partially deaf.

The potency of vitamin A is usually calculated in International Units, of which it has been estimated that the dog requires about 35 per day for each pound of his body weight. Such parts as are not utilized are not lost, but are stored in the liver for future use in time of shortage. A dog well fortified with this particular vitamin can well go a month or more without harm with none of it in his diet. At such times he draws upon his liver for its surplus.

It is for its content of vitamins A and D that cod-liver oil (and the oils from the livers of other fish) is fed to puppies and growing children. Fish liver oils are an excellent source of vitamin A, and if a small amount of them is included in the diet no anxiety about deficiency of vitamin A need be entertained. In buying cod-liver oil, it pays to obtain the best grade. The number of International Units it contains per teaspoonful is stated on most labels. The vitamin content of cod-liver oil is impaired by exposure to heat, light, and air. It should be kept in a dark, cool place and the bottle should be firmly stopped.

Another source of vitamin A is found in carrots but it is almost impossible to get enough carrots in a dog to do him any good. It is better and easier to use a preparation known as carotene, three drops of which contains almost the vitamin A in a bushel of carrots.

Other natural sources of vitamin A are liver, kidney, heart, cheese, egg yolks, butter and milk. If these foods, or any one of them, are generously included in the adult dog's maintenance ration, all other sources of vitamin A may be dispensed with. The ration for all puppies, however, and for pregnant and lactating bitches should be copiously fortified either with fish liver oil or with tablets containing vitamin A.

Vitamin B. What was formerly known as a single vitamin B has now been found to be a complex of many different factors. Some of them are, in minute quantities, very important parts of the diets of any kind of animals. The various factors of this complex, each a separate vitamin, are designated by the letter B followed by an inferior number, as B_1, B_2, or B_6.

The absence or insufficiency in the diet of Vitamin B_1, otherwise known as thiamin, has been blamed for retarded growth, loss of weight, decreased fertility, loss of appetite, and impaired digestion. A prolonged shortage of B_1 may result in paralysis, the accumulation of fluid in the tissues, and finally in death, apparently from heart failure.

It is not easy to estimate just how much B_1 a dog requires per pound of body weight, since dogs as individuals vary in their needs, and the activity of an animal rapidly depletes the thiamin in his body. The feeding of 50 International Units per day per pound of body weight is probably wasteful but harmless. That is at least enough.

Thiamin is not stored in the system for any length of time and requires a daily dosage. It is destroyed in part by heat above the boiling point. It is found in yeast (especially in brewer's yeast), liver, wheat germ, milk, eggs, and in the coloring matter of vegetables. However, few dogs or persons obtain an optimum supply of B_1 from their daily diet, and it is recommended that it be supplied to the dog daily.

Brewer's yeast, either in powdered or tablet form affords a cheap and rather efficient way to supply the average daily requirements. An overdose of yeast is likely to cause gas in the dog's stomach.

Another factor of the vitamin B complex, riboflavin, affects particularly the skin and hair. Animals fed a diet in which it is deficient are prone to develop a scruffy dryness of the skin, especially about the eyes and mouth, and the hair becomes dull and dry, finally falling out, leaving the skin rough and dry. In experiments with rats deprived of riboflavin the toes have fallen off.

Riboflavin is present in minute quantities in so many foods that a serious shortage in any well balanced diet is unlikely. It is especially to be found in whey, which is the explanation of the smooth skin and lively hair of so many dogs whose ration contains cottage cheese.

33

While few dogs manifest any positive shortage of riboflavin, experiments on various animals have shown that successively more liberal amounts of it in their diets, up to about four times as much as is needed to prevent the first signs of deficiency, result in increased positive health.

Riboflavin deteriorates with exposure to heat and light. Most vitamin products contain it in ample measure.

Dogs were immediately responsible for the discovery of the existence of vitamin B_2, or nicotinic acid, formerly known as vitamin G. The canine disease of black tongue is analogous with the human disease called pellagra, both of which are prevented and cured by sufficient amounts of nicotinic acid in the diet. Black tongue is not a threat for any dog that eats a diet which contains even a reasonable quantity of lean meat, but it used to be prevalent among dogs fed exclusively upon corn bread or corn-meal mush, as many were.

No definite optimum dosage has been established. However, many cases of vaguely irritated skin, deadness of coat, and soft, spongy, or bleeding gums have been reported to be remedied by administration of nicotinic acid.

It has been demonstrated that niacin is essential if a good sound healthy appetite is to be maintained. Pantothenic acid is essential to good nerve health. Pyridoxin influences proper gastro-intestinal functions. Vitamin B_{12}, the "animal protein factor," is essential for proper growth and health in early life. And the water soluble B factor affects the production of milk.

Vitamin C, the so-called anti-scorbutic vitamin, is presumed to be synthesized by the dog in his own body. The dog is believed not to be subject to true scurvy. Vitamin C, then, can well be ignored as pertains to the dog. It is the most expensive of the vitamins, and, its presence in the vitamin mixture for the dog will probably do no good.

Vitamin D, the anti-rachitic vitamin, is necessary to promote the assimilation of calcium and phosphorus into the skeletal structure. One may feed all of those minerals one will, but without vitamin D they will pass out of the system unused. It is impossible to develop sound bones and teeth without its presence. Exposure to sunshine unimpeded by glass enables the animal to manufacture vitamin D in his system, but sunshine is not to be depended upon for an entire supply.

Vitamin D is abundant in cod-liver oil and in the liver oils of some other fish, or it may be obtained in a dry form in combination with other vitamins. One International Unit per pound of body weight per day is sufficient to protect a dog from rickets. From a teaspoonful to a tablespoonful of cod-liver oil a day will serve well instead for any dog.

This is the only one of the vitamins with which overdosage is possible and harmful. While a dog will not suffer from several times the amount stated and an excess dosage is unlikely, it is only fair to warn the reader that it is at least theoretically possible.

Vitamin E is the so-called fertility vitamin. Whether it is required for dogs has not as yet been determined. Rats fed upon a ration from which vitamin E was wholly excluded became permanently sterile, but the finding is not believed to pertain to all animals. Some dog keepers, however, declare that the feeding of wheat germ oil, the most abundant source of vitamin E, has prevented early abortions of their bitches, has resulted in larger and more vigorous litters of puppies, has increased the fertility of stud dogs, has improved the coats of their dogs and furthered the betterment of their general health. Whether vitamin E or some other factor or factors in the wheat germ oil is responsible for these alleged benefits is impossible to say.

Vitamin E is so widely found in small quantities in well nigh all foods that the hazard of its omission from any normal diet is small.

Numerous other vitamins have been discovered and isolated in recent years, and there are suspected to be still others as yet unknown. The ones here discussed are the only ones that warrant the use of care to include them in the dog's daily ration. It is well to reiterate that vitamins are not medicine, but are food, a required part of the diet. Any person interested in the complete nutrition of his dog will not neglect them.

It should go without saying that a dog should have access to clean, fresh, pure drinking water at all times, of which he should be permitted to drink as much or as little as he chooses. The demands of his system for drinking water will depend in part upon the moisture content of his food. Fed upon dry dog biscuits, he will probably drink considerable water to moisten it; with a diet which contains much milk or soup, he will need little additional water.

That he chooses to drink water immediately after a meal is harmless. The only times his water should be limited (but not entirely withheld from him) is after violent exercise or excitement, at which times his thirst should be satisfied only gradually.

The quantities of food required daily by dogs are influenced and determined by a number of factors: the age, size, individuality, and physical condition of the animal; the kind, quality, character, and proportions of the various foods in the ration; the climate, environment and methods of management; and the type and amount of work done, or the degree of exercise. Of these considerations, the age and size of the dog and the kind and amount of work are particularly important in determining food requirements. During early puppyhood a dog may require two or three (or even more) times as much food per pound of body weight as the same dog will require at maturity.

Any statement we should make here about the food requirements of a dog as to weight or volume would be subject to modification. Dogs vary in their metabolism. One dog might stay fat and sleek on a given amount of a given ration, whereas his litter brother in an adjoining kennel might require twice or only half as much of the same ration to maintain him in the same state of flesh.

The only sound determiners of how much to feed a dog are his appetite and his condition. As a general rule, a dog should have as much food for maintenance as he will readily clean up in five or ten minutes, unless he tends to lay on unwanted fat, in which case his intake of food should be reduced, especially its content of fats and carbohydrates. A thin dog should have his ration increased and be urged to eat it. The fats in his ration should be increased, and he may be fattened with a dessert of candy, sugar, or sweet cake following his main meal. These should never be used before a meal, lest they impair the appetite, and they should not be given to a fat dog at all. Rightly employed, they are useful and harmless, contrary to the prevalent belief.

Growing puppies require frequent meals, as will be discussed later. Pregnant and lactating bitches and frequently used stud dogs should have at least two meals, and better three, each day. For the mere maintenance of healthy adult dogs, one large meal a day appears to suffice as well as more smaller ones. Many tenderhearted dog keepers choose to divide the ration into two parts and to feed their dogs twice each day. There can be no objection offered to such a program except that it involves additional work for the keeper. Whether one meal or two, they should be given at regular hours, to which dogs soon adjust and expect their dinner at a given time.

It is better to determine upon an adequate ration, with plenty of meat in it, and feed it day after day, than to vary the diet in the assumption that a dog tires of eating the same thing. There is no evidence that he does, and it is a burden upon his carnivorous digestion to be making constant adjustments and readjustments to a new diet.

Today there are available for dogs many brands of canned foods, some good and others not so good. But it is safe to feed your dog exclusively—if you do not object to the cost—a canned dog food which has been produced by a reliable concern. Many of the producers of canned dog foods are subject to Federal inspection because they also process meat and meat products for human consumption. The Federal regulations prohibit the use of diseased or unsuitable by-products in the preparation of dog food. Some of the canned dog foods on the market are mostly cereal. A glance at the analysis chart on the label will tell you whether a particular product is a good food for your dog.

If fish is fed, it should be boned—thoroughly. The same is true of fowl and rabbit meats. Small bones may be caught in the dog's throat or may puncture the stomach or intestines. Large, raw shank bones of beef may be given to the dog with impunity, but they should be renewed at frequent intervals before they spoil. A dog obtains much amusement from gnawing a raw bone, and some nutrition. Harm does not accrue from his swallowing of bone fragments, which are dissolved by the hydrochloric acid in his stomach. If the dog is fed an excessive amount of bones, constipation may result. When this occurs, the best way to relieve the condition is by the use of the enema bag. Medicinal purges of laxatives given at this time may cause irreparable damage.

Meat for dogs may be fed raw, or may be roasted, broiled, or boiled. It is not advisable to feed fried foods to dogs. All soups, gravies and juices from cooked meat must be conserved and included in the food, since they contain some of the minerals and vitamins extracted from the meat.

37

A well-known German physician selected a medium sized, strong, healthy bitch, and after she had been mated, he fed her on chopped horse meat from which the salts were to a large extent extracted by boiling for two hours in distilled water. In addition to this she was given each day a certain quantity of fried fat. As drink she had only distilled water. She gave birth to six healthy puppies, one of which was killed immediately, and its bones found to be strong and well built and free from abnormalities. The other puppies did not thrive, but remained weak, and could scarcely walk at the end of a month, when four died from excessive feebleness. And the sixth was killed two weeks later. The mother in the meantime had become very lean but was tolerably lively and had a fair appetite. She was killed one hundred and twenty-six days after the beginning of the experiment, and it was then found that the bones of her spine and pelvis were softened—a condition known to physicians as osteomalacia.

The results of this experiment are highly interesting and instructive, showing clearly as they do that the nursing mother sends out to her young, in her milk, a part of her store of lime, which is absolutely essential to their welfare. They show also that if proper food is denied her, when in whelp and when nursing, not only her puppies but she as well must suffer greatly in consequence. And in the light of these facts is uncovered one of the most potential causes of rickets, so common among large breeds.

It may therefore be accepted that bitches in whelp must have goodly quantities of meat; moreover, that while cooking may be the rule if the broth is utilized, it is a wise plan to give the food occasionally in the raw state.

There is little choice among the varieties of meat, except that pork is seldom relished by dogs, usually contains too much fat, and should be cooked to improve its digestibility when it is used at all. Beef, mutton, lamb, goat, and horse flesh are equally valuable. The choice should be made upon the basis of their comparative cost and their availability in the particular community. A dog suddenly changed from another diet to horse flesh may develop a harmless and temporary diarrhea, which can be ignored. Horse flesh is likely to be deficient in fats, which may be added in the form of suet, lard or pure corn oil.

The particular cuts of whatever meat is used is of little consequence. Liver and kidney are especially valuable and when it is possible they should be included as part of the meat used. As the only meat in the ration, liver and kidney tend to loosen the bowels. It is better to include them as a part of each day's ration than to permit them to serve as the sole meat content one or two days a week.

It makes no difference whether meat is ground or is fed to the dog in large or medium sized pieces. He is able to digest pieces of meat as large as he can swallow. The advantage of grinding meat is that it can be better mixed with whatever else it is wished to include in the ration, the dog being unable to pick out the meat and reject the rest. There is little harm in his doing so, except for the waste, since it is the meat upon which we must depend for the most part for his nutrition.

Fresh ground meat can be kept four or five days under ordinary refrigeration without spoiling. It may be kept indefinitely if solidly frozen. Frozen ground horse meat for dogs is available in many markets, is low in price, and is entirely satisfactory for the purpose intended.

A suggested ration is made as follows: Two-thirds to three-quarters by weight of ground meat including ten to twenty percent of fat and a portion of liver or kidney, with the remainder thoroughly cooked rice or oatmeal, or shredded wheat, or dog biscuit, or wheat germ, with a sprinkling of calcium phosphate diabasic. Vitamins may be added, or given separately.

If it is desired to offer the dog a second meal, it may be of shredded wheat or other breakfast cereal with plenty of milk, with or without one or more soft boiled eggs. Evaporated canned milk or powdered milk is just as good food for the dog as fresh milk. Cottage cheese is excellent for this second meal.

These are not the only possible rations for the dog, but they will prove adequate. Leavings from the owner's table can be added to either ration, but can hardly be depended upon for the entire nourishment of the dog.

The dog's food should be at approximately body heat, tepid but never hot.

Little consideration is here given to the costs of the various foods. Economies in rations and feeding practices are admittedly desirable, but not if they are made at the expense of the dog's health.

39

SOME BRIEF PRECEPTS ABOUT FEEDING

Many dogs are overfed. Others do not receive adequate rations. Both extremes should be avoided, but particularly overfeeding of grown dogs. Coupled with lack of exercise, overfeeding usually produces excessive body weight and laziness, and it may result in illness and sterility. Prolonged undernourishment causes loss of weight, listlessness, dull coats, sickness, and death.

An adequate ration will keep most mature dogs at a uniform body weight and in a thrifty, moderately lean condition. Observation of condition is the best guide in determining the correct amount of food.

The axiom, "One man's meat is another man's poison," is applicable to dogs also. Foods that are not tolerated by the dog or those that cause digestive and other disturbances should be discontinued. The use of moldy, spoiled, or rotten food is never good practice. Food should be protected from fouling by rats or mice, especially because rats are vectors of leptospirosis. The excessive use of food of low energy content and low biological values will often result in poor condition and may cause loss of weight and paunchiness.

All feeding and drinking utensils must be kept scrupulously clean. They should be washed after each using.

It is usually desirable to reduce the food allotment somewhat during hot weather. Dogs should be fed at regular intervals, and the best results may be expected when regular feeding is accompanied by regular, but not exhausting, exercise.

Most dogs do not thrive on a ration containing large amounts of sloppy foods, and excessive bulk is to be avoided especially for hardworking dogs, puppies, and pregnant or lactating bitches. If the ration is known to be adequate and the dog is losing weight or is not in good condition, the presence of intestinal parasites is to be suspected. However, dogs sometimes go "off feed" for a day or two. This is cause for no immediate anxiety, but if it lasts more than two or three days, a veterinarian should be consulted.

FOOD FOR THE STUD DOG

The stud dog that is used for breeding only at infrequent intervals requires only the food needed for his maintenance in good health, as set forth in the foregoing pages. He should be well fed with ample meat in his diet, moderately exercised to keep his flesh firm and hard, and not permitted to become too thin or too fat.

More care is required for the adequate nutrition of the dog offered at public stud and frequently employed for breeding. A vigorous stud dog may very handily serve two bitches a week over a long period without a serious tax upon his health and strength if he is fully nourished and adequately but not excessively exercised. Such a dog should have at least two meals a day, and they should consist of even more meat, milk (canned is as good as fresh), eggs, cottage cheese, and other foods of animal origin than is used in most maintenance rations. Liver and some fat should be included, and the vitamins especially are not to be forgotten. In volume this will be only a little more than the basic maintenance diet, the difference being in its richness and concentration.

An interval of an hour or two should intervene between a dog's meal and his employment for breeding. He may be fed, but only lightly, immediately after he has been used for breeding.

The immediate reason that a stud dog should be adequately fed and exercised is the maintenance of his strength and virility. The secondary reason is that a popular stud dog is on exhibition at all times, between the shows as well as at the shows. Clients with bitches to be bred appear without notice to examine a dog at public stud, and the dog should be presented to them in the best possible condition—clean, hard, in exactly the most becoming state of flesh, and with a gleaming, lively coat. These all depend largely upon the highly nutritious diet the dog receives.

FOOD FOR THE BROOD BITCH

Often a well fed bitch comes through the ordeal of rearing a large litter of puppies without any impairment of her vitality and flesh. In such case she may be returned to a good maintenance ration until she is ready to be bred again. About the time she weans her puppies her coat will be dead and ready to drop out, but if she is healthy and well fed a new and vigorous coat will grow in, and she will be no worse off for her maternal ordeal. Some bitches, either from a deficient nutrition or a constitutional disposition to contribute too much of their own strength and substance to the nutrition of the puppies, are thin and exhausted at the time of weaning. Such a bitch needs the continuance of at least two good and especially nutritious meals a day for a month or more until her flesh and strength are restored before she is returned to her routine maintenance ration, upon which she may be kept until time comes to breed her again.

At breeding time a bitch's flesh should be hard, and she should be on the lean side rather than too fat. No change in her regular maintenance diet need be made until about the fourth or fifth week of her pregnancy. The growth of the fetus is small up until the middle of the pregnancy, after which it becomes rapid.

The bitch usually begins to "show in whelp" in four to six weeks after breeding, and her food consumption should be then gradually stepped up. If she has been having only one meal a day, she should be given two; if she has had two, both should be larger. Henceforth until her puppies are weaned, she must eat not merely for two, as is said of the pregnant woman, but for four or five, possibly for ten or twelve. She is not to be encouraged to grow fat. Especial emphasis should be laid upon her ration's content of meat, including liver, milk, calcium phosphate, and vitamins A and D, both of which are found in cod-liver oil.

Some breeders destroy all but a limited number of puppies in a litter in the belief that a bitch will be unable adequately to nourish all the puppies she has whelped. In some extreme cases it may be necessary to do this or to obtain a foster mother or wet nurse to share the burden of rearing the puppies. However, the healthy bitch with normal metabolism can usually generate enough milk to feed adequately all the puppies she has produced, provided she is well enough fed and provided the puppies are fed additionally as soon as they are able to eat.

After whelping until the puppies are weaned, throughout the lactating period, the bitch should have all the nourishing food she can be induced to eat—up to four or five meals a day. These should consist largely of meat and liver, some fat, a small amount of cereals, milk, eggs, cottage cheese, calcium phosphate, and vitamins, with especial reference to vitamins A and D. At that time it is hardly possible to feed a bitch too much or to keep her too fat. The growth of the puppies is much more rapid after they are born than was their growth in the dam's uterus, and the large amount of food needed to maintain that rapid growth must pass through the bitch and be transformed to milk, while at the same time she must maintain her own body.

THE FEEDING OF PUPPIES

If the number of puppies in a litter is small, if the mother is vigorous, healthy, and a good milker, the youngsters up until their weaning time may require no additional food over and above the milk they suck from their dam's breasts. If the puppies are numerous or if the dam's milk is deficient in quality or quantity, it is wise to begin feeding the puppies artificially as soon as they are able and willing to accept food. This is earlier than used to be realized.

It is for the sake of the puppies' vigor rather than for the sake of their ultimate size that their growth is to be promoted as rapidly as possible. Vigorous and healthy puppies attain early maturity if they are given the right amounts of the right quality of food. The ultimate size of the dog at maturity is laid down in his germ plasm, and he can be stunted or dwarfed, if at all, only at the expense of his type. If one tries to prevent the full growth of a dog by withholding from him the food he needs, one will wind up with a rachitic, cowhocked dog, one with a delicate digestive apparatus, a sterile one, one with all of these shortcomings combined, or even a dead dog.

Growth may be slowed with improper food, sometimes without serious harm, but the dog is in all ways better off if he is forced along with the best food and encouraged to attain his full size at an early age. Dogs of the smaller breeds usually reach their full maturity several months earlier than those of the larger breeds. A well grown dog reaches his sexual maturity and can be safely used for limited breeding at one year of age.

As soon as teeth can be felt with the finger in a puppy's mouth, which is usually at about seventeen or eighteen days of age, it is safe to begin to feed him. His first food (except for his mother's milk) should be of scraped raw beef at body temperature. The first day he may have ¼ to 2 teaspoonfuls, according to size. He will not need to learn to eat this meat; he will seize upon it avidly and lick his chops for more. The second day he may have ⅓ to 3 teaspoonfuls, according to size, with two feedings 12 hours apart. Thereafter, the amount and frequency of this feeding may be rapidly increased. By the twenty-fifth day the meat need not be scraped, but only finely ground. This process of the early feeding of raw meat to puppies not only gives them a good start in life, but

44

it also relieves their mother of a part of her burden of providing milk for them.

At about the fourth week, some cereal (thoroughly cooked oatmeal, shredded wheat, or dried bread) may be either moistened and mixed with the meat or be served to the puppies with milk, fresh or canned. It may be necessary to immerse their noses into such a mixture to teach them to eat it. Calcium phosphate and a small amount of cod-liver oil should be added to such a mixture, both of which substances the puppies should have every day until their maturity. At the fourth week, while they are still at the dam's breast, they may be fed three or four times a day upon this extra ration, or something similar, such as cottage cheese or soft boiled egg. By the sixth week their dam will be trying to wean them, and they may have four or five meals daily. One of these may be finely broken dog biscuit thoroughly soaked in milk. One or two of the meals should consist largely or entirely of meat with liver.

The old advice about feeding puppies "little and often" should be altered to "much and often." Each puppy at each meal should have all the food he will readily clean up. Food should not be left in front of the puppies. They should be fed and after two or three minutes the receptacle should be taken away. Young puppies should be roly-poly fat, and kept so up to at least five or six months of age. Thereafter they should be slightly on the fat side, but not pudgy, until maturity.

The varied diet of six-week-old puppies may be continued, but at eight or nine weeks the number of meals may be reduced to four, and at three months, to three large rations per day. After six months the meals may be safely reduced again to two a day, but they must be generous meals with meat, liver, milk, cod-liver oil, and calcium phosphate. At full maturity, one meal a day suffices, or two may be continued.

The secret of turning good puppies into fine, vigorous dogs is to keep them growing through the entire period of their maturation. The most important item in the rearing of puppies is adequate and frequent meals of highly nourishing foods. Growth requires two or three times as much food as maintenance. Time between meals should be allowed for digestion, but puppies should never be permitted to become really hungry. Water in a shallow dish should be available to puppies at all times after they are able to walk.

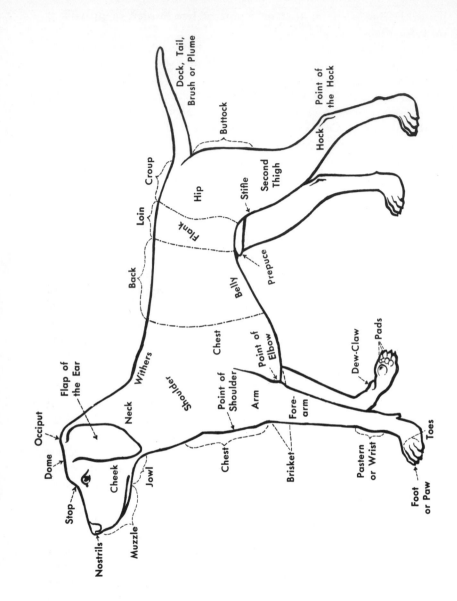

46

The Breeding
of Dogs

HERE, if anywhere in the entire process of the care and management of dogs, the exercise of good judgment is involved. Upon the choice of the two dogs, male and female, to be mated together depends the future success or failure of one's dogs. If the two to be mated are ill chosen, either individually or as pertains to their fitness as mates, one to the other, all the painstaking care to feed and rear the resultant puppies correctly is wasted. The mating together of two dogs is the drafting of the blueprints and the writing of the specifications of what the puppies are to be like. The plans, it is true, require to be executed; the puppies, when they arrive, must be adequately fed and cared for in order to develop them into the kinds of dogs they are in their germ plasm designed to become. However, if the plans as determined in the mating are defective, just so will the puppies that result from them be defective, in spite of all the good raising one can give them.

The element of luck in the breeding of dogs cannot be discounted, for it exists. The mating which on paper appears to be the best possible may result in puppies that are poor and untypical of their breed. Even less frequently, a good puppy may result from a chance mating together of two ill chosen parents. These results are fortuitous and unusual, however. The best dogs as a lot come from parents carefully chosen as to their individual excellences and as to their suitability as mates for each other. It is as unwise as

47

it is unnecessary to trust to luck in the breeding of dogs. Careful planning pays off in the long run, and few truly excellent dogs are produced without it.

Some breeders without any knowledge of genetics have been successful, without knowing exactly why they succeeded. Some of them have adhered to beliefs in old wives' tales and to traditional concepts that science has long since exploded and abandoned. Such as have succeeded have done so in spite of their lack of knowledge and not because of it.

There is insufficient space at our disposal in this book to discuss in detail the science of genetics and the application of that science to the breeding of dogs. Whole books have been written about the subject. One of the best, clearest, and easiest for the layman to understand is *The New Art of Breeding Better Dogs,* by Philip Onstott, which may be obtained from Howell Book House, the publisher. In it and in other books upon the subject of genetics will be found more data about the practical application of science to the breeding of livestock than can be included here.

The most that can be done here is to offer some advice soundly based upon the genetic laws. Every feature a dog may or can possess is determined by the genes carried in the two reproductive cells, one from each parent, from the union of which he was developed. There are thousands of pairs of these determiners in the life plan of every puppy, and often a complex of many genes is required to produce a single recognizable attribute of the dog.

These genes function in pairs, one member of each pair being contributed by the father and the other member of the pair coming from the mother. The parents obtained these genes they hand on from their parents, and it is merely fortuitous which half of any pair of genes present in a dog's or a bitch's germ plasm may be passed on to any one of the progeny. Of any pair of its own genes, a dog or a bitch may contribute one member to one puppy and the other member to another puppy in the same litter or in different litters. The unknown number of pairs of genes is so great that there is an infinite number of combinations of them, which accounts for the differences we find between two full brothers or two full sisters. In fact, it depends upon the genes received whether a dog be a male or a female.

We know that the male dog contributes one and the bitch the

48

other of every pair of genes that unite to determine what the puppy will be like and what he will grow into. Thus, the parents make exactly equal contributions to the germ plasm or zygote from which every puppy is developed. It was long believed that the male dog was so much more important than the bitch in any mating that the excellence or shortcomings of the bitch might be disregarded. This theory was subsequently reversed and breeders considered the bitch to be more important than the dog. We now know that their contribution in every mating and in every individual puppy is exactly equal, and neither is to be considered more than the other.

There are two kinds of genes—the recessive genes and the dominant. And there are three kinds of pairs of genes: a recessive from the sire plus a recessive from the dam; a dominant from the sire plus a dominant from the dam; and a dominant from one parent plus a recessive from the other. It is the last combination that is the source of our trouble in breeding. When both members of a pair of genes are recessive, the result is a recessive attribute in the animal that carries them; when both members of the pair are dominant, the result is a pure dominant attribute; but when one member of the pair is recessive and the other member dominant, the result will be a wholly or only partially dominant attribute, which will breed true only half of the time. This explains why a dog or a bitch may fail to produce progeny that looks at all like itself.

If all the pairs of a dog's genes were purely dominant, we could expect him to produce puppies that resembled himself in all particulars, no matter what kind of mate he was bred to. Or if all his genes were recessive and he were mated to a bitch with all recessive genes, the puppies might be expected to look quite like the parents. However, a dog with mixed pairs of genes bred to a bitch with mixed pairs of genes may produce anything at all, puppies that bear no resemblance to either parent.

Long before the Mendelian laws were discovered, some dogs were known to be "prepotent" to produce certain characters, that is the characters would show up in their puppies irrespective of what their mates might be like. For instance, some dogs, themselves with dark eyes, might be depended upon never to produce a puppy with light eyes, no matter how light eyed the mate to which he was bred. This was true despite the fact that the dog's litter brother which had equally dark eyes, when bred to a light eyed bitch might produce a large percentage of puppies with light eyes.

Before it is decided to breed a bitch, it is well to consider whether she is worth breeding, whether she is good enough as an individual and whether she came from a good enough family to warrant the expectations that she will produce puppies worth the expense and trouble of raising. It is to be remembered that the bitch contributes exactly half the genes to each of her puppies; if she has not good genes to contribute, the time and money involved in breeding her and rearing her puppies will be wasted.

It is conceded that a bad or mediocre bitch when bred to an excellent dog will probably produce puppies better than herself. But while one is "grading up" from mediocre stock, other breeders are also grading upward from better stock and they will keep just so far ahead of one's efforts that one can never catch up with them. A merely pretty good bitch is no good at all for breeding. It is better to dispose of a mediocre bitch or to relegate her to the position of a family pet than to breed from her. It is difficult enough, with all the care and judgment one is able to muster, to obtain superlative puppies even from a fine bitch, without cluttering the earth with inferior puppies from just any old bitch.

If one will go into the market and buy the best possible bitch from the best possible family one's purse can afford and breed her sensibly to the best and most suitable stud dog one can find, success is reasonably sure. Even if for economy's sake, the bitch is but a promising puppy backed up by the best possible pedigree, it will require only a few months until she is old enough to be bred. From such a bitch, one may expect first-rate puppies at the first try, whereas in starting with an inferior bitch one is merely lucky if in two or three generations he obtains a semblance of the kind of dog he is trying to produce.

Assuming it is decided that the bitch is adequate to serve as a brood bitch, it becomes necessary to choose for her a mate in collaboration with which she may realize the ultimate of her possibilities. It is never wise to utilize for stud the family pet or the neighbor's pet just because he happens to be registered in the studbook or because his service costs nothing. Any dog short of the best and most suitable (wherever he may be and whoever may own him) is an extravagance. If the bitch is worth breeding at all, she is worth shipping clear across the continent, if need be, to obtain for her a mate to enable her to realize her possibilities. Stud fees may range from fifty to one hundred dollars or even more. The average value of each puppy, if well reared, should at the time of weaning approximate the legitimate stud fee of its sire. With a good bitch it is therefore profitable to lay out as much as may be required to obtain the services of the best and most suitable stud dog—always assuming that he is worth the price asked. However, it is never wise to choose an inferior or unsuitable dog just because he is well ballyhooed and commands an exorbitant stud fee.

There are three considerations by which to evaluate the merits of a stud dog—his outstanding excellence as an individual, his pedigree and the family from which he derived, and the excellence or inferiority of the progeny he is known to have produced.

As an individual a good stud dog may be expected to be bold and aggressive (not vicious) and structurally typical of his breed, but without any freakish exaggerations of type. He must be sound, a free and true mover, possess fineness and quality, and be a gentleman of his own breed. Accidentally acquired scars or injuries such as broken legs should not be held against him, because he can transmit only his genes to his puppies and no such accidents impair his genes.

A dog's pedigree may mean much or little. One of two litter brothers, with pedigrees exactly alike, may prove to be a superlative show and stud dog, and the other worth exactly nothing for either purpose. The pedigree especially is not to be judged on its length, since three generations is at most all that is required, although further extension of the pedigree may prove interesting to a curious owner. No matter how well-bred his pedigree may show a dog to be, if he is not a good dog the ink required to write the pedigree was wasted.

The chief value of a pedigree is to enable us to know from which of a dog's parents, grandparents, or great-grandparents, he derived his merits, and from which his faults. In choosing a mate for him (or for her, as the case may be) one seeks to reinforce the one and to avoid the other. Let us assume that one of the grandmothers was upright in shoulder, whereas the shoulder should be well laid back; we can avoid as a mate for such a dog one with any

51

tendency to straight shoulders or one from straight shouldered ancestry. The same principle would apply to an uneven mouth, a light eye, a soft back, splayed feet, cowhocks, or to any other inherited fault. Suppose, on the other hand, that the dog himself, the parents, and all the grandparents are particularly nice in regard to their fronts; in a mate for such a dog, one desires as good a front as is obtainable, but if she, or some of her ancestors are not too good in respect to their fronts, one may take a chance anyway and trust to the good fronted dog with his good fronted ancestry to correct the fault. That then is the purpose of the pedigree as a guide to breeding.

A stud dog can best be judged, however, by the excellence of the progeny he is known to have produced, if it is possible to obtain all the data to enable the breeder to evaluate that record. A complete comparative evaluation is perhaps impossible to make, but one close enough to justify conclusions is available. Not only the number but the quality of the bitches to which the dog has been bred must enter into the consideration. A young dog may not have had the opportunity to prove his prowess in the stud. He may have been bred to few bitches and those few of indifferent merits, or his get may not be old enough as yet to hit the shows and establish a record for themselves or for their sire. Allowance may be made for such a dog.

On the other hand, a dog may have proved himself to be phenomenal in the show ring, or may have been made to seem phenomenal by means of the owner's ballyhoo and exploitation. Half of the top bitches in the entire country may have been bred to him upon the strength of his winning record. Merely from the laws of probability such a dog, if he is not too bad, will produce some creditable progeny. It is necessary to take into consideration the opportunities a dog has had in relation to the fine progeny he has produced.

That, however, is the chief criterion by which a good stud dog may be recognized. A dog which can sire two or three excellent puppies in every litter from a reasonably good bitch may be considered as an acceptable stud. If he has in his lifetime sired one or two champions each year, and especially if one or two of the lot are superlative champions, top members of their breed, he is a great stud dog. Ordinarily and without other considerations, such a dog is to be preferred to one of his unproved sons, even though the son be as good or better an individual. In this way one employs genes one knows to produce what one wants. The son may be only hybrid dominant for his excellent qualities.

In the choice of a stud dog no attention whatever need be paid to claims that he sires numerically big litters. Unless the sire is deficient in sperm, the number of puppies in the litter, provided there are any puppies at all, depends entirely upon the bitch. At one service, a dog deposits enough spermatozoa to produce a million puppies, if there were so many ova to be fertilized. In any event, the major purpose should be to obtain good puppies, not large numbers of them.

There are three methods of breeding employed by experienced breeders—outcrossing, inbreeding, and line breeding. By outcrossing is meant the breeding together of mates of which no blood relationship can be traced. It is much favored by novice breeders, who feel that the breeding together of blood relatives is likely to result in imbecility, constitutional weakness, or some other kind of degeneration. Inbreeding is the mating together of closely related animals—father to daughter, mother to son, brother to sister, half brother to half sister. Some of the best animals ever produced have been bred from some such incestuous mating, and the danger from such practices, if they are carried out by persons who know what they are about, is minimal. Line breeding is the mating together of animals related one to another, but less closely—such as first cousins, grandsire to granddaughter, granddam to grandson, uncle to niece, or aunt to nephew.

Absolute outcrossing is usually impossible, since all the good dogs in any breed are more or less related—descended from some common ancestor in the fifth or sixth or seventh generation of their pedigrees. In any event, it is seldom to be recommended, since the results from it in the first generation of progeny are usually not satisfactory. It may be undertaken by some far-sighted and experienced breeder for the purpose of bringing into his strain some particular merit lacking in it and present in the strain of the unrelated dog. While dogs so bred may obtain an added vigor from what is known in genetics as *heterosis,* they are likely to manifest a coarseness and a lack of uniformity in the litter which is not to be found in more closely bred puppies. Good breeders never out-

53

cross if it is possible to obtain the virtues they want by sticking to their own strain. And when they do outcross, it is for the purpose of utilizing the outcrossed product for further breeding. It is not an end in itself.

Inbreeding (or incest breeding, as it is sometimes called) involves no such hazards as are and in the past have been attributed to it. It produces some very excellent dogs when correctly employed, some very bad ones even when correctly employed, and all bad ones when carelessly used. All the standard breeds of dogs were established as uniform breeds through intense inbreeding and culling over many generations. Inbreeding brings into manifestation undesirable recessive genes, the bearers of which can be discarded and the strain can thus be purged of its bad recessives.

Dogs of great soundness and excellence, from excellent parents and grandparents, all of them much alike, may be safely mated together, no matter how closely they may be related, with reasonable hope that most of the progeny will be sound and typical with a close resemblance to all the members of their ancestry. However, two such superlative and well-bred dogs are seldom to be found. It is the way to make progress rapidly and to establish a strain of dogs much alike and which breeds true. The amateur with the boldness and courage to try such a mating in the belief that his dogs are good enough for it is not to be discouraged. But if his judgment is not justified by the results, let him not complain that he has not been warned.

Line breeding is the safest course between the Scylla of outcrossing and the Charybdis of inbreeding for the inexperienced navigator in the sea of breeding. It, too, is to be used with care, because when it succeeds it partakes much of the nature of inbreeding. At any rate, its purpose is the pairing of like genes.

Here the pedigrees come into use. We examine the pedigree of the bitch to be bred. We hope that all the dogs named in it are magnificent dogs, but we look them over and choose the best of the four grandparents. We check this grandparent's breeding and find it good, as it probably is if it is itself a dog or bitch of great excellence. We shall assume that this best dog in the bitch's pedigree is the maternal grandsire. Then our bitch may be bred back to this particular grandsire, to his full brother if he has one of equal excellence, to his best son or best grandson. In such a fashion we compound the genes of this grandsire, and hope to obtain some puppies with his excellences intensified.

The best name in the pedigree may be some other dog or bitch, in which case it is his or her germ plasm that is to be doubled to serve for the foundation of the pedigrees of the puppies of the projected litter.

In making a mating, it is never wise to employ two dogs with the same positive fault. It is wise to use two dogs with as many of the same positive virtues as it is possible to obtain. Neither should faults balance each other, as one with a front too wide, the other with a front too narrow; one with a sway back, the other roach backed. Rather, one member of the mating should be right where the other is wrong. We cannot trust to obtain the intermediate, if we overcompensate the fault of one mate with a fault of the other.

NEGOTIATIONS TO USE THE STUD DOG

Plans to use a stud dog should be laid far enough in advance to enable one to make sure that the services of the dog will be available when they are required. Most men with a dog at public stud publish "stud cards," on which are printed the dog's pedigree and pertinent data pertaining to its record. These should be requested for all the dogs one contemplates using. Most such owners reserve the right to refuse to breed their dogs to bitches they deem unsuitable for them; they wish to safeguard their dog's reputation as a producer of superior puppies, by choosing the bitches to which he shall be bred. Therefore, it is advisable to submit a description of the bitch, with or without a picture of her, and her pedigree to the stud dog's owner at the time the application to use him is made.

Notification should be sent to the owner of the dog as soon as the bitch begins to show in heat, and she should be taken or sent by air or by railway express to the dog's owner about the time she is first recognized to be in full heat and ready to breed. The stud dog's owner should be advised by telegram or telephone just how she has been sent and just when she may be expected, and instruction should be given about how she is to be returned.

Extreme care should be used in securely crating a bitch for shipment when she is in heat. Such bitches are prone to chew their way out of insecure boxes and escape to be bred by some vagrant mongrel. A card containing a statement of the bitch's condition should be attached to the crate as a warning to the carrier to assure her greater security.

MATING

The only time the bitch may become pregnant is during her period of oestruation, a time also variously referred to as the "oestrus," "the season," and as being in "heat." A bitch's first season usually occurs when she is between six and nine months of age, with the average age being eight months. In rare instances it may occur as early as five months or as late as thirteen months of age. After the first season, oestrus usually recurs at intervals of approximately six months, though this too is subject to variation. Also, the bitch's cycle may be influenced by factors such as a change of environment or a change of climate, and her cycle will, of course, be changed if it is interrupted by pregnancy. Most bitches again come in season four to six months after whelping.

There is a decided controversy among breeders as to the wisdom of breeding a bitch during her first season. Some believe a really fine bitch should be bred during her first season in order that she may produce as many puppies as possible during the fertile years of her life span. Others feel that definite physical harm results from breeding a bitch at her first season. Since a normal healthy bitch can safely produce puppies until she is about nine years old, she can comfortably yield eight to ten litters with rests between them in her life. Any breeder should be satisfied with this production from one animal. It seems wiser, therefore, to avoid the risk of any harm and pass her first season. Bitches vary in temperament and in the ages at which they reach sufficient maturity for motherhood and its responsibilities. As with the human animal, stability comes with age and a dam is much more likely to be a good mother if she is out of the puppy phase herself. If the bitch is of show quality, she might become a champion between her first and second heats if not bred.

Usually, oestruation continues for a period of approximately three weeks, but this too is subject to variation. Prior to the beginning of the oestrus, there may be changes in the bitch's actions and demeanor; she may appear restless, or she may become increasingly affectionate. Often there is increased frequency of urination and the bitch may be inclined to lick her external parts. The breeder should be alert for any signs of the approach of oestrus since the bitch must be confined and protected at this time in order to preclude the possibility of the occurrence of a mating with any but the selected stud.

The first physical sign of oestrus is a bloody discharge of watery consistency. The mucous membrane lining the vulva becomes congested, enlarged, and reddened, and the external parts become puffy and swollen. The color of the discharge gradually deepens during the first day or two until it is a rich red color; then it gradually becomes lighter until by the tenth to twelfth day it has only a slightly reddish, or straw-colored, tinge. During the next day or so it becomes almost clear. During this same period, the swelling and hardness of the external parts gradually subside, and by the time the discharge has lost most of its color, the parts are softened and spongy. It is at this time that ovulation, the production of ripened ova (or eggs), takes place, although physical manifestations of oestrus may continue for another week.

A normal bitch has two ovaries which contain her ova. All the eggs she will produce during her lifetime are present in the ovaries at birth. Ordinarily, some of the ova ripen each time the bitch comes in season. Should a bitch fail to ovulate (produce ripened ova), she cannot, of course, become pregnant. Actually, only one ovary is necessary for ovulation, and loss of or damage to one ovary without impairment of the other will not prevent the bitch from producing puppies.

If fertilization does not occur, the ova (and this is also true of the sperm of the male) live only a short time—probably a couple of days at the most. Therefore, if mating takes place too long before or after ovulation, a bitch will not conceive, and the unfertilized ova will pass through the uterus into the vagina. Eventually they will either be absorbed or will pass out through the vulva by the same opening through which urination takes place. If fertilization does occur, the fertilized eggs become implanted on the inner surface of the uterus and grow to maturity.

Obviously, the breeder must exercise great care in determining when the dog and the bitch should be put together. Because the length of time between the beginning of the oestrus and the time of ovulation varies in different bitches, no hard and fast rule can be established, although the twelfth to fourteenth day is in most cases the correct time. The wise breeder will keep a daily record of the changes in the bitch's condition and will arrange to put the bitch

58

and dog together when the discharge has become almost clear and the external parts are softened and spongy. If the bitch refuses the advances of the dog, it is preferable to separate the two, wait a day, then again permit the dog to approach the bitch.

Ordinarily, if the bitch is willing to accept the dog, fertilization of the ovum will take place. Usually one good service is sufficient, although two at intervals of twenty-four to forty-eight hours are often allowed.

Male dogs have glands on the penis which swell after passing the sphincter muscle of the vagina and "tie" the two animals together. The time may last for a period of a few minutes, a half hour, or occasionally up to an hour or more, but will end naturally when the locking glands have deflated the needful amount. While tying may increase the probability of success, in many cases no tie occurs, yet the bitches become pregnant.

Sperm are produced in the dog's testicles and are stored in the epididymis, a twisting tube at the side of the testicle. The occasional male dog whose testicles are not descended (a cryptorchid) is generally conceded to be sterile, although in a few instances it has been asserted that cryptorchids were capable of begetting progeny. The sterility in cryptorchids is believed to be due to the fact that the sperm are destroyed if the testicle remains within the abdominal cavity because the temperature is much higher there than in the normally descended testicle. Thus all sperm produced by the dog may be destroyed if both testicles are undescended. A monorchid (a dog with one testicle descended, the other undescended) may be fertile. Nevertheless, it is unwise to use a monorchid for stud purposes, because monorchidism is believed to be a heritable trait, and the monorchid, as well as the cryptorchid, is ineligible for the show ring.

After breeding, a bitch should be confined for a week to ten days to avoid mismating with another dog.

WHELPING CALENDAR

Find the month and date on which your bitch was bred in one of the left-hand columns. Directly opposite that date, in the right-hand column, is her expected date of whelping, bearing in mind that 61 days is as common as 63.

Bred Jan	Whelp Mar	Bred Feb	Whelp Apr	Bred Mar	Whelp May	Bred Apr	Whelp Jun	Bred May	Whelp Jul	Bred Jun	Whelp Aug	Bred Jul	Whelp Sep	Bred Aug	Whelp Oct	Bred Sep	Whelp Nov	Bred Oct	Whelp Dec	Bred Nov	Whelp Jan	Bred Dec	Whelp Feb
1	5	1	5	1	3	1	3	1	3	1	3	1	2	1	3	1	3	1	3	1	3	1	2
2	6	2	6	2	4	2	4	2	4	2	4	2	3	2	4	2	4	2	4	2	4	2	3
3	7	3	7	3	5	3	5	3	5	3	5	3	4	3	5	3	5	3	5	3	5	3	4
4	8	4	8	4	6	4	6	4	6	4	6	4	5	4	6	4	6	4	6	4	6	4	5
5	9	5	9	5	7	5	7	5	7	5	7	5	6	5	7	5	7	5	7	5	7	5	6
6	10	6	10	6	8	6	8	6	8	6	8	6	7	6	8	6	8	6	8	6	8	6	7
7	11	7	11	7	9	7	9	7	9	7	9	7	8	7	9	7	9	7	9	7	9	7	8
8	12	8	12	8	10	8	10	8	10	8	10	8	9	8	10	8	10	8	10	8	10	8	9
9	13	9	13	9	11	9	11	9	11	9	11	9	10	9	11	9	11	9	11	9	11	9	10
10	14	10	14	10	12	10	12	10	12	10	12	10	11	10	12	10	12	10	12	10	12	10	11
11	15	11	15	11	13	11	13	11	13	11	13	11	12	11	13	11	13	11	13	11	13	11	12
12	16	12	16	12	14	12	14	12	14	12	14	12	13	12	14	12	14	12	14	12	14	12	13
13	17	13	17	13	15	13	15	13	15	13	15	13	14	13	15	13	15	13	15	13	15	13	14
14	18	14	18	14	16	14	16	14	16	14	16	14	15	14	16	14	16	14	16	14	16	14	15
15	19	15	19	15	17	15	17	15	17	15	17	15	16	15	17	15	17	15	17	15	17	15	16
16	20	16	20	16	18	16	18	16	18	16	18	16	17	16	18	16	18	16	18	16	18	16	17
17	21	17	21	17	19	17	19	17	19	17	19	17	18	17	19	17	19	17	19	17	19	17	18
18	22	18	22	18	20	18	20	18	20	18	20	18	19	18	20	18	20	18	20	18	20	18	19
19	23	19	23	19	21	19	21	19	21	19	21	19	20	19	21	19	21	19	21	19	21	19	20
20	24	20	24	20	22	20	22	20	22	20	22	20	21	20	22	20	22	20	22	20	22	20	21
21	25	21	25	21	23	21	23	21	23	21	23	21	22	21	23	21	23	21	23	21	23	21	22
22	26	22	26	22	24	22	24	22	24	22	24	22	23	22	24	22	24	22	24	22	24	22	23
23	27	23	27	23	25	23	25	23	25	23	25	23	24	23	25	23	25	23	25	23	25	23	24
24	28	24	28	24	26	24	26	24	26	24	26	24	25	24	26	24	26	24	26	24	26	24	25
25	29	25	29	25	27	25	27	25	27	25	27	25	26	25	27	25	27	25	27	25	27	25	26
26	30	26	30	26	28	26	28	26	28	26	28	26	27	26	28	26	28	26	28	26	28	26	27
27	31	27	1 (May)	27	29	27	29	27	29	27	29	27	28	27	29	27	29	27	29	27	29	27	28
28	1 (Apr)	28	2	28	30	28	30	28	30	28	30	28	29	28	30	28	30	28	30	28	30	28	1 (Mar)
29	2			29	31	29	1 (July)	29	31	29	31	29	30	29	31	29	1 (Dec)	29	31	29	31	29	2
30	3			30	1 (June)	30	2	30	1 (Aug)	30	1 (Sep)	30	1 (Oct)	30	1 (Nov)	30	2	30	1 (Jan)	30	1 (Feb)	30	3
31	4			31	2			31	2			31	2	31	2			31	2			31	4

THE PREGNANCY AND WHELPING
OF THE BITCH

The "period of gestation" of the bitch, by which is meant the duration of her pregnancy, is usually estimated at sixty-three days. Many bitches, especially young ones, have their puppies as early as sixty days after they are bred. Cases have occurred in which strong puppies were born after only fifty-seven days, and there have been cases that required as many as sixty-six days. However, if puppies do not arrive by the sixty-fourth day, it is time to consult a veterinarian.

For the first five to six weeks of her pregnancy, the bitch requires no more than normal good care and unrestricted exercise. For that period, she needs no additional quantity of food, although her diet must contain sufficient amounts of all the food factors, as is stated in the division of this book that pertains to food. After the fifth to sixth week, the ration must be increased and the violence of exercise restricted. Normal running and walking are likely to be better for the pregnant bitch than a sedentary existence but she should not be permitted to jump, hunt, or fight during the latter half of her gestation. Violent activity may cause her to abort her puppies.

About a week before she is due to whelp, a bed should be prepared for her and she be persuaded to use it for sleeping. This bed may be a box of generous size, big enough to accommodate her with room for activity. It should be high enough to permit her to stand upright, and is better for having a hinged cover. An opening in one side will afford her ingress and egress. This box should be placed in a secluded location, away from any possible molestation by other dogs, animals, or children. The bitch must be made confident of her security in her box.

A few hours, or perhaps a day or two, before her whelping, the bitch will probably begin arranging the bedding of the box to suit herself, tearing blankets or cushions and nosing the parts into the corners. Before the whelping actually starts, however, it is best to substitute burlap sacking, securely tacked to the floor of the box. This is to provide traction for the puppies to reach the dam's breast.

The whelping may take place at night without any assistance from the owner. The box may be opened in the morning to reveal

61

the happy bitch nursing a litter of complacent puppies. But she may need some assistance in her parturition. If whelping is recognized to be in process, it is best to help the bitch.

As the puppies arrive, one by one, the enveloping membranes should be removed as quickly as possible, lest the puppies suffocate. Having removed the membrane, the umbilical cord should be severed with clean scissors some three or four inches from the puppy's belly. (The part of the cord attached to the belly will dry up and drop off in a few days.) There is no need for any medicament or dressing of the cord after it is cut.

The bitch should be permitted to eat the afterbirth if she so desires, and she normally does. If she has no assistance, she will probably remove the membrane and sever the cord with her teeth. The only dangers are that she may delay too long or may bite the cord too short. Some bitches, few of them, eat their newborn puppies (especially bitches not adequately fed during pregnancy). This unlikelihood should be guarded against.

As they arrive, it is wise to remove all the puppies except one, placing them in a box or basket lined and covered by a woolen cloth, somewhere aside or away from the whelping bed, until all have come and the bitch's activity has ceased. The purpose of this is to prevent her from walking or lying on the whelps, and to keep her from being disturbed by the puppies' whining. A single puppy should be left with the bitch to ease her anxiety.

It is best that the "midwife" be somebody with whom the bitch is on intimate terms and in whom she has confidence. Some bitches exhibit a jealous fear and even viciousness while they are whelping. Such animals are few, and most appear grateful for gentle assistance through their ordeal.

The puppies arrive at intervals of a few minutes to an hour until all are delivered. It is wise to call a veterinarian if the interval is greater than one hour. Though such service is seldom needed, an experienced veterinarian can usually be depended upon to withdraw with obstetrical forceps an abnormally presented puppy. It is possible, but unlikely, that the veterinarian will recommend a Caesarian section. This surgery in the dog is not very grave, but it should be performed only by an expert veterinarian. It is unnecessary to describe the process here, or the subsequent management of the patient, since, if a Caesarian section should be necessary, the veterinarian will provide all the needed instructions.

Some bitches, at or immediately after their whelping period, go into a convulsive paralysis, which is called *eclampsia*. This is unlikely if the bitch throughout her pregnancy has had an adequate measure of calcium in her rations. The remedy for eclampsia is the intravenous or intramuscular administration of parenteral calcium. The bitch suspected of having eclampsia should be attended by a veterinarian.

Assuming that the whelping has been normal and without untoward incident, all of the puppies are returned to the bitch, and put, one by one, to the breast, which strong puppies will accept with alacrity. The less handling of puppies for the first four or five hours of their lives, the better. However, the litter should be looked over carefully for possible defectives and discards, which should be destroyed as soon as possible. There is no virtue in rearing hare-lipped, crippled, or mismarked puppies.

It is usually unwise to destroy sound, healthy puppies just to reduce the number in the litter, since it is impossible to sort young puppies for excellence and one may be destroying the best member of the litter, a future champion. Unless a litter is extraordinarily numerous, the dam, if well fed, can probably suckle them all. If it is found that her milk is insufficient, the litter may be artificially fed or may be divided, and the surplus placed on a foster mother if it is possible to obtain one. The foster mother need not be of the same breed as the puppies, a mongrel being as good as any. She should be approximately the same size as the actual mother of the puppies, clean, healthy, and her other puppies should be of as nearly the same age as the ones she is to take over as possible. She should be removed from her own puppies (which may well be destroyed) and her breasts be permitted to fill with milk until she is somewhat uncomfortable, at which time her foster puppies can be put to her breasts and will usually be accepted without difficulty. Unless the services of the foster mother are really required, it is better not to use her.

The whelping bitch may be grateful for a warm meal even between the arrivals of her puppies. As soon as her chore is over, she should be offered food in her box. This should be of cereal and milk or of meat and broth, something sloppy. She will probably not leave her puppies to eat and her meals must be brought to her.

63

It is wise to give a mild laxative for her bowels, also milk of magnesia. She will be reluctant to get out of her box even to relieve herself for about two days, but she should be urged, even forced, to do so regularly. A sensible bitch will soon settle down to care for her brood and will seldom give further trouble. She should be fed often and well, all that she can be induced to eat during her entire lactation.

As a preventive for infections sometimes occurring after whelping, some experienced breeders and veterinarians recommend injecting the bitch with penicillin or another antibiotic immediately following the birth of the last puppy. Oral doses of the same drug may be given daily thereafter for the first week. It is best to consult your veterinarian about this treatment.

ACID MILK

Occasionally a bitch produces early milk (colostrum) so acid that it disagrees with, sometimes kills, her puppies. The symptoms of the puppies are whining, disquiet, frequently refusal to nurse, frailty, and death. It is true that all milk is slightly acid, and it should be, turning blue litmus paper immersed in it a very light pink. However, milk harmfully on the acid side will readily turn litmus paper a vivid red. It seems that only the first two or three days milk is so affected. Milk problems come also from mastitis and other infections in the bitch.

This is not likely to occur with a bitch that throughout her pregnancy has received an adequate supply of calcium phosphate regularly in her daily ration. That is the best way to deal with the situation—to see to the bitch's correct nutrition in advance of her whelping. The owner has only himself to blame for the bitch's too acid milk, since adequate calcium in advance would have neutralized the acid.

If it is found too late that her milk is too acid, the puppies must be taken from her breast and either given to a foster mother or artificially fed from bottle or by medicine dropper. Artificial feeding of very young puppies seldom is successful. Sometimes the acidity of the dam's milk can be neutralized by giving her large doses of bicarbonate of soda (baking soda), but the puppies should not be restored to her breasts until her milk ceases to turn litmus paper red.

If it is necessary to feed the puppies artificially, "Esbilac," a commercial product, or the following orphan puppy formula, may be used.

7 oz. whole milk
1 oz. cream (top milk)
1 egg yolk
2 tbsp. corn syrup
2 tbsp. lime water

REARING THE PUPPIES

Puppies are born blind and open their eyes at approximately the ninth day thereafter. If they were whelped earlier than the full sixty-three days after the breeding from which they resulted, the difference should be added to the nine days of anticipated blindness. The early eye color of young puppies is no criterion of the color to which the eyes are likely to change, and the breeder's anxiety about his puppies' having light eyes is premature.

In breeds that require the docking of the tail, this should be done on the third day and is a surgical job for the veterinarian. Many a dog has had his tail cut off by an inexperienced person, ruining his good looks and his possibility for a win in the show ring. Dew claws should be removed at the same time. There is little else to do with normal puppies except to let them alone and permit them to grow. The most important thing about their management is their nutrition, which is discussed in another chapter. The first two or three weeks, they will thrive and grow rapidly on their mother's milk, after which they should have additional food as described.

Puppies sleep much of the time, as do other babies, and they should not be frequently awakened to be played with. They grow more and more playful as they mature.

After the second week their nails begin to grow long and sharp. The mother will be grateful if the puppies' nails are blunted with scissors from time to time so that in their pawing of the breast they do not lacerate it. Sharp nails tend to prompt the mother to wean the whelps early, and she should be encouraged to keep them with her as long as she will tolerate them. Even the small amount of milk they can drain from her after the weaning process is begun is the best food they can obtain. It supplements and makes digestible the remainder of their ration.

Many bitches, after their puppies are about four weeks of age, eat and regurgitate food, which is eaten by the puppies. This food is warmed and partly digested in the bitch's stomach. This practice, while it may appear digusting to the novice keeper of dogs, is perfectly normal and should not be discouraged. However, it renders it all the more necessary that the food of the bitch be sound, clean, and nutritious.

It is all but impossible to rear a litter of puppies without their becoming infested with roundworms. Of course, the bitch should be wormed, if she harbors such parasites, before she is bred, and her teats should be thoroughly washed with mild soap just before she whelps to free them from the eggs of roundworms. Every precaution must be taken to reduce the infestation of the puppies to a minimum. But, in spite of all it is possible to do, puppies will have roundworms. These pests hamper growth, reduce the puppies' normal resistance to disease, and may kill them outright unless the worms are eliminated. The worming of puppies is discussed in the chapter entitled "Intestinal Parasites and Their Control."

External Vermin
and Parasites

U NDER this heading the most common external parasites will be given consideration. Fleas, lice, ticks, and flies are those most commonly encountered and causing the most concern. The external parasite does not pose the problem that it used to before we had the new "miracle" insecticides. Today, with DDT, lindane, and chlordane, the course of extermination and prevention is much easier to follow. Many of the insecticide sprays have a four to six weeks residual effect. Thus the premises can be sprayed and the insect pests can be quite readily controlled.

FLEAS

Neglected dogs are too often beset by hundreds of blood-thirsty fleas, which do not always confine their attacks to the dogs but also sometimes feast upon their masters. Unchecked, they overrun kennels, homes, and playgrounds. Moreover, they are the intermediate hosts for the development of the kind of tapeworm most frequently found in dogs, as will be more fully discussed under the subject of *Intestinal Parasites*. Fleas are all-round bad actors and nuisances. Although it need hardly concern us in America, where the disease is not known to exist, fleas are the recognized and only vectors of bubonic plague.

There are numerous kinds and varieties of fleas, of which we shall discuss here only the three species often found on dogs. These are the human flea (*Pulex irritans*), the dog flea (*Ctenocephalides canis*), and the so-called chicken flea or sticktight flea (*Echidnophaga gallinacea*).

Of these the human flea prefers the blood of man to that of the dog, and unless humans are also bothered, are not likely to be found on the dog. They are small, nearly black insects, and occur mostly in the Mississippi Valley and in California. Their control is the same as for the dog flea.

The dog flea is much larger than his human counterpart, is dark brown in color and seldom bites mankind. On an infested dog these dog fleas may be found buried in the coat of any part of the anatomy, but their choicest habitat is the area of the back just forward from the tail and over the loins. On that part of a badly neglected dog, especially in summer, fleas by the hundreds will be found intermixed with their dung and with dried blood. They may cause the dog some discomfort or none. It must not be credited that because a dog is not kept in a constant or frequent agitation of scratching that he harbors no fleas. The coats of pet animals are soiled and roughened by the fleas and torn by the scratching that they sometimes induce. Fleas also appear to be connected with summer eczema of dogs; at least the diseased condition of the skin often clears up after fleas are eradicated.

Although the adults seldom remain long away from the dog's body, fleas do not reproduce themselves on the dog. Rather, their breeding haunts are the debris, dust, and sand of the kennel floor, and especially the accumulations of dropped hair, sand, and loose soil of unclean sleeping boxes. Nooks and cracks and crannies of the kennel may harbor the eggs or maggot-like larvae of immature fleas.

This debris and accumulation must be eliminated—preferably by incineration—after which all possible breeding areas should be thoroughly sprayed with a residual effect spray.

The adult dog may be combed well, then bathed in a detergent solution, rinsed thoroughly in warm water, and allowed to drip fairly dry. A solution of Pine Oil (1 oz. to a quart of water) is then used as a final rinse. This method of ridding the dog of its fleas is ideal in warm weather. The Pine Oil imparts a pleasant odor to the dog's coat and the animal will enjoy being bathed and groomed.

The same procedure may be followed for young puppies except that the Pine Oil solution should be rinsed off. When bathing is not feasible, then a good flea powder—one containing lindane—should be used.

Sticktight fleas are minute, but are to be found, if at all, in patches on the dog's head and especially on the ears. They remain quiescent and do not jump, as the dog fleas and human fleas do. Their tiny heads are buried in the dog's flesh. To force them loose from the area decapitates them and the heads remain in the skin which is prone to fester from the irritation. They may be dislodged by placing a cotton pad or thick cloth well soaked in ether or alcohol over the flea patch, which causes them immediately to relinquish their hold, after which they can be easily combed loose and destroyed.

These sticktights abound in neglected, dirty, and abandoned chicken houses, which, if the dogs have access to them, should be cleaned out thoroughly and sprayed with DDT.

Fleas, while a nuisance, are only a minor problem. They should be eliminated not only from the dog but from all the premises he inhabits. Dogs frequently are reinfested with fleas from other dogs with which they play or come in contact. Every dog should be occasionally inspected for the presence of fleas, and, if any are found, immediate means should be taken to eradicate them.

LICE

There are even more kinds of lice than of fleas, although as they pertain to dogs there is no reason to differentiate them. They do not infest dogs, except in the events of gross neglect or of unforeseen accident. Lice reproduce themselves on the body of the dog. To rid him of the adult lice is easy. The standard Pine Oil solution used to kill fleas will also kill lice. However, the eggs or "nits" are harder to remove. Weather permitting, it is sometimes best to have the dog clipped of all its hair. In heavily infested dogs this is the only sure way to cope with the situation. When the hair is clipped, most of the "nits" are removed automatically. A good commercial flea and louse powder applied to the skin will then keep the situation under control.

Rare as the occurrence of lice upon dogs may be, they must be promptly treated and eradicated. Having a dog with lice can prove to be embarrassing, for people just do not like to be around anything lousy. Furthermore, the louse may serve as the intermediate host of the tapeworm in dogs.

The dog's quarters should be thoroughly sprayed with a residual spray of the same type recommended for use in the control of fleas. The problem of disinfecting kennel and quarters is not as great as it is in the case of fleas, for the louse tends to stay on its host, not leaving the dog as the flea does.

TICKS

The terms "wood ticks" and "dog ticks," as usually employed, refer to at least eight different species, whose appearances and habits are so similar that none but entomologists are likely to know them apart. It is useless to attempt to differentiate between these various species here, except to warn the reader that the Rocky Mountain spotted fever tick (*Dermacentor andersoni*) is a vector of the human disease for which it is named, as well as of rabbit fever (tularemia), and care must be employed in removing it from dogs lest the hands be infected. Some one or more of these numerous species are to be found in well nigh every state in the Union, although there exist wide areas where wood ticks are seldom seen and are not a menace to dogs.

All the ticks must feed on blood in order to reproduce themselves. The eggs are always deposited on the ground or elsewhere after the female, engorged with blood, has dropped from the dog or other animal upon which she has fed. The eggs are laid in masses in protected places on the ground, particularly in thick clumps of grass. Each female lays only one such mass, which contains 2500 to 5000 eggs. The development of the American dog tick embraces four stages: the egg, the larva or seed tick, the nymph, and the adult. The two intermediate stages in the growth of the tick are spent on rodents, and only in the adult stage does it attach itself to the dog. Both sexes affix themselves to dogs and to other animals and feed on their blood; the males do not increase in size, although the female is tremendously enlarged as she gorges. Mating occurs while the female is feeding. After some five to thirteen days, she drops from her host, lays her eggs and dies. At no time do ticks feed on anything except the blood of animals.

The longevity and hardihood of the tick are amazing. The larvae and nymphs may live for a full year without feeding, and the adults survive for more than two years if they fail to encounter a host to which they may attach. In the Northern United States the adults are most active in the spring and summer, few being found after July. But in the warmer Southern states they may be active the year around.

Although most of the tick species require a vegetative cover and wild animal hosts to complete their development, at least one species, the brown tick (*Rhipicephalus sanguinius*), is adapted to life in the dryer environment of kennels, sheds, and houses, with the dog as its only necessary host. This tick is the vector of canine piroplasmosis, although this disease is at this time almot negligible in the United States.

This brown dog tick often infests houses in large numbers, both immature and adult ticks lurking around baseboards, window casings, furniture, the folds of curtains, and elsewhere. Thus, even dogs kept in houses are sometimes infested with hundreds of larvae, nymphs, and adults of this tick. Because of its ability to live in heated buildings, the species has become established in many Northern areas. Unlike the other tick species, the adult of the brown dog tick does not bite human beings. However, also unlike the other ticks, it is necessary not only to rid the dogs of this particular tick but also to eliminate the pests from their habitat, especially the dogs' beds and sleeping boxes. A spray with a 10% solution of DDT suffices for this purpose. Fumigation of premises seldom suffices, since not only are brown dog ticks very resistant to mere fumigation, but the ticks are prone to lurk around entry ways, porches and outbuildings, where they cannot be reached with a fumigant. The spraying with DDT may not penetrate to spots where some ticks are in hiding, and it must be repeated at intervals until all the pests are believed to be completely eradicated.

Dogs should not be permitted to run in brushy areas known to be infested with ticks, and upon their return from exercise in a place believed to harbor ticks, dogs should be carefully inspected for their presence.

If a dog's infestation is light, the ticks may be picked individually from his skin. To make tick release its grip, dab with alcohol or a drop of ammonia. If the infestation is heavy, it is easier and quicker to saturate his coat with a derris solution (one ounce of soap and two ounces of derris powder dissolved in one gallon of water). The derris should be of an excellent grade containing at least 3% of rotenone. The mixture may be used and reused, since it retains its strength for about three weeks if it is kept in a dark place.

If possible, the dip should be permitted to dry on the dog's coat. It should not get into a dog's eyes. The dip will not only kill the ticks that are attached to the dog, but the powder drying in the hair will repel further infestation for two or three days and kill most if not all the boarders. These materials act slowly, requiring sometimes as much as twenty-four hours to complete the kill.

If the weather is cold or the use of the dip should be otherwise inconvenient, derris powder may be applied as a dust, care being taken that it penetrates the hair and reaches the skin. Breathing or swallowing derris may cause a dog to vomit, but he will not be harmed by it. The dust and liquid should be kept from his eyes.

Since the dog is the principal host on which the adult tick feeds and since each female lays several thousand eggs after feeding, treating the dog regularly will not only bring him immediate relief but will limit the reproduction of the ticks. Keeping underbrush, weeds, and grass closely cut tends to remove protection favorable to the ticks. Burning vegetation accomplishes the same results.

Many of the ticks in an infested area may be killed by the thorough application of a spray made as follows: Four tablespoonfuls of nicotine sulphate (40% nicotine) in three gallons of water. More permanent results may be obtained by adding to this solution four ounces of sodium fluorides, but this will injure the vegetation.

Besides the ticks that attach themselves to all parts of the dog, there is another species that infests the ear specifically. This pest, the spinose ear tick, penetrates deep into the convolutions of the ear and often causes irritation and pain, as evidenced by the dog's scratching its ears, shaking its head or holding it on one side. One part derris powder (5% rotenone) mixed with ten parts medicinal mineral oil and dropped into the ear will kill spinose ear ticks. Only a few drops of the material is required, but it is best to massage the base of the ear to make sure the remedy penetrates to the deepest part of the ear to reach all the ticks.

FLIES

Flies can play havoc with dogs in outdoor kennels, stinging them and biting the ears until they are raw. Until recently the only protection against them was the screening of the entire kennel. The breeding places of flies, which are damp filth and stagnant garbage, are in most areas now happily abated, but the chief agent for control of the pest is DDT.

A spray of a 10% solution of DDT over all surfaces of the kennel property may be trusted to destroy all the flies that light on those surfaces for from two weeks to one month. It must, of course, be repeated from time to time when it is seen that the efficacy of the former treatment begins to diminish.

Intestinal Parasites and Their Control

THE varieties of worms that may inhabit the alimentary tract of the dog are numerous. Much misapprehension exists, even among experienced dog keepers, about the harm these parasites may cause and about the methods of getting rid of them. Some dog keepers live in terror of these worms and continually treat their dogs for them whether they are known to be present or not; others ignore the presence of worms and do nothing about them. Neither policy is justified.

Promiscuous dosing, without the certainty that the dog harbors worms or what kind he may have, is a practice fraught with danger for the well-being of the animal. All drugs for the expulsion or destruction of parasites are poisonous or irritant to a certain degree and should be administered only when it is known that the dog is infested by parasites and what kind. It is hardly necessary to say that when a dog is known to harbor worms he should be cleared of them, but in most instances there is no such urgency as is sometimes manifested.

It may be assumed that puppies at weaning time are more or less infested with intestinal roundworms or ascarids (*Toxocara canis*) and that such puppies need to be treated for worms. It is all but impossible to rear a litter of puppies to weaning age free from those parasites. Once the puppies are purged of them, it is amazing to see the spurt of their growth and the renewal of their thriftiness.

74

Many neglected puppies surmount the handicap of their worms and at least some of them survive. This, however, is no reason that good puppies—puppies that are worth saving—should go unwormed and neglected.

The ways to find out that a dog actually has worms are to see some of the worms themselves in the dog's droppings or to submit a sample of his feces to a veterinarian or to a biological laboratory for microscopic examination. From a report of such an examination, it is possible to know whether or not a dog is a host to intestinal parasites at all and intelligently to undertake the treatment and control of the specific kind he may harbor.

All of the vermifuges, vermicides, and anthelmintic remedies tend to expel other worms besides the kind for which they are specifically intended, but it is better to employ the remedy particularly effective against the individual kind of parasite the dog is known to have, and to refrain from worm treatment unless or until it is known to be needed.

ROUNDWORMS

The ascarids, or large intestinal roundworms, are the largest of the worm parasites occurring in the digestive tract of the dog, varying in length from 1 to 8 inches, the females being larger than the males. The name "spool worms," which is sometimes applied to them, is derived from their tendency to coil in a springlike spiral when they are expelled, either from the bowel or vomited, by their hosts. There are at least two species of them which frequently parasitize dogs: *Toxocara canis* and *Toxascaris leonina,* but they are so much alike except for some minor details in the life histories of their development that it is not practically necessary for the dog keeper to seek to distinguish between them.

Neither specie requires an intermediate host for its development. Numerous eggs are deposited in the intestinal tract of the host animal; these eggs are passed out by the dog in his feces and are swallowed by the same or another animal, and hatching takes place in its small intestine. Their development requires from twelve to sixteen days under favorable circumstances.

It has been shown that puppies before their birth may be infested by roundworms from their mother. This accounts for the occasional finding of mature or nearly mature worms in very young puppies. It cannot occur if the mother is entirely free from worms, as she should be.

These roundworms are particularly injurious to young puppies. The commonest symptoms of roundworm infestation are general unthriftiness, digestive disturbances, and bloat after feeding. The hair grows dead and lusterless, and the breath may have a peculiar sweetish odor. Large numbers of roundworms may obstruct the intestine, and many have been known to penetrate the intestinal wall. In heavy infestations the worms may wander into the bile ducts, stomach, and even into the lungs and upper respiratory passages where they may cause pneumonia, especially in very young animals.

The control of intestinal roundworms depends primarily upon prompt disposal of feces, keeping the animals in clean quarters and on clean ground, and using only clean utensils for feed and water. Dampness of the ground favors the survival of worm eggs and larvae. There is no known chemical treatment feasible for the destruction of eggs in contaminated soil, but prolonged exposure to sunlight and drying has proved effective.

Numerous remedies have been in successful use for roundworms, including turpentine, which has a recognized deleterious effect upon the kidneys; santonin, an old standby; freshly powdered betel nut and its derivative, arecoline, both of which tend to purge and sicken the patient; oil of chenopodium, made from American wormseed; carbon tetrachloride, widely used as a cleaning agent; tetrachlorethylene, closely related chemically to the former, but less toxic; and numerous other medicaments. While all of them are effective as vermifuges or vermicides, if rightly employed, to each of them some valid objection can be interposed.

In addition to the foregoing, there are other vermifuges available for treatment of roundworms. Some may be purchased without a prescription, whereas others may be procured only when prescribed by a veterinarian.

HOOKWORMS

Hookworms are the most destructive of all the parasites of dogs. There are three species of them—*Ancylostoma caninum*, *A. braziliense*, and *Uncinaria stenocephalia*—all to be found in dogs in some parts of the United States. The first named is the most widespread; the second found only in the warmer parts of the South and Southwest; the last named, in the North and in Canada. All are similar one to another and to the hookworm that infests mankind (*Ancylostoma uncinariasis*). For purposes of their eradication, no distinction need be made between them.

It is possible to keep dogs for many years in a dry and well drained area without an infestation with hookworms, which are contracted only on infested soils. However, unthrifty dogs shipped from infested areas are suspect until it is proved that hookworm is not the cause of their unthriftiness.

Hookworm males seldom are longer than half an inch, the females somewhat larger. The head end is curved upward, and is equipped with cutting implements, which may be called teeth, by which they attach themselves to the lining of the dog's intestine and suck his blood.

The females produce numerous eggs which pass out in the dog's feces. In two weeks or a little more these eggs hatch, the worms pass through various larval stages, and reach their infective stage. Infection of the dog may take place through his swallowing the organism, or by its penetration of his skin through some lesion. In the latter case the worms enter the circulation, reach the lungs, are coughed up, swallowed, and reach the intestine where their final development occurs. Eggs appear in the dog's feces from three to six weeks after infestation.

Puppies are sometimes born with hookworms already well developed in their intestines, the infection taking place before their birth. Eggs of the hookworm are sometimes found in the feces of puppies only thirteen days old. Assumption is not to be made that all puppies are born with hookworms or even that they are likely to become infested, but in hookworm areas the possibility of either justifies precautions that neither shall happen.

Hookworm infestation in puppies and young dogs brings about a condition often called kennel anemia. There may be digestive

78

disturbances and blood streaked diarrhea. In severe cases the feces may be almost pure blood. Infested puppies fail to grow, often lose weight, and the eyes are sunken and dull. The loss of blood results in an anemia with pale mucous membranes of the mouth and eyes. This anemia is caused by the consumption of the dog's blood by the worms and the bleeding that follows the bites. The worms are not believed to secrete a poison or to cause damage to the dog except loss of blood.

There is an admitted risk in worming young puppies before weaning time, but it is risk that must be run if the puppies are known to harbor hookworms. The worms, if permitted to persist, will ruin the puppies and likely kill them. No such immediacy is needful for the treatment of older puppies and adult dogs, although hookworm infestation will grow steadily worse until it is curbed. It should not be delayed and neglected in the belief or hope that the dog can cure himself.

If treatment is attempted at home, there are available three fairly efficacious and safe drugs that may be used: normal butyl chloride, hexaresorcinal, and methyl benzine.

If a dog is visibly sick and a diagnosis of hookworm infestation has been made, treatment had best be under professional guidance.

Brine made by stirring common salt (sodium chloride) into boiling water, a pound and a half of salt to the gallon of water, will destroy hookworm infestation in the soil. A gallon of brine should be sufficient to treat eight square feet of soil surface. One treatment of the soil is sufficient unless it is reinfested.

TAPEWORMS

The numerous species of tapeworm which infest the dog may, for practical purposes, be divided into two general groups, the armed forms and the unarmed forms. Species of both groups resemble each other in their possession of a head and neck and a chain of segments. They are, however, different in their life histories, and the best manner to deal with each type varies. This is unfortunately not well understood, since to most persons a tapeworm is a tapeworm.

The armed varieties are again divided into the single pored forms of the genera *Taenia, Multiceps,* and *Echinococcus,* and the double pored tapeworm, of which the most widespread and prevalent among dogs in the United States is the so-called dog tapeworm, *Dipylidium caninum.* This is the variety with segments shaped like cucumber-seeds. The adult rarely exceeds a foot in length, and the head is armed with four or five tiny hooks. For the person with well cared for and protected dogs, this is the only tapeworm of which it is necessary to take particular cognizance.

The dog tapeworm requires but a single intermediate host for its development, which in most cases is the dog flea or the biting louse. Thus, by keeping dogs free from fleas and lice the major danger of tapeworm infestation is obviated.

The tapeworm is bi-sexual and requires the intermediate host in order to complete its life cycle. Segments containing the eggs of the tapeworm pass out with the stool, or the detached proglottid may emerge by its own motile power and attach itself to the contiguous hair. The flea then lays its eggs on this segment, thus affording sustenance for the larva. The head of the tapeworm develops in the lung chamber of the baby flea. Thus, such a flea, when it develops and finds its way back to a dog, is the potential carrier of tapeworm. Of course, the cycle is complete when the flea bites the dog and the dog, in biting the area to relieve the itching sensation, swallows the flea.

Since the egg of the tapeworm is secreted in the segment that breaks off and passes with the stool, microscopic examination of the feces is of no avail in attempting to determine whether tapeworms infest a dog. It is well to be suspicious of a finicky eater— a dog that refuses all but the choicest meat and shows very little appetite. The injury produced by this armed tapeworm to the dog that harbors it is not well understood. Frequently it produces no symptoms at all, and it is likely that it is not the actual cause of many of the symptoms attributed to it. At least, it is known that a dog may have one or many of these worms over a long period of time and apparently be no worse for their presence. Nervous symptoms or skin eruptions, or both, are often charged to the presence of tapeworm, which may or may not be the cause of the morbid condition.

Tapeworm-infested dogs sometimes involuntarily pass segments of worms and so soil floors, rugs, furniture, or bedding. The passage by dogs of a segment or a chain of segments via the anus is a frequent cause of the dog's itching, which he seeks to allay by sitting and dragging himself on the floor by his haunches. The segments or chains are sometimes mistakenly called pinworms, but pinworms are a kind of roundworm to which dogs are not subject.

Despite that they may do no harm, few dogs owners care to tolerate tapeworms in their dogs. These worms, it has been definitely established, are not transmissible from dog to dog or to man. Without the flea or the louse, it is impossible for the adult dog tapeworm to reproduce itself, and by keeping dogs free from fleas and lice it is possible to keep them also free from dog tapeworm.

The various unarmed species of tapeworm find their intermediate hosts in the flesh and other parts of various animals, fish, crustacians and crayfish. Dogs not permitted to eat raw meats which have not been officially inspected, never have these worms, and it is needless here to discuss them at length. Hares and rabbits are the intermediate hosts to some of these worms and dogs should not be encouraged to feed upon those animals.

Little is known of the effects upon dogs of infestations of the unarmed tapeworms, but they are believed to be similar to the effects (if any) of the armed species.

The prevention of tapeworm infestation may be epitomized by saying: Do not permit dogs to swallow fleas or lice nor to feed upon uninspected raw meats. It is difficult to protect dogs from such contacts if they are permitted to run at large, but it is to be presumed that persons interested enough in caring for dogs to read this book will keep their dogs at home and protect them.

The several species of tapeworm occurring in dogs are not all removable by the same treatment. The most effective treatment for the removal of the armed species, which is the one most frequently found in the dogs, is arecoline hydrobromide. This drug is a drastic purgative and acts from fifteen to forty-five minutes after its administration. The treatment should be given in the morning after the dog has fasted overnight, and food should be withheld for some three hours after dosing.

Arecoline is not so effective against the double-pored tapeworm as against the other armed species, and it may be necessary to repeat the dose after a few days waiting, since some of the tapeworm heads may not be removed by the first treatment and regeneration of the tapeworm may occur in a few weeks. The estimatedly correct dosage is not stated here, since the drug is so toxic that the dosage should be estimated for the individual dog by a competent veterinarian, and it is better that he should be permitted to administer the remedy and control the treatment.

WHIPWORMS

The dog whipworm (*Trichuris vulpis*) is so called from its fancied resemblance to a tiny blacksnake whip, the front part being slender and hairlike and the hinder part relatively thick. It rarely exceeds three inches in its total length. Whipworms in dogs exist more or less generally throughout the world, but few dogs in the United States are known to harbor them. They are for the most part confined to the caecum, from which they are hard to dislodge, but sometimes spill over into the colon, whence they are easy to dislodge.

The complete life history of the whipworm is not well established, but it is known that no intermediate host is required for its development. The eggs appear to develop in much the same way as the eggs of the large roundworm, but slower, requiring from two weeks to several months for the organisms to reach maturity.

It has not as yet been definitely established that whipworms are the true causes of all the ills of which they are accused. In many instances they appear to cause little damage, even in heavy infestations. A great variety of symptoms of an indefinite sort have been ascribed to whipworms, including digestive disturbances, diarrhea, loss of weight, nervousness, convulsions, and general unthriftiness, but it remains to be proved that whipworms were responsible.

To be effective in its removal of whipworms, a drug must enter the caecum and come into direct contact with them; but the entry of the drug into this organ is somewhat fortuitous, and to increase the chances of its happening, large doses of a drug essentially harmless to the dog must be used. Normal butyl chloride meets this requirement, but it must be given in large doses. Even then, complete clearance of whipworms from the caecum may not be expected; the best to be hoped is that their numbers will be reduced and the morbid symptoms will subside.

Before treatment the dog should be fasted for some eighteen hours, although he may be fed two hours after being treated. It is wise to follow the normal butyl chloride in one hour with a purgative dose of castor oil. This treatment, since it is not expected to be wholly effective, may be repeated at monthly intervals.

The only known means of the complete clearance of whipworms from the dog is the surgical removal of the caecum, which of course should be undertaken only by a veterinary surgeon.

HEART WORMS

Heart worms (*Dirofilaria immitis*) in dogs are rare. They occur largely in the South and Southeast, but their incidence appears to be increasing and cases have been reported along the Atlantic Seaboard as far north as New York. The various species of mosquitoes are known to be vectors of heart worms, although the flea is also accused of spreading them.

The symptoms of heart worm infestation are somewhat vague, and include coughing, shortness of breath and collapse. In advanced cases, dropsy may develop. Nervous symptoms, fixity of vision, fear of light, and convulsions may develop. However, all such symptoms may occur from other causes and it must not be assumed because a dog manifests some of these conditions that he has heart worms. The only way to be sure is a microscopic examination of the blood and the presence or absence of the larvae. Even in some cases where larvae have been found in the blood, post mortem examinations have failed to reveal heart worms in the heart.

Both the diagnosis and treatment of heart worm are functions of the veterinarian. They are beyond the province of the amateur. The drug used is a derivative from antimony known as fuadin, and many dogs are peculiarly susceptible to antimony poisoning. If proper treatment is used by a trained veterinarian, a large preponderance of cases make a complete recovery. But even the most expert of veterinarians may be expected to fail in the successful treatment of a percentage of heart worm infestations. The death of some of the victims is to be anticipated.

LESS FREQUENTLY FOUND WORMS

Besides the intestinal worms that have been enumerated, there exist in some dogs numerous other varieties and species of worms which are of so infrequent occurrence that they require no discussion in a book for the general dog keeper. These include, esophageal worms, lungworms, kidney worms, and eye worms. They are in North America, indeed, so rare as to be negligible.

COCCIDIA

Coccidia are protozoic, microscopic organisms. The forms to which the dog is a host are *Isospora rivolta*, *I. bigeminia* and *I. felis*. Coccidia eggs, called *oocysts*, can be carried by flies and are picked up by dogs as they lick themselves or eat their stools.

These parasides attack the intestinal wall and cause diarrhea. They are particularly harmful to younger puppies that have been weaned, bringing on fever, running eyes, poor appetite and debilitation as well as the loose stools.

The best prevention is scrupulous cleanliness of the puppy or dog, its surroundings and its playmates whether canine or human. Flies should be eliminated as described in the preceding chapter and stools removed promptly where the dog cannot touch it.

Infection can be confirmed by microscopic examination of the stool. Treatment consists of providing nourishing food, which should be force-fed if necessary, and whatever drug the veterinarian recommends. Puppies usually recover, though occasionally their teeth may be pitted as in distemper.

A dog infected once by one form develops immunity to that form but may be infected by another form.

Skin Troubles

THERE is a tendency on the part of the amateur dog keeper to consider any lesion of the dog's skin to be mange. Mange is an unusual condition in clean, well fed, and well cared for dogs. Eczema occurs much more frequently and is often more difficult to control.

MANGE OR SCABIES

There are at least two kinds of mange that effect dogs—sarcoptic mange and demodectic or red mange, the latter rare indeed and difficult to cure.

Sarcoptic mange is caused by a tiny spider-like mite (*Sarcoptes scabiei canis*) which is similar to the mite that causes human scabies or "itch." Indeed, the mange is almost identical with scabies and is transmissible from dog to man. The mite is approximately 1/100th of an inch in length and without magnification is just visible to acute human sight.

Only the female mites are the cause of the skin irritation. They burrow into the upper layers of the skin, where each lays twenty to forty eggs, which in three to seven days hatch into larvae. These larvae in turn develop into nymphs which later grow into adults. The entire life cycle requires from fourteen to twenty-one days for completion. The larvae, nymphs, and males do not burrow into the skin, but live under crusts and scabs on the surface.

The disease may make its first appearance on any part of the dog's body, although it is usually first seen on the head and muzzle, around the eyes, or at the base of the ears. Sometimes it is first noticed in the armpits, the inner parts of the thighs, the lower abdomen or on the front of the chest. If not promptly treated it may cover the whole body and an extremely bad infestation may cause the death of the dog after a few months.

Red points which soon develop into small blisters are the first signs of the disease. These are most easily seen on the unpigmented parts of the skin, such as the abdomen. As the female mites burrow into the skin, there is an exudation of serum which dries and scabs. The affected parts soon are covered with bran-like scales followed with grayish crusts. The itching is intense, especially in hot weather or after exercise. The rubbing and scratching favor secondary bacterial infections and the formation of sores. The hair may grow matted and fall out, leaving bare spots. The exuded serum decomposes and gives rise to a peculiar mousy odor which increases as the disease develops and which is especially characteristic.

Sarcoptic mange is often confused with demodectic (red) mange, ringworm, or with simple eczema. If there is any doubt about the diagnosis, a microscopic examination of the scrapings of the lesions will reveal the true facts.

It is easy to control sarcoptic mange if it is recognized in its earlier stages and treatment is begun immediately. Neglected, it may be very difficult to eradicate. If it is considered how rapidly the causative mites reproduce themselves, the necessity for early treatment becomes apparent. That treatment consists not only of medication of the dog but also of sterilization of his bedding, all tools and implements used on him, and the whole premises upon which he has been confined. Sarcoptic mange is easily and quickly transmissible from dog to dog, from area to area on the same dog, and even from dog to human.

In some manner which is not entirely understood, an inadequate or unbalanced diet appears to predispose a dog to sarcoptic mange, and few dogs adequately fed and cared for ever contract it. Once a dog has contracted mange, however, improvement in the amount of quality of his food seems not to hasten his recovery.

There are various medications recommended for sarcoptic mange, sulphur ointment being the old standby. However, it is messy, difficult to use, and not always effective. For the treatment of sarcoptic mange, there are available today such insecticides as lindane, chlordane, and DDT. The use of these chemicals greatly facilitates treatment and cure of the dogs affected with mange and those exposed to it.

A bath made by dissolving four ounces of derris powder (containing at least 5% rotenone) and one ounce of soap in one gallon of water has proved effective, especially if large areas of the surface of the dog's skin are involved. All crusts and scabs should be removed before its application. The solution must be well scrubbed into the skin with a moderately stiff brush and the whole animal thoroughly soaked. Only the surplus liquid should be taken off with a towel and the remainder must be permitted to dry on the dog. This bath should be repeated at intervals of five days until all signs of mange have disappeared. Three such baths will usually suffice.

The advantage of such all over treatment is that it protects uninfected areas from infection. It is also a precautionary measure to bathe in this solution uninfected dogs which have been in contact with the infected one.

Isolated mange spots may be treated with oil of lavender. Roll a woolen cloth into a swab with which the oil of lavender can be applied and rubbed in thoroughly for about five minutes. This destroys all mites with which the oil of lavender comes into contact.

Even after a cure is believed to be accomplished, vigilance must be maintained to prevent fresh infestations and to treat new spots immediately if they appear.

DEMODECTIC OR RED MANGE

Demodectic mange, caused by the wormlike mite *Demodex canis,* which lives in the hair follicles and the sebaceous glands of the skin, is difficult to cure. It is a baffling malady of which the prognosis is not favorable. The life cycle of the causative organism is not well understood, the time required from the egg to maturity being so far unknown. The female lays eggs which hatch into young of appearance similar to that of the adult, except that they are smaller and have but three pairs of legs instead of four.

One peculiar feature about demodectic mange is that some dogs appear to be genetically predisposed to it while others do not contract it whatever their contact with infected animals may be. Young animals seem to be especially prone to it, particularly those with short hair. The first evidence of its presence is the falling out of the hair on certain areas of the dog. The spots may be somewhat reddened, and they commonly occur near the eyes, on the hocks, elbows, or toes, although they may be on any part of the dog's body. No itching occurs at the malady's inception, and it never grows so intense as in sarcoptic mange.

In the course of time, the hairless areas enlarge, and the skin attains a copper hue; in severe cases it may appear blue or leadish gray. During this period the mites multiply and small pustules develop. Secondary invasions may occur to complicate the situation. Poisons are formed by the bacteria in the pustules, and the absorption of toxic materials deranges the body functions and eventually affects the whole general health of the dog, leading to emaciation, weakness, and the development of an acrid, unpleasant odor.

This disease is slow and subtle in its development, runs a casual course, and frequently extends over a period of two or even three years. Unless it is treated, it usually terminates in death, although spontaneous recovery occasionally occurs, especially if the dog has been kept on a nourishing diet. As in other skin diseases, correct nutrition plays a major part in recovery from demodectic mange, as it plays an even larger part in its prevention.

It is possible to confuse demodectic mange with sarcoptic mange, fungus infection, acne, or eczema. A definite diagnosis is possible only from microscopic examination of skin scrapings and of material from the pustules. The possibility of demodectic mange, particularly in its earlier stages, is not negated by the failure to find the mites under the microscope, and several examinations may be necessary to arrive at a definite diagnosis.

The prognosis is not entirely favorable. It may appear that the mange is cured and a new and healthy coat may be re-established only to have the disease manifest itself in a new area, and the whole process of treatment must be undertaken afresh.

In the treatment of demodectic mange, the best results have been obtained by the persistent use of benzine hexachloride, chlordane, rotenone, and 2-mercapto benzothiazole. Perseverance is necessary, but even then failure is possible.

EAR MITES OR EAR MANGE

The mites responsible for ear mange (*Ododectes cynotis*) are considerably larger than the ones which cause sarcoptic mange. They inhabit the external auditory canal and are visible to the unaided eye as minute, slowly moving, white objects. Their life history is not known, but is probably similar to that of the mite that causes sarcoptic mange.

These mites do not burrow into the skin, but are found deep in the ear canal, near the eardrum. Considerable irritation results from their presence, and the normal secretions of the ear are interfered with. The ear canal is filled with inflammatory products, modified ear wax, and mites, causing the dog to scratch and rub its ears and to shake its head. While ear mange is not caused by incomplete washing or inefficient drying of the ears, it is encouraged by such negligence.

The ear mange infestation is purely local and is no cause for anxiety. An ointment containing benzine hexachloride is very effective in correcting this condition. The ear should be treated every third or fourth day.

ECZEMA

Eczema is probably the most common of all ailments seen in the dog. Oftentimes it is mistaken for mange or ringworm, although there is no actual relationship between the conditions. Eczema is variously referred to by such names as "hot spots," "fungitch," and "kennel itch."

Some years ago there was near-unanimity of opinion among dog people that the food of the animal was the major contributing factor of eczema. Needless to say, the manufacturers of commercial dog foods were besieged with complaints. Some research on the cause of eczema placed most of the blame on outside environmental factors, and with some help from other sources it was found that a vegetative organism was the causative agent in a great majority of the cases.

Some dogs do show an allergic skin reaction to certain types of protein given to them as food, but this is generally referred to as the "foreign protein" type of dermatitis. It manifests itself by raising numerous welts on the skin, and occasionally the head, face, and ears will become alarmingly swollen. This condition can be controlled by the injection of antihistamine products and subsequent dosage with antihistaminic tablets or capsules such as chlortrimenton or benedryl. Whether "foreign protein" dermatitis is due to an allergy or whether it is due to some toxin manufactured and elaborated by the individual dog is a disputed point.

Most cases of eczema start with reddening of the skin in certain parts. The areas most affected seem to be the region along the spine and at the base of the tail. In house dogs this may have its inception from enlarged and plugged anal glands. The glands when full and not naturally expressed are a source of irritation. The dog will rub his hind parts on the grass in order to alleviate the itching sensation. Fleas, lice, and ticks may be inciting factors, causing the dog to rub and roll in the grass in an attempt to scratch the itchy parts.

In hunting dogs, it is believed that the vegetative cover through which the dogs hunt causes the dermatitis. In this class of dogs the skin becomes irritated and inflamed in the armpits, the inner surfaces of the thighs, and along the belly. Some hunting dogs are bedded down in straw or hay, and such dogs invariably show a

91

general reddening of the skin and a tendency to scratch.

As a general rule, the difference between moist and dry eczema lies in the degree to which the dog scratches the skin with his feet or chews it with his teeth. The inflammation ranges from a simple reddening of the skin to the development of papules, vesicles, and pustules with a discharge. Crusts and scabs like dandruff may form, and if the condition is not treated, it will become chronic and then next to impossible to treat with any success. In such cases the skin becomes thickened and may be pigmented. The hair follicles become infected, and the lesions are constantly inflamed and exuding pus.

When inflammation occurs between the toes and on the pads of the feet, it closely resembles "athletes foot" in the human. Such inflammation generally causes the hair in the region to turn a reddish brown. The ears, when they are affected, emit a peculiar moldy odor and exude a brownish black substance. It is thought that most cases of canker of the ear are due to a primary invasion of the ear canal by a vegetative fungus. If there is a pustular discharge, it is due to the secondary pus-forming bacteria that gain a foothold after the resistance of the parts is lowered by the fungi.

Some breeds of dogs are more susceptible to skin ailments than are others. However, all breeds of dogs are likely to show some degree of dermatitis if they are exposed to causative factors.

Most cases of dermatitis are seen in the summer time, which probably accounts for their being referred to as "summer itch" or "hot spots." The warm moist days of summer seem to promote the growth and development of both fleas and fungi. When the fleas bite the dog, the resulting irritation causes the dog to scratch or bite to alleviate the itch. The area thus becomes moist and makes a perfect place for fungi spores to propagate. That the fungi are the cause of the trouble seems evident, because most cases respond when treated externally with a good fungicide. Moreover, the use of a powder containing both an insecticide and a fungicide tends to prevent skin irritation. Simply dusting the dog once or twice a week with a good powder of the type mentioned is sound procedure in the practice of preventive medicine.

(Editor's note: I have had some success with hydrogen peroxide in treating mild skin troubles. Saturate a cotton pad with a mixture of 2 parts 3% hydrogen peroxide to 1 part boiled water. Apply, but do NOT rub, to affected skin. Let dry naturally and when *completely* dry apply an antiseptic talcum powder like Johnson & Johnson's Medicated Powder. When this treatment was suggested to my veterinarian, he confirmed that he had had success with it. If the skin irritation is not noticeably better after two of these treatments, once daily, the case should be referred to a veterinarian.)

RINGWORM

Ringworm is a communicable disease of the skin of dogs, readily transmissible to man and to other dogs and animals. The disease is caused by specific fungi, which are somewhat similar to ordinary molds. The lesions caused by ringworm usually first appear on the face, head, or legs of the dog, but they may occur on any part of the surface of his body.

The disease in dogs is characterized by small, circular areas of dirty gray or brownish-yellow crusts or scabs partially devoid of hair, the size of a dime. As the disease progresses, the lesions increase both in size and in number and merge to form larger patches covered with crusts containing broken off hair. A raw, bleeding surface may appear when crusts are broken or removed by scratching or rubbing to relieve itching. In some cases, however, little or no itching is manifested. Microscopic examination and culture tests are necessary for accurate diagnosis.

If treatment of affected dogs is started early, the progress of the disease can be immediately arrested. Treatment consists of clipping the hair from around the infected spots, removing the scabs and painting the spots with tincture of iodine, five percent salicylic acid solution, or other fungicide two or three times weekly until recovery takes place. In applying these remedies it is well to cover the periphery of the circular lesion as well as its center, since the spots tend to expand outward from their centers. Scabs, hair, and debris removed from the dog during his treatments should be burned to destroy the causative organisms and to prevent reinfection. Precautions in the handling of animals affected with ringworm should be observed to preclude transmission to man and other animals. Isolation of affected dogs is not necessary if the treatment is thorough.

COAT CARE

Skin troubles can often be checked and materially alleviated by proper grooming. Every dog is entitled to the minimum of weekly attention to coat, skin and ears; ideally, a daily stint with brush and comb is highly recommended. Frequent examination may catch skin disease in its early stages and provide a better chance for a quick cure.

The outer or "guard" hairs of a dog's coat should glint in the sunlight. There should be no mats or dead hair in the coat. Wax in the outer ear should be kept at a minimum.

It is helpful to stand the dog on a flat, rigid surface off the floor at a height convenient to the groomer. Start at the head and ears brushing briskly *with* the lay of short hair, *against* the lay of long hair at first then with it. After brushing, use a fine comb with short teeth on fine, short hair and a coarse comb with long teeth on coarse or long hair. If mats cannot be readily removed with brush or comb, use barber's thinning shears and cut into the matted area several times until mat pulls free easily. Some mats can be removed with the fingers if one has the patience to separate the hair a bit at a time.

After brushing and combing, run your palms over the dog's coat from head to tail. Natural oils in your skin will impart sheen to your dog's coat.

The ears of some dogs secrete and exude great amounts of wax. Frequent examination will determine when your dog's ears need cleaning. A thin coating of clean, clear wax is not harmful. But a heavy accumulation of dirty, dark wax needs removal by cotton pads soaked in diluted hydrogen peroxide (3% cut in half with boiled water), or alcohol or plain boiled water if wax is not too thick.

There are sprays, "dry" bath preparations and other commercial products for maintaining your dog's coat health. Test them first, and if they are successful, you may find them beneficial time-savers in managing your dog's coat.

First Aid

JOHN STEINBECK, the Nobel Prize winning author, in *Travels with Charley in Search of America* bemoans the lack of a good, comprehensive book of home dog medicine. Charley is the aged Poodle that accompanies his illustrious author-owner on a motor tour of the U.S.A.

As in human medicine, most treatment and dosing of dogs are better left in the experienced, trained hands and mind of a professional—in this case, the veterinarian. However, there are times and situations when professional aid is not immediately available and an owner's prompt action may save a life or avoid permanent injury. To this purpose, the following suggestions are given.

The First Aid Kit

For instruments keep on hand a pair of tweezers, a pair of pliers, straight scissors, a rectal thermometer, a teaspoon, a tablespoon, and swabs for cotton.

For dressings, buy a container of cotton balls, a roll of cotton and a roll of 2″ gauze. Strips of clean, old sheets may come in handy.

For medicines, stock ammonia, aspirin, brandy, 3% hydrogen peroxide, bicarbonate of soda, milk of bismuth, mineral oil, salt, tea, vaseline, kaopectate, baby oil and baby talcum powder.

Handling the Dog for Treatment

Approach any injured or sick dog calmly with reassuring voice and gentle, steady hands. If the dog is in pain, slip a gauze or sheet strip noose over its muzzle tying the ends first under the throat and then back of the neck. Make sure the dog's lips are not caught between his teeth, but make noose around muzzle *tight*.

If the dog needs to be moved, grasp the loose skin on the back of the neck with one hand and support chest with the other hand. If the dog is too large to move in this manner, slide him on a large towel, blanket or folded sheet which may serve as a stretcher for two to carry.

If a pill or liquid is to be administered, back the dog in a corner in a sitting position. For a pill, pry back of jaws apart with thumb and forefinger of one hand and with the same fingers of your other hand place pill as far back in dog's throat as possible; close and hold jaws, rubbing throat to cause swallowing. If dog does not gulp, hold one hand over nostrils briefly; he will gulp for air and swallow pill. For liquids, lift the back of the upper lip and tip spoon into the natural pocket formed in the rear of the lower lip; it may be necessary to pull this pocket out with forefinger. Do not give liquids by pouring directly down the dog's throat; this might choke him or make the fluid go down the wrong way.

After treatment keep dog quiet, preferably in his bed or a room where he cannot injure himself or objects.

Bites and Wounds

Clip hair from area. Wash gently with pure soap and water or hydrogen peroxide. If profuse bleeding continues, apply sheet strip or gauze tourniquet between wound and heart but nearest the wound. Release tourniquet briefly at ten-minute intervals. Cold water compresses may stop milder bleeding.

For insect bites and stings, try to remove stinger with tweezers or a dab of cotton, and apply a few drops of ammonia. If dog is in pain, give aspirin at one grain per 10 pounds. (An aspirin tablet is usually 5 grains.)

Burns

Clip hair from area. Apply strong, lukewarm tea (for its tannic acid content) on a sheet strip compress. Vaseline may be used for slight burns. Give aspirin as recommended if dog is in pain. Keep him warm if he seems to be in shock.

Constipation

Give mineral oil: one-quarter teaspoon up to 10 pounds; half teaspoon from 10 to 25 pounds; full teaspoon from 25 to 75 pounds; three-quarters tablespoon over 75 pounds.

Diarrhea

Give kaopectate in same doses by size as indicated for mineral oil above, but repeat within four and eight hours.

Fighting

Do not try forcibly to separate dogs. If available throw a pail of cold water on them. A sharp rap on the rump of each combatant with a strap or stick may help. A heavy towel or blanket dropped over the head of the aggressor, or a newspaper twisted into a torch, lighted and held near them, may discourage the fighters. If a lighted newspaper is used, be careful that sparks do not fall or blow on dogs.

Fits

Try to get the dog into a room where he cannot injure himself. If possible, cover him with a towel or blanket. When the fit ends, give aspirin one grain for every 10 pounds.

Nervousness

Remove cause or remove the dog from the site of the cause. Give the recommended dose of aspirin. Aspirin acts as a tranquilizer.

97

Poisoning

If container of the poison is handy, use recommended antidote printed thereon. Otherwise, make a strong solution of household salt in water and force as much as possible into the dog's throat using the lip pocket method. Minutes count with several poisons; if veterinarian cannot be reached immediately, try to get dog to an MD or registered nurse.

Shock

If dog has chewed electric cord, protect hand with rubber glove or thick dry towel and pull cord from socket. If dog has collapsed, hold ammonia under its nose or apply artificial respiration as follows: place dog on side with its head low, press on abdomen and rib cage, releasing pressure at one- or two-second intervals. Keep dog warm.

Stomach Upsets

For mild stomach disorders, milk of bismuth in same doses as recommended for mineral oil under *Constipation* will be effective. For more severe cases brandy in the same doses but diluted with an equal volume of water may be helpful.

Swallowing Foreign Objects

If object is still in mouth or throat, reach in and remove it. If swallowed, give strong salt solution as for *Poisoning*. Some objects that are small, smooth or soft may not give trouble.

Porcupines and Skunks

Using tweezers or pliers, twist quills one full turn and pull out. Apply hydrogen peroxide to bleeding wounds. For skunk spray, wash dog in tomato juice.

WARNING! Get your dog to a veterinarian *soonest* for severe bites, wounds, burns, poisoning, fits and shock.

Internal Canine Diseases
and Their Management

THE word *management* is employed in this chapter heading rather than *treatment,* since the treatment of disease in the dog is the function of the veterinarian, and the best counsel it is possible to give the solicitous owner of a sick dog is to submit the case to the best veterinarian available and to follow his instructions implicitly. In general, it may be said, the earlier in any disease the veterinarian is consulted, the more rapid is the sick animal's recovery and the lower the outlay of money for the services of the veterinarian and for the medicine he prescribes.

Herein are presented some hints for the prevention of the various canine maladies and for their recognition when they occur. In kennel husbandry, disease is a minor problem, and, if preventive methods are employed, it is one that need not be anticipated.

DISTEMPER

Distemper, the traditional bugbear of keeping dogs, the veritable scourge of dog-kind, has at long last been well conquered. Compared with some years ago when "over distemper" was one of the best recommendations for the purchase of a dog, the incidence of distemper in well-bred and adequately cared for dogs is now minimal.

The difference between then and now is that we now have available preventive sera, vaccines, and viruses, which may be employed to forestall distemper before it ever appears. There are valid differences of opinion about which of these measures is best to use and at what age of the dog they are variously indicated. About the choice of preventive measures and the technique of administering them, the reader is advised to consult his veterinarian and to accept his advice. There can be no doubt, however, that any person with a valued or loved young dog should have him immunized.

For many years most veterinarians used the so-called "three-shot" method of serum, vaccine and virus, spaced two weeks apart after the puppy was three or four months old, for permanent immunization. For temporary immunization lasting up to a year, some veterinarians used only vaccine; this was repeated annually if the owner wished, though since a dog was considered most susceptible to distemper in the first year of his life, the annual injection was often discontinued. Under both these methods, serum was used at two-week intervals from weaning to the age when permanent or annual immunization was given.

Until 1950 living virus, produced by the methods then known to and used by laboratories, was considered too dangerous to inject without the preparation of the dog for it by prior use of serum or vaccine (killed virus). Then, researchers in distemper developed an attenuated or weakened live virus by injecting strong virus into egg embryos and other intermediate hosts. The weakened virus is now often used for permanent, one-shot distemper immunization of puppies as young as eight weeks.

Today certain researchers believe that the temporary immunity given by the bitch to her young depends on her own degree of immunity. If she has none, her puppies have none; if she has maximum immunity, her puppies may be immune up to the age of 12 weeks or more. By testing the degree of the bitch's immunity early in her pregnancy, these researchers believe they can determine the proper age at which her puppies should receive their shots.

The veterinarian is best qualified to determine the method of distemper immunization and the age to give it.

Canine distemper is an acute, highly contagious, febrile disease caused by a filterable virus. It is characterized by a catarrhal inflammation of all the mucous membranes of the body, frequently

100

accompanied by nervous symptoms and pustular eruptions of the skin. Its human counterpart is influenza, which, though not identical with distemper, is very similar to it in many respects. Distemper is so serious and complicated a disease as to require expert attention; when a dog is suspected of having it, a veterinarian should be consulted immediately. It is the purpose of this discussion of the malady rather to describe it that its recognition may be possible than to suggest medication for it or means of treating it.

Distemper is known in all countries and all parts of the United States in all seasons of the year, but it is most prevalent during the winter months and in the cold, damp weather of early spring and late autumn. No breed of dogs is immune. Puppies of low constitutional vigor, pampered, overfed, unexercised dogs, and those kept in overheated, unventilated quarters contract the infection more readily and suffer more from it than hardy animals, properly fed and living in a more natural environment. Devitalizing influences which decrease the resistance of the dog, such as rickets, parasitic infestations, unsanitary quarters, and especially an insufficient or unbalanced diet, are factors predisposing to distemper.

While puppies as young as ten days or two weeks have been known to have true cases of distemper, and very old dogs in rare instances, the usual subjects of distemper are between two months (after weaning) and full maturity at about eighteen months. The teething period of four to six months is highly critical. It is believed that some degree of temporary protection from distemper is passed on to a nursing litter through the milk of the mother.

As was first demonstrated by Carré in 1905 and finally established by Laidlaw and Duncan in their work for the Field Distemper Fund in 1926 to 1928, the primary causative agent of distemper is a filterable virus. The clinical course of the disease may be divided into two parts, produced respectively by the primary Carré filterable virus and by a secondary invasion of bacterial organisms which produce serious complicating conditions usually associated with the disease. It is seldom true that uncomplicated Carré distemper would cause more than a fever with malaise and indisposition if the secondary bacterial invasion could be avoided. The primary disease but prepares the ground for the secondary invasion which produces the havoc and all too often kills the patient.

Although it is often impossible to ascertain the source of infection

101

in outbreaks of distemper, it is known that the infection may spread from affected to susceptible dogs by either direct or indirect contact. The disease, while highly infectious throughout its course, is especially easy to communicate in its earliest stages, even before clinical symptoms are manifested. The virus is readily destroyed by heat and by most of the common disinfectants in a few hours, but it resists drying and low temperatures for several days, and has been known to survive freezing for months.

The period of incubation (the time between exposure to infection and the development of the first symptoms) is variable. It has been reported to be as short as three days and as long as two weeks. The usual period is approximately one week. The usual course of the disease is about four weeks, but seriously complicated cases may prolong themselves to twelve weeks.

The early symptoms of distemper, as a rule, are so mild and subtle as to escape the notice of any but the most acute observer. These first symptoms may be a rise in temperature, a watery discharge from the eyes and nose, an impaired appetite, a throat-clearing cough, and a general sluggishness. In about a week's time the symptoms become well marked, with a discharge of mucus or pus from the eyes and nose, and complications of a more or less serious nature, such as broncho-pneumonia, hemorrhagic inflammation of the gastro-intestinal tract, and disturbances of the brain and spinal cord, which may cause convulsions. In the early stages of distemper the body temperature may suddenly rise from the normal 101°F. to 103°. Shivering, dryness of the nostrils, a slight dry cough, increased thirst, a drowsy look, reluctance to eat, and a desire to sleep may follow. Later, diarrhea (frequently streaked with blood or wholly of blood), pneumonia, convulsions, paralysis, or chorea (a persistent twitching condition) may develop. An inflammation of the membranes of the eye may ensue; this may impair or destroy the sight through ulceration or opacity of the cornea. Extreme weakness and great loss of body weight occur in advanced stages.

All, any, or none of these symptoms may be noticeable. It is believed that many dogs experience distemper in so mild a form as to escape the owner's observation. Because of its protean and obscure nature and its strong similarity to other catarrhal affections, the diagnosis of distemper, especially in its early stages, is difficult. In young dogs that are known to have been exposed to the disease, a rise of body temperature, together with shivering, sneezing, loss of appetite, eye and nasal discharge, sluggishness, and diarrhea (all or any of these symptoms), are indicative of trouble.

There is little specific that can be done for a dog with primary distemper. The treatment is largely concerned with alleviating the symptoms. No drug or combination of drugs is known at this time that has any specific action on the disease. Distemper runs a definite course, no matter what is done to try to cure it.

Homologous anti-distemper serum, administered subcutaneously or intravenously by the veterinarian, is of value in lessening the severity of the attack. The veterinarian may see fit to treat the secondary pneumonia with penicillin or one of the sulpha drugs, or to allay the secondary intestinal infection with medication. It is best to permit him to manage the case in his own way. The dog is more prone to respond to care in his own home and with his own people, if suitable quarters and adequate nursing are available to him. Otherwise, he is best off in a veterinary hospital.

The dog affected with distemper should be provided with clean, dry, warm but not hot, well ventilated quarters. It should be given moderate quantities of nourishing, easily digested food—milk, soft boiled eggs, cottage cheese, and scraped lean beef. The sick dog should not be disturbed by children or other dogs. Discharges from eyes and nose should be wiped away. The eyes may be bathed with boric acid solution, and irritation of the nose allayed with greasy substances such as petrolatum. The dog should not be permitted to get wet or chilled, and he should have such medication as the veterinarian prescribes and no other.

When signs of improvement are apparent, the dog must not be given an undue amount of food at one meal, although he may be fed at frequent intervals. The convalescing dog should be permitted to exercise only very moderately until complete recovery is assured.

In the control of distemper, affected animals should be promptly isolated from susceptible dogs. After the disease has run its course, whether it end in recovery or death, the premises where the patient has been kept during the illness should be thoroughly cleaned and disinfected, as should all combs, brushes, or other utensils used on the dog, before other susceptible dogs are brought in. After an apparent recovery has been made in the patient, the germs are present for about four weeks and can be transmitted to susceptible dogs.

CHOREA OR ST. VITUS DANCE

A frequent sequela of distemper is chorea, which is characterized by a more or less pronounced and frequent twitching of a muscle or muscles. There is no known remedy for the condition. It does not impair the usefulness of a good dog for breeding, and having a litter of puppies often betters or cures chorea in the bitch. Chorea is considered a form of unsoundness and is penalized in the show ring. The condition generally becomes worse.

ECLAMPSIA OR WHELPING TETANY

Convulsions of bitches before, during, or shortly after their whelping are called eclampsia. It seldom occurs to a bitch receiving a sufficient amount of calcium and vitamin D in her diet during her pregnancy. The symptoms vary in their severity for nervousness and mild convulsions to severe attacks which may terminate in coma and death. The demands of the nursing litter for calcium frequently depletes the supply in the bitch's system.

Eclampsia can be controlled by the hypodermic administration of calcium gluconate. Its recurrence is prevented by the addition to the bitch's ration of readily utilized calcium and vitamin D.

RICKETS, OR RACHITIS

The failure of the bones of puppies to calcify normally is termed rickets, or more technically rachitis. Perhaps more otherwise excellent puppies are killed or ruined by rickets than by any other disease. It is essentially a disease of puppies, but the malformation of the skeleton produced by rickets persists through the life of the dog.

The symptoms of rickets include lethargy, arched neck, crouched stance, knobby and deformed joints, bowed legs, and flabby muscles. The changes characteristic of defective calcification in the puppy are most marked in the growth of the long bones of the leg, and at the cartilaginous junction of the ribs. In the more advanced stages of rickets the entire bone becomes soft and easily deformed or broken. The development of the teeth is also retarded.

Rickets results from a deficiency in the diet of calcium, phosphorus, or vitamin D. It may be prevented by the inclusion of sufficient amounts of those substances in the puppy's diet. It may also be cured, if not too far advanced, by the same means, although distortions in the skeleton that have already occurred are seldom rectified. The requirements of vitamin D to be artificially supplied are greater for puppies raised indoors and with limited exposure to sunlight or to sunlight filtered through window glass.

(It is possible to give a dog too much vitamin D, but very unlikely without deliberate intent.)

Adult dogs that have had rickets in puppyhood and whose recovery is complete may be bred from without fear of their transmission to their puppies of the malformations of their skeletons produced by the disease. The same imbalance or absence from their diet that produced rickets in the parent may produce it in the progeny, but the disease in such case is reproduced and not inherited.

The requirements of adult dogs for calcium, phosphorus, and vitamin D are much less than for puppies and young dogs, but a condition called osteomalacia, or late rickets, is sometimes seen in grown dogs as the result of the same kind of nutritional deficiency that causes rickets in puppies. In such cases a softening of the bones leads to lameness and deformity. The remedy is the same as in the rickets of puppyhood, namely the addition of calcium, phosphorus, and vitamin D to the diet. It is especially essential that bitches during pregnancy and lactation have included in their diets ample amounts of these elements, both for their own nutrition and for the adequate skeletal formations of their fetuses and the development of their puppies.

BLACKTONGUE

Blacktongue (the canine analogue of pellagra in the human) is no longer to be feared in dogs fed upon an adequate diet. For many years, it was a recognized scourge among dogs, and its cause and treatment were unknown. It is now known to be caused solely by the insufficiency in the ration of vitamin B complex and specifically by an insufficiency of nicotinic acid. (Nicotinic acid is vitamin B_2, formerly known as vitamin G.)

Blacktongue may require a considerable time for its full development. It usually begins with a degree of lethargy, a lack of appetite for the kind of food the dog has been receiving, constipation, often with spells of vomiting, and particularly with a foul odor from the mouth. As the disease develops, the mucous membranes of the mouth, gums, and tongue grow red and become inflamed, with purple splotches of greater or lesser extent, especially upon the front part of the tongue, and with ulcers and pustules on the lips and the lining of the cheeks. Constipation may give way to diarrhea as the disease develops. Blacktongue is an insidious malady, since its development is so gradual.

This disease is unlikely to occur except among dogs whose owners are so unenlightened, careless, or stingy as to feed their dogs exclusively on a diet of cornmeal mush, salt pork, cowpeas, sweet potatoes, or other foodstuffs that are known to be responsible for the development of pellagra in mankind. Blacktongue is not infectious or contagious, although the same deficiency in the diet of dogs may produce the malady in all the inmates throughout a kennel.

Correct treatment involves no medication as such, but consists wholly in the alteration of the diet to include foods which are good sources of the vitamin B complex, including nicotinic acid; such food as the muscles of beef, mutton, or horse, dried yeast, wheat germ, milk, eggs, and especially fresh liver. As an emergency treatment, the hypodermic injection of nicotinic acid may be indicated. Local treatments of the mouth, its cleansing and disinfection, are usually included, although they will avail nothing without the alteration in the diet.

LEPTOSPIROSIS OR CANINE TYPHUS

Leptospirosis, often referred to as canine typhus, is believed to be identical with Weil's disease (infectious jaundice) in the human species. It is not to be confused with non-infectious jaundice in the dog, which is a mere obstruction in the bile duct which occurs in some liver and gastric disorders. Leptospirosis is a comparatively rare disease as yet, but its incidence is growing and it is becoming more widespread.

It is caused by either of two spirocheates, *Leptospira canicola* or *Leptospira icterohenorrhagiae*. These causative organisms are found in the feces or urine of infected rats, and the disease is transmitted to dogs by their ingestion of food fouled by those rodents. It is therefore wise in rat infested houses to keep all dog food in covered metal containers to which it is impossible for rats to gain access. It is also possible for an ill dog to transmit the infection to a well one, and, it is believed, to man. Such cases, however, are rare.

Symptoms of leptospirosis include a variable temperature, vomiting, loss of appetite, gastroenteritis, diarrhea, jaundice and depression. Analysis of blood and urine may be helpful toward diagnosis. The disease is one for immediate reference to the veterinarian whenever suspected.

Prognosis is not entirely favorable, especially if the disease is neglected in its earlier stages. Taken in its incipience, treatment with penicillin has produced excellent results, as has antileptospiral serum and vaccine.

Control measures include the extermination of rats in areas where the disease is known to exist, and the cleaning and disinfection of premises where infected dogs have been kept.

INFECTIOUS HEPATITIS

This is a virus disease attacking the liver. Apparently it is not the same virus that causes hepatitis in humans. Symptoms include an unusual thirst, loss of appetite, vomiting, diarrhea, pain causing the dog to moan, anemia and fever. The afflicted dog may try to hide.

The disease runs a fast course and is often fatal. A dog recovering from it may carry the virus in his urine for a long period, thus infecting other dogs months later.

Serum and vaccine are available to offer protection. A combination for distemper and hepatitis is now offered.

TURNED-IN OR TURNED-OUT EYELIDS

When the eyelid is inverted, or turned-in, it is technically termed entropion. When the eyelid is turned-out, it is referred to as extropion. Both conditions seem to be found in certain strains of dogs and are classified as being heritable. Both conditions may be corrected by competent surgery. It is possible to operate on such

107

cases and have complete recovery without scar formation. However, cognizance should be taken of either defect in a dog to be used for breeding purposes.

CONJUNCTIVITIS OR INFLAMMATION
OF THE EYE

Certain irritants, injuries or infections, and many febrile diseases, such as distemper, produce conjunctivitis, an inflammation of the membranes lining the lids of the dog's eyes. At first there is a slight reddening of the membranes and a watery discharge. As the condition progresses, the conjunctivae become more inflamed looking and the color darkens. The discharge changes consistency and color, becoming muco-purulent in character and yellow in color. The eyelids may be pasted shut and granulation of the lids may follow.

When eye infection persists for an extended period of time, the cornea sometimes becomes involved. Ulcers may develop, eventually penetrating the eyeball. When this happens, the condition becomes very painful and, even worse, often leads to the loss of vision.

Home treatment, to be used only until professional care may be had, consists of regular cleaning of the eye with a 2% boric acid solution and the application of one of the antibiotic eye ointments.

When anything happens to the dog's eye, it is always best to seek professional help and advice.

RABIES

This disease, caused by a virus, is transmissible to all warm blooded animals, and the dog seems to be the number one disseminator of the virus. However, outbreaks of rabies have been traced to wild animals—the wolf, coyote, or fox biting a dog which in turn bites people, other dogs, or other species of animals.

The virus, which is found in the saliva of the rabid animal, enters the body only through broken skin. This usually is brought about by biting and breaking the skin, or through licking an open cut on the skin. The disease manifests itself clinically in two distinct forms. One is called the "furious type" and the other the "dumb type." Both types are produced by the same strain of virus.

The disease works rather peculiarly on the dog's disposition and character. The kindly old dog may suddenly become ferocious; just the reverse may also occur, the mean, vicious dog becoming gentle and biddable. At first the infected dog wants to be near his master, wants to lick his hand or his boots; his appetite undergoes a sudden change, becoming voracious, and the animal will eat anything— stones, bits of wood, even metal. Soon there develops a sense of wanderlust, and the dog seems to wish to get as far away as possible from his owner.

In all rabid animals there is an accentuation of the defense mechanisms. In other words, the dog will bite, the cat will hiss and claw, the horse will bite and kick, and the cow will attack anything that moves.

An animal afflicted with rabies cannot swallow because there is usually a paralysis of the muscles of deglutinition. The animal, famished for a drink, tries to bite the water or whatever fluid he may be attempting to drink. The constant champing of the jaws causes the saliva to become mixed and churned with air, making it appear whipped and foamy. In the old days when a dog "frothed at the mouth," he was considered "mad." There is no doubt but what some uninfected dogs have been suspected of being rabid and shot to death simply because they exhibited these symptoms.

One of the early signs of rabies in the dog is the dropping of the lower jaw. This is a sign of rabies of the so-called "dumb type." The animal has a "faraway" look in his eyes, and his voice or bark has an odd pitch. Manifesting these symptoms, the dog is often taken to the clinic by the owner, who is sure the dog has a bone in the throat. The hind legs, and eventually the whole hindquarters, subsequently become paralyzed, and death ensues.

Many commonwealths have passed laws requiring that all dogs be vaccinated against rabies, and usually, a vaccination certificate must be presented before a dog license may be issued. The general enforcement of this law alone would go a long way toward the eradication of rabies.

Some will ask why a dog must be impounded as a biter when he has taken a little "nip" at someone and merely broken the skin— if this must be done, they cannot understand the "good" of the vaccination. But the vaccination does not give the dog the right to bite. Statistics show that rabies vaccination is effective in about 88% of the cases. All health authorities wish it were 100% effective, thus eliminating a good deal of worry from their minds. Because the vaccination is not 100% effective, we cannot take a chance on the vaccine alone. The animal must be impounded and under the daily supervision of a qualified observer, generally for a period of fourteen days. It is pretty well recognized that if the bite was provocated by rabies, the biting animal will develop clinical symptoms in that length of time; otherwise, he will be released as "clinically normal."

THE SPAYING OF BITCHES

The spaying operation, technically known as an ovariectomy, is the subject of a good deal of controversy. It is an operation that has its good and its bad points.

Spayed bitches cannot be entered in the show ring, and of course can never reproduce their kind. However, under certain circumstances, the operation is recommended by veterinarians. If the operation is to be performed, the bitch should preferably be six to eight months of age. At this age, she has pretty well reached the adolescent period; time enough has been allowed for the endocrine balance to become established and the secondary sex organs to develop.

Mechanical difficulties sometimes arise in the urinary systems of bitches that have been operated on at three or four months of age. In a very small percentage of the cases, loss of control of the sphincter muscles of the bladder is observed. But this can readily be corrected by an injection of the female hormone stilbestrol.

There are many erroneous ideas as to what may happen to the female if she is spayed. Some people argue that the disposition will be changed, that the timid dog may become ferocious, and, strangely enough, that the aggressive animal will become docile. Some breeders say that the spayed bitch will become fat, lazy, and lethargic. According to the records that have been kept on bitches following the spaying operation, such is not the case. It is unjust to accuse the spaying operation when really the dog's owner is at fault—he just feeds the dog too much.

THE CASTRATION OF DOGS

This operation consists of the complete removal of the testes. Ordinarily the operation is not encouraged. Circumstances may attenuate the judgment, however. Castration may be necessary to correct certain pathological conditions such as a tumor, chronic prostatitis, and types of perineal troubles. Promiscuous wetting is sometimes an excuse for desexing.

It must be remembered that as with the spayed bitch, the castrated dog is barred from the show ring.

ANAL GLANDS

On either side of the anus of the dog is situated an anal gland, which secretes a lubricant that better enables the dog to expel the contents of the rectum. These glands are subject to being clogged, and in them accumulates a fetid mass. This accumulation is not, strictly speaking, a disease—unless it becomes infected and purulent. Almost all dogs have it, and most of them are neglected without serious consequences. However, they are better if they are relieved. Their spirits improve, their eyes brighten, and even their coats gradually grow more lively if the putrid mass is occasionally squeezed out of the anus.

This is accomplished by seizing the tail with the left hand, en circling its base with the thumb and forefinger of the right hand, and pressing the anus firmly between thumb and finger. The process results in momentary pain to the dog and often causes him to flinch, which may be disregarded. A semi-liquid of vile odor is extruded from the anus. The operation should be repeated at intervals of from one week to one month, depending on the rapidity of glandular accumulation. No harm results from the frequency of such relief, although there may be no apparent results if the anal glands are kept free of their accumulations.

If this process of squeezing out of the glands is neglected, the glands sometimes become infected and surgery becomes necessary. This is seldom the case, but, if needful at all, it must be entrusted to a skillful veterinary surgeon.

111

METRITIS

Metritis is the acute or chronic inflammation of the uterus of the bitch and may result from any one of a number of things. Perhaps the most common factor, especially in eight- to twelve-year-old bitches, is pseudocyesis, or false pregnancy. Metritis often follows whelping; it may be the result of a retained placenta, or of infection of the uterus following the manual or instrument removal of a puppy.

The term pyometria is generally restricted to cases where the uterus is greatly enlarged and filled with pus. In most such cases surgery must be resorted to in order to effect a cure.

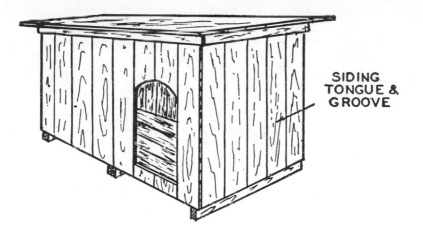

SIDING
TONGUE &
GROOVE

ASSEMBLED VIEW

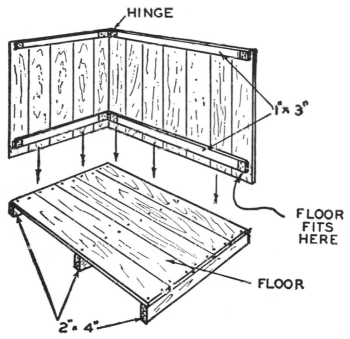

HINGE

1" x 3"

FLOOR
FITS
HERE

FLOOR

2" x 4"

Housing for Dogs

EVERY owner will have, and will have to solve, his own problems about providing his dog or dogs with quarters best suited to the dog's convenience. The special circumstances of each particular owner will determine what kind of home he will provide for his dogs. Here it is impossible to provide more than a few generalities upon the subject.

Little more need be said than that fit quarters for dogs must be secure, clean, dry, and warm. Consideration must be given to convenience in the care of kennel inmates by owners of a large number of dogs, but by the time one's activities enlarge to such proportions one will have formulated one's own concept of how best to house one's dogs. Here, advice will be predicated upon the maintenance of not more than three or four adult dogs with accommodations for an occasional litter of puppies.

First, let it be noted that dogs are not sensitive to aesthetic considerations in the place they are kept; they have no appreciation of the beauty of their surroundings. They do like soft beds of sufficient thickness to protect them from the coldness of the floors. These beds should be secluded and covered to conserve body heat. A box or crate of adequate size to permit the dog to lie full length in it will suffice. The cushion may be a burlap bag stuffed with shredded paper, *not straw, hay, or grass*. Paper is recommended, for its use will reduce the possibility of the dog's developing skin trouble.

Most dogs are allergic to fungi found on vegetative matter such as straw, hay, and grass. Wood shavings and excelsior may be used with impunity.

The kennel should be light, except for a retiring place; if sunshine is available at least part of the day, so much the better. Boxes in a shed or garage with secure wire runs to which the dogs have ready access suffice very well, are very inexpensive, and are easy to plan and to arrange. The runs should be made of wire fencing strong enough that the dogs are unable to tear it with their teeth and high enough that the dogs are unable to jump or climb over it. In-turning flanges of wire netting at the tops of the fences tend to obviate jumping. Boards, rocks, or cement buried around the fences forestall burrowing to freedom.

These pens need not be large, if the dogs are given frequent respites from their captivity and an opportunity to obtain needed exercise. However, they should be large enough to relieve them of the aspect of cages. Concrete floors for such pens are admittedly easy to keep clean and sanitary. However, they have no resilience, and the feet of dogs confined for long periods on concrete floors are prone to spread and their shoulders to loosen. A further objection to concrete is that it grows hot in the summer sunshine and is very cold in winter. If it is used for flooring at all, a low platform of wood, large enough to enable the dogs to sprawl out on it full length, should be provided in each pen.

A well drained soil is to be preferred to concrete, if it is available; but it must be dug out to the depth of three inches and renewed occasionally, if it is used. Otherwise, the accumulation of urine will make it sour and offensive. Agricultural limestone, applied monthly and liberally, will "sweeten" the soil.

Gates, hinges, latches, and other hardware must be trustworthy. The purpose of such quarters is to confine the dogs and to keep them from running at large; unless they serve such a purpose they are useless. One wants to know when one puts a dog in his kennel, the dog will be there when one returns. An improvised kennel of old chicken wire will not suffice for one never knows whether it will hold one's dogs or not.

Frequently two friendly bitches may be housed together, or a dog housed with a bitch. Unless one is sure of male friendships, it is seldom safe to house two adult male dogs together. It is better, if possible, to provide a separate kennel for each mature dog. But, if the dogs can be housed side by side with only a wire fence between them, they can have companionship without rancor. Night barking can be controlled by confining the dogs indoors or by shutting them up in their boxes.

Adult dogs require artificial heat in only the coldest of climates, if they are provided with tight boxes placed under shelter. Puppies need heat in cold weather up until weaning time, and even thereafter if they are not permitted to sleep together. Snuggled together in a tight box with shredded paper, they can withstand much cold without discomfort. All dogs in winter without artificial heat should have an increase of their rations—especially as pertains to fat content.

Whatever artificial heat is provided for dogs should be safe, foolproof, and dog-proof. Caution should be exercised that electric wiring is not exposed, that stoves cannot be tipped over, and that it is impossible for sparks from them to ignite the premises. Many fires in kennels, the results of defective heating apparatus or careless handling of it, have brought about the deaths of the inmates. It is because of them that this seemingly unnecessary warning is given.

No better place for a dog to live can be found than the home of its owner, sharing even his bed if permitted. So is the dog happiest. There is a limit, however, to the number of dogs that can be tolerated in the house. The keeper of a small kennel can be expected to alternate his favorite dogs in his own house, thus giving them a respite to confinement in a kennel. Provision must be made for a place of exercise and relief at frequent intervals for dogs kept in the house. An enclosed dooryard will serve such a purpose, or the dog may be exercised on a lead with as much benefit to the owner as to the dog.

That the quarters of the dog shall be dry is even more important than that they shall be warm. A damp, drafty kennel is the cause of much kennel disease and indisposition. It is harmless to permit a dog to go out into inclement weather of his own choice, if he is provided with a sheltered bed to which he may retire to dry himself.

By cleanness, sanitation is meant—freedom from vermin and bacteria. A little coat of dust or a degree of disorder does not discommode the dog or impair his welfare, but the best dog keepers are orderly persons. They at least do not permit bedding and old bones to accumulate in a dog's bed, and they take the trouble to spray with antiseptic or wash with soap and water their dog's house at frequent intervals. The feces in the kennel runs should be picked up and destroyed at least once, and better twice, daily. Persistent filth in kennels can be counted on as a source of illness sooner or later. This warning appears superfluous, but it isn't; the number of ailing dogs kept in dirty, unsanitary kennels is amazing. It is one of the axioms of keeping dogs that their quarters must be sanitary or disease is sure to ensue.

GOOD DOG KEEPING PRACTICES

Pride of ownership is greatly enhanced when the owner takes care to maintain his dog in the best possible condition at all times. And meticulous grooming not only will make the dog look better but also will make him feel better. As part of the regular, daily routine, the grooming of the dog will prove neither arduous nor time consuming; it will also obviate the necessity for indulging in a rigorous program designed to correct the unkempt state in which too many owners permit their dogs to appear. Certainly, spending a few minutes each day will be well worth while, for the result will be a healthier, happier, and more desirable canine companion.

THAT DOGGY ODOR

Many persons are disgusted to the point of refusal to keep a dog by what they fancy is a "doggy odor." Of course, almost everything has a characteristic odor everyone is familiar with the smell of the rose. No one would want the dog to smell like a rose, and, conversely, the world wouldn't like it very well if the rose smelled doggy. The dog must emit a certain amount of characteristic odor or he woudn't be a dog. That seems to be his God-given grant. However, when the odor becomes too strong and obnoxious, then it is time to look for the reason. In most cases it is the result of clogged anal glands. If this be the case, all one must do to rid the pet of his odor is to express the contents of these glands and apply to the anal region a little soap and water.

If the odor is one of putrefaction, look to his mouth for the trouble. The teeth may need scaling, or a diseased root of some

117

one or two teeth that need to be treated may be the source of the odor. In some dogs there is a fold or a crease in the lower lip near the lower canine tooth, and this may need attention. This spot is favored by fungi that cause considerable damage to the part. The smell here is somewhat akin to the odor of human feet that have been attacked by the fungus of athlete's foot.

The odor may be coming from the coat if the dog is heavily infested with fleas or lice. Too, dogs seem to enjoy the odor of dead fish and often roll on a foul smelling fish that has been cast up on the beach. The dog with a bad case of otitis can fairly "drive you out of the room" with this peculiar odor. Obviously, the way to rid the dog of odor is to find from whence it comes and then take steps to eliminate it. Some dogs have a tendency toward excessive flatulence (gas). These animals should have a complete change of diet and with the reducing of the carbohydrate content, a teaspoon of granular charcoal should be added to each feeding.

BATHING THE DOG

There is little to say about giving a bath to a dog, except that he shall be placed in a tub of warm (not hot) water and thoroughly scrubbed. He may, like a spoiled child, object to the ordeal, but if handled gently and firmly he will submit to what he knows to be inevitable.

The water must be only tepid, so as not to shock or chill the dog. A bland, unmedicated soap is best, for such soaps do not irritate the skin or dry out the hair. Even better than soap is one of the powdered detergents marketed especially for this purpose. They rinse away better and more easily than soap and do not leave the coat gummy or sticky.

It is best to begin with the face, which should be thoroughly and briskly washed with a cloth. Care should be taken that the cleaning solvent does not get into the dog's eyes, not because of the likelihood of causing permanent harm, but because such an experience is unpleasant to the dog and prone to prejudice him against future baths. The interior of the ear canals should be thoroughly cleansed until they not only look clean but also until no unpleasant odor comes from them. The head may then be rinsed and dried before proceeding to the body. Especial attention should be given to the drying of the ears, inside and outside. Many ear infections arise from failure to dry the canals completely.

With the head bathed and the surplus water removed from that part, the body must be soaked thoroughly with water, either with a hose or by dipping the water from the bath and pouring it over the dog's back until he is totally wetted. Thereafter, the soap or detergent should be applied and rubbed until it lathers freely. A stiff brush is useful in penetrating the coat and cleansing the skin. It is not sufficient to wash only the back and sides—the belly, neck, legs, feet, and tail must all be scrubbed thoroughly.

If the dog is very dirty, it may be well to rinse him lightly and repeat the soaping process and scrub again. Thereafter, the dog must be rinsed with warm (tepid) water until all suds and soil come away. If a bath spray is available, the rinsing is an easy matter. If the dog must be rinsed in standing water, it will be needful to renew it two or three times.

When he is thoroughly rinsed, it is well to remove such surplus water as may be squeezed with the hand, after which he is enveloped with a turkish towel, lifted from the tub, and rubbed until he is dry. This will probably require two or three dry towels. In the process of drying the dog, it is well to return again and again to the interior of the ears.

THE DOG'S TEETH

The dog, like the human being, has two successive sets of teeth, the so-called milk teeth or baby teeth, which are shed and replaced later by the permanent teeth. The temporary teeth, which begin to emerge when the puppy is two and a half to three weeks of age, offer no difficulty. The full set of milk teeth (consisting usually of six incisors and two canines in each jaw, with four molars in the upper jaw and six molars in the lower jaw) is completed usually just before weaning time. Except for some obvious malformation, the milk teeth may be ignored and forgotten about.

At about the fourth month the baby teeth are shed and gradually replaced by the permanent teeth. This shedding and replacement process may consume some three or four months. This is about the most critical period of the dog's life—his adolescence. Some constitutionally vigorous dogs go through their teething easily, with no seeming awareness that the change is taking place. Others, less vigorous, may suffer from soreness of the gums, go off in flesh, and require pampering. While they are teething, puppies should be particularly protected from exposure to infectious diseases and should be fed on nutritious foods, especially meat and milk.

The permanent teeth normally consist of 42—six incisors and two canines (fangs) in each jaw, with twelve molars in the upper jaw and fourteen in the lower jaw. Occasionally the front molars fail to emerge; this deficiency is considered by most judges to be only a minor fault, if the absence is noticed at all.

Dentition is a heritable factor in the dog, and some dogs have soft, brittle and defective permanent teeth, no matter how excellent the diet and the care given them. The teeth of those dogs which are predisposed to have excellent sound ones, however, can be ruined by an inferior diet prior to and during the period of their eruption. At this time, for the teeth to develop properly, a dog must have an adequate supply of calcium phosphate and vitamin D, besides all the protein he can consume.

Often the permanent teeth emerge before the shedding of the milk teeth, in which case the dog may have parts of both sets at the same time. The milk teeth will eventually drop out, but as long as they remain they may deflect or displace the second teeth in the process of their growth. The incisors are the teeth in which a malformation may result from the late dropping of the baby teeth. When it is realized just how important a correct "bite" may be deemed in the show ring, the hazards of permitting the baby teeth to deflect the permanent set will be understood.

The baby teeth in such a case must be dislodged and removed. The roots of the baby teeth are resorbed in the gums, and the teeth can usually be extracted by firm pressure of thumb and finger, although it may be necessary to employ forceps or to take the puppy to the veterinarian.

The permanent teeth of the puppy are usually somewhat overshot, by which is meant that the upper incisors protrude over and do not play upon the lower incisors. Maturity may be trusted to remedy this apparent defect unless it is too pronounced.

An undershot mouth in a puppy, on the other hand, tends to grow worse as the dog matures. Whether or not it has been caused by the displacement of the permanent teeth by the persistence of the milk teeth, it can sometimes be remedied (or at least bettered) by frequent hard pressure of the thumb on the lower jaw, forcing the lower teeth backward to meet the upper ones. Braces on dog teeth have seldom proved efficacious, but pressure and massage are worth trying on the bad mouth of an otherwise excellent puppy.

High and persistent fevers, especially from the fourth to the ninth month, sometimes result in discolored, pitted, and defective teeth, commonly called "distemper teeth." They often result from maladies other than distemper. There is little that can be done for them. They are unpleasant to see and are subject to penalty in the show ring, but are serviceable to the dog. Distemper teeth are not in themselves heritable, but the predisposition for their development appears to be. At least, at the teething age, the offspring from distemper toothed ancestors seem to be especially prone to fevers which impair their dentition.

Older dogs, especially those fed largely upon carbohydrates, tend to accumulate more or less tartar upon their teeth. The tartar generally starts at the gum line on the molars and extends gradually to the cusp. To rectify this condition, the dog's teeth should be scaled by a veterinarian.

The cleanliness of a dog's mouth may be brought about and the formation of tartar discouraged by the scouring of the teeth with a moist cloth dipped in a mixture of equal parts of table salt and baking soda.

A large bone given the dog to chew on or play with tends to prevent tartar from forming on the teeth. If tartar is present, the chewing and gnawing on the bone will help to remove the deposit mechanically. A bone given to puppies will act as a teething ring and aid in the cutting of the permanent teeth. So will beef hide strips you can buy in pet shops.

CARE OF THE NAILS

The nails of the dog should be kept shortened and blunted right down to the quick—never into the quick. If this is not done, the toes may spread and the foot may splay into a veritable pancake. Some dogs have naturally flat feet, which they have inherited. No pretense is made that the shortening of the nails of such a foot will obviate the fault entirely and make the foot beautiful or serviceable.

It will only improve the appearance and make the best of an obvious fault. Short nails do, however, emphasize the excellence of a good foot.

Some dogs keep their nails short by digging and friction. Their nails require little attention, but it is a rare dog whose foot cannot be bettered by artificially shortening the nails.

Nail clippers are available, made especially for the purpose. After using them, the sides of the nail should be filed away as much as is possible without touching the quick. Carefully done, it causes the dog no discomfort. But, once the quick of a dog's nail has been injured, he may forever afterward resent and fight having his feet treated or even having them examined.

The obvious horn of the nail can be removed, after which the quick will recede to permit the removal of more horn the following week. This process may be kept up until the nail is as short and blunt as it can be made, after which nails will need attention only at intervals of six weeks or two months.

Some persons clip the nails right back to the toes in one fell swoop, disregarding injury to the quick and pain of the dog. The nails bleed and the dog limps for a day or two, but infection seldom develops. Such a procedure should not be undertaken without a general anesthetic. If an anesthetic is used, this forthright method does not prejudice the dog against having his feet handled.

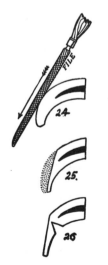

NAIL TRIMMING ILLUSTRATED

The method here illustrated is to take a sharp file and stroke the nail downwards in the direction of the arrow, as in Figure 24, until it assumes the shape in Figure 25, the shaded portion being the part removed, a three-cornered file should then be used on the underside just missing the quick, as in Figure 26, and the operation is then complete, the dog running about quickly wears the nail to the proper shape.

Care for
the Old Dog

First, how old is old, in a dog? Some breeds live longer than others, as a general rule. The only regularity about dog ages at death is their irregularity breed to breed and dog to dog.

The dog owner can best determine senility in his canine friend by the dog's appearance and behavior. Old dogs "slow down" much as humans do. The stairs are a little steeper, the breath a little shorter, the eye dimmer, the hearing usually a little harder.

As prevention is always better than cure, a dog's life may be happily and healthfully extended if certain precautionary steps are taken. As the aging process becomes quite evident, the owner should become more considerate of his dog's weaknesses, procrastinations and lapses. A softer, drier, warmer bed may be advisable; a foam rubber mattress will be appreciated. If a kennel dog has been able to endure record-breaking hot or cold, torrential or desert-dry days, he may in his old age appreciate spending his nights at least in a warm, comfy human house. And if the weather outside is frightful during the day, he should—for minimum comfort and safety—be brought inside before pneumonia sets in.

The old dog should NOT be required or expected to chase a ball, or a pheasant, or one of his species of different sex. The old bitch should not continue motherhood.

If many teeth are gone or going, foods should be softer. The diet should be blander—delete sweet or spicy or heavy tidbits—and there should be less of it, usually. The older dog needs less fat, less carbohydrate and less minerals unless disease and convalescence dictate otherwise. DON'T PERMIT AN OLD DOG TO GET FAT! It's cruel. The special diet known as PD or KD may be in order, if the dog has dietary troubles or a disease concomitant with old age. The veterinarian should be asked about PD or KD diets. Vitamin B-12 and other vitamin reinforcements may help.

The dog diseases of old age parallel many of the human illnesses. Senior male dogs suffer from prostate trouble, kidney disease and cancer. Senior bitches suffer from metritis and cancer. Both sexes suffer blindness, deafness and paralysis. Dogs suffer from heart disease; I know one old dog that is living an especially happy old age through the courtesy of digitalis. If the symptoms of any disease manifest themselves in an old dog the veterinarian MUST be consulted.

Many dog owners are selfish about old dogs. In their reluctance to lose faithful friends, they try to keep their canine companions alive in terminal illnesses, such as galloping cancer. If the veterinarian holds little or no promise for recovery of a pet from an illness associated with old age, or if the pet suffers, the kindest act the owner can perform is to request euthanasia. In this sad event, the kindest step the owner may take in *his* interest is to acquire a puppy or young dog of the same breed immediately. Puppies have a wonderful way of absorbing grief!

Glossary of Dog Terms

Achilles tendon: The large tendon attaching the muscle of the calf in the second thigh to the bone below the hock; the hamstring.

A.K.C.: The American Kennel Club.

Albino: An animal having a congenital deficiency of pigment in the skin, hair, and eyes.

American Kennel Club: A federation of member show-giving and specialty clubs which maintains a stud book, and formulates and enforces rules under which dog shows and other canine activities in the United States are conducted. Its address is 51 Madison Ave., New York, N. Y. 10010.

Angulation: The angles of the bony structure at the joints, particularly of the shoulder with the upper arm (front angulation), or the angles at the stifle and the hock (rear angulation).

Anus: The posterior opening of the alimentary canal through which the feces are discharged.

Apple head: A rounded or domed skull.

Balance: A nice adjustment of the parts one to another; no part too big or too small for the whole organism; symmetry.

Barrel: The ribs and body.

Bitch: The female of the dog species.

Blaze: A white line or marking extending from the top of the skull (often from the occiput), between the eyes, and over the muzzle.

Brisket: The breast or lower part of the chest in front of and between the forelegs, sometimes including the part extending back some distance behind the forelegs.

Burr: The visible, irregular inside formation of the ear.

Butterfly nose: A nose spotted or speckled with flesh color.

Canine: (Noun) Any animal of the family *Canidae,* including dogs, wolves, jackals, and foxes.
(Adjective) Of or pertaining to such animals; having the nature and qualities of a dog.

Canine tooth: The long tooth next behind the incisors in each side of each jaw; the fang.

Castrate: (Verb) Surgically to remove the gonads of either sex, usually said of the testes of the male.

Character: A combination of points of appearance, behavior, and disposition

125

contributing to the whole dog and distinctive of the individual dog or of its particular breed.

Cheeky: Having rounded muscular padding on sides of the skull.

Chiseled: (Said of the muzzle) modeled or delicately cut away in front of the eyes to conform to breed type.

Chops: The mouth, jaws, lips, and cushion.

Close-coupled: Short in the loins.

Cobby: Stout, stocky, short-bodied; compactly made; like a cob (horse).

Coupling: The part of the body joining the hindquarters to the parts of the body in front; the loin; the flank.

Cowhocks: Hocks turned inward and converging like the presumed hocks of a cow.

Croup: The rear of the back above the hind limbs; the line from the pelvis to the set-on of the tail.

Cryptorchid: A male animal in which the testicles are not externally apparent, having failed to descend normally, not to be confused with a castrated dog.

Dentition: The number, kind, form, and arrangement of the teeth.

Dewclaws: Additional toes on the inside of the leg above the foot; the ones on the rear legs usually removed in puppyhood in most breeds.

Dewlap: The pendulous fold of skin under the neck.

Distemper teeth: The discolored and pitted teeth which result from some febrile disease.

Down in (or on) pastern: With forelegs more or less bent at the pastern joint.

Dry: Free from surplus skin or flesh about mouth, lips, or throat.

Dudley nose: A brown or flesh-colored nose, usually accompanied by eye-rims of the same shade and light eyes.

Ewe-neck: A thin sheep-like neck, having insufficient, faulty, or concave arch.

Expression: The combination of various features of the head and face, particularly the size, shape, placement and color of eyes, to produce a certain impression, the outlook.

Femur: The heavy bone of the true thigh.

Fetlock or Fetlock joint: The joint between the pastern and the lower arm; sometimes called the "knee," although it does not correspond to the human knee.

Fiddle front: A crooked front with bandy legs, out at elbow, converging at pastern joints, and turned out pasterns and feet, with or without bent bones of forearms.

Flews: The chops; pendulous lateral parts of the upper lips.

Forearm: The part of the front leg between the elbow and pastern.

Front: The entire aspect of a dog, except the head, when seen from the front; the forehand.

Guard hairs: The longer, smoother, stiffer hairs which grow through the undercoat and normally conceal it.

Hackney action: The high lifting of the front feet, like that of a Hackney horse, a waste of effort.

Hare-foot: A long, narrow, and close-toed foot, like that of the hare or rabbit.

Haw: The third eyelid, or nictitating membrane, especially when inflamed.

Height: The vertical distance from withers at top of shoulder blades to floor.

Hock: The lower joint in the hind leg, corresponding to the human ankle; sometimes, incorrectly, the part of the hind leg, from the hock joint to the foot.

Humerus: The bone of the upper arm.

Incisors: The teeth adapted for cutting; specifically, the six small front teeth in each jaw between the canines or fangs.

Knuckling over: Projecting or bulging forward of the front legs at the pastern joint; incorrectly called knuckle knees.

Leather: Pendant ears.

Lippy: With lips longer or fuller than desirable in the breed under consideration.

Loaded: Padded with superfluous muscle (said of such shoulders).

Loins: That part on either side of the spinal column between the hipbone and the false ribs.

Molar tooth: A rear, cheek tooth adapted for grinding food.

Monorchid: A male animal having but one testicle in the scrotum; monorchids may be potent and fertile.

Muzzle: The part of the face in front of the eyes.

Nictitating membrane: A thin membrane at the inner angle of the eye or beneath the lower lid, capable of being drawn across the eyeball. This membrane is frequently surgically excised in some breeds to improve the expression.

Occiput or occipital protuberance: The bony knob at the top of the skull between the ears.

Occlusion: The bringing together of the opposing surfaces of the two jaws; the relation between those surfaces when in contact.

Olfactory: Of or pertaining to the sense of smell.

Out at elbow: With elbows turned outward from body due to faulty joint and front formation, usually accompanied by pigeon-toes; loose-fronted.

Out at shoulder: With shoulder blades loosely attached to the body, leaving the shoulders jutting out in relief and increasing the breadth of the front.

Overshot: Having the lower jaw so short that the upper and lower incisors fail to meet; pig-jawed.

Pace: A gait in which the legs move in lateral pairs, the animal supported alternatively by the right and left legs.

Pad: The cushion-like, tough sole of the foot.

Pastern: That part of the foreleg between the fetlock or pastern joint and the foot; sometimes incorrectly used for pastern joint or fetlock.

Period of gestation: The duration of pregnancy, about 63 days in the dog.

Puppy: Technically, a dog under a year in age.

Quarters: The two hind legs taken together.

Roach-back: An arched or convex spine, the curvature rising gently behind the withers and carrying over the loins; wheel-back.

Roman nose: The convex curved top line of the muzzle.

Scapula: The shoulder blade.

Scissors bite: A bite in which the incisors of the upper jaw just overlap and play upon those of the lower jaw.

Slab sides: Flat sides with insufficient spring of ribs.

Snipey: Snipe-nosed, said of a muzzle too sharply pointed, narrow, or weak.

Spay: To render a bitch sterile by the surgical removal of her ovaries; to castrate a bitch.

Specialty club: An organization to sponsor and forward the interests of a single breed.

Specialty show: A dog show confined to a single breed.

Spring: The roundness of ribs.

Stifle or stifle joint: The joint next above the hock, and near the flank, in the hind leg; the joint corresponding to the knee in man.

Stop: The depression or step between the forehead and the muzzle between the eyes.

Straight hocks: Hocks lacking bend or angulation.

Straight shoulders: Shoulder formation with blades too upright, with angle greater than 90° with bone of upper arm.

Substance: Strength of skeleton, and weight of solid musculature.

Sway-back: A spine with sagging, concave curvature from withers to pelvis.

Thorax: The part of the body between the neck and the abdomen, and supported by the ribs and sternum.

Throaty: Possessing a superfluous amount of skin under the throat.

Undercoat: A growth of short, fine hair, or pile, partly or entirely concealed by the coarser top coat which grows through it.

Undershot: Having the lower incisor teeth projecting beyond the upper ones when the mouth is closed; the opposite to overshot; prognathous; underhung.

Upper arm: The part of the dog between the elbow and point of shoulder.

Weaving: Crossing the front legs one over the other in action.

Withers: The part between the shoulder bones at the base of the neck; the point from which the height of a dog is usually measured.

(End of Part II. Please see Contents page for total number of pages in book.)